Out of

After working in advertising, James Irvine Robertson turned his hand to pig and diary farming, but also found time to contribute to agricultural journals, newspapers and magazines, and to write a highly successful series of comic novels as well as the acclaimed *The Lady of Kynachan*. He has edited the *Clan Donnachaidh Annual* for fourteen years, edited the magazine of the Stewart Society and written and lectured extensively on the history of Perthshire and the Highlands. He lives in Stirling.

Out of Atholl

James Irvine Robertson

BIRLINN

First published in 2008 by
Birlinn Limited
West Newington House
10 Newington Road
Edinburgh
EH9 1QS

www.birlinn.co.uk

ISBN13: 978 1 84158 766 0
ISBN10: 1 84158 766 4

British Library Cataloguing-in-Publication Data
A catalogue record for this book is available from the British Library

Typeset by Brinnoven, Livingston
Printed and bound by MPG Books, Bodmin

Contents

List of Illustrations

Contemporary cartoon of Colonel David

Jessie Irvine, *née* Stewart

Jessie Irvine in old age

The Manse at Little Dunkeld, built for Revd Alexander Irvine in 1816

Col. Alexander Robertson of Struan, 'name father' of Sandy Irvine

Inventory of the Jamaica estate of Charles Stewart, 1787

Baptismal certificate of Anne Stewart

Medal awarded to John Stewart by the Second Company of St John's Regiment of Militia of Grenada, 1816

Letter announcing Clemmie Irvine's death, 1840

Revd Alexander (Sandy) Irvine

Revd Sandy Irvine

Dr William Irvine

Foss Kirk, Sandy Irvine's first charge

Foss manse, built for Sandy Irvine

Captain David Campbell, playing golf at St Andrews

Captain Campbell, aka Old Schiehallion, in his garden in St Andrews

Amelia Campbell, *née* Stewart Menzies of Foss

The Manse at Blair Atholl, Sandy Irvine's final home

Mrs Jean Robertson, *née* Stewart

Shierglass House, 2008

Struan Kirk, burial ground of the Robertsons of Kindrochit and the clan chiefs

Kindrochit House in the mid 19th century

Kindrochit House, 2008

Captain Duncan Robertson of Kindrochit

Dr William Robertson of Montreal

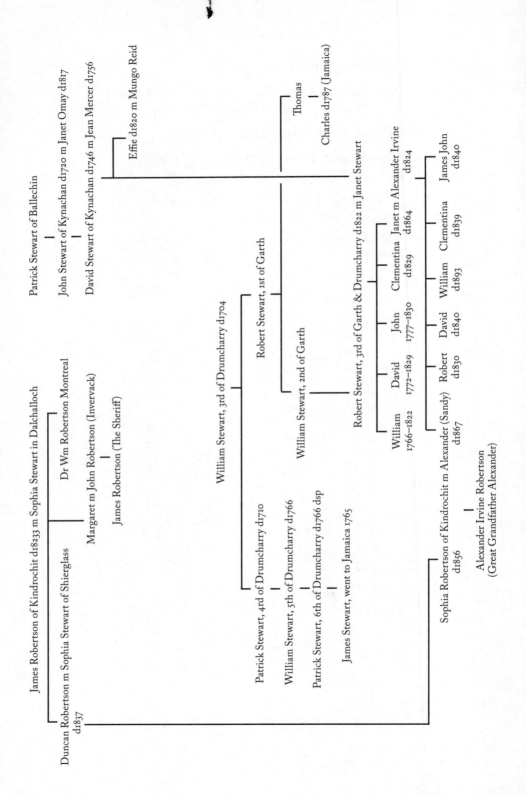

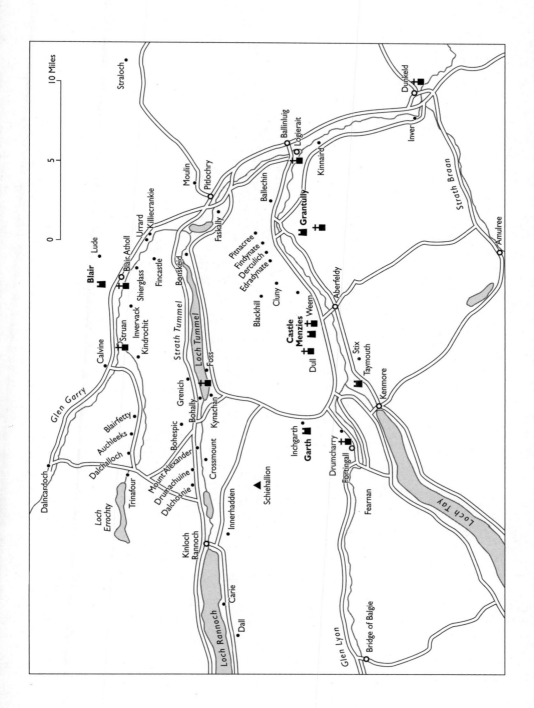

Introduction

The ancient and forbidding castle of Garth guards the pass of Glen Goulandie between the straths of the rivers Tay and Tummel in Highland Perthshire. Set on a peak of rock at the top of a precipitous three-mile track, the stark keep is surrounded by trees and deep gorges. The burns draining the mountain Schiehallion roar softly from their depths. Alexander Stewart, Earl of Buchan, known as the Wolf of Badenoch, built this place before 1400, and my great-great-great-grandmother, his descendant, finally sold it in 1834. Cromwell's troops reduced it to ruins in the 1650s, but it was restored some 50 years ago and is now a comfortable residence. I am sitting in its great hall with the windows and doors wide open. The nearest human being is half a mile away. I should feel surrounded by ghosts – after all, the castle has a grim history and a sinister reputation in the surrounding communities. But give it the courtesy of a few moments' stillness, and the peace of the place steals in.

This book is about some of the people who were once owners of this fortress and their kinsfolk from nearby estates. Often the culture of their times was so different from our own that it is scarcely possible to understand. How, for instance, could a minister of the Church of Scotland justify the ownership of a slave plantation in Trinidad? Or a woman sue her five-year-old son? Or a man regret the end of the Napoleonic wars? Or yet another amputate a prisoner's arms before hanging him?

Some things, however, have not changed. Pause a few seconds after reading the following words by a grieving father: 'Janet, born 18 July 1817, – and died 20 January 1819 twelve minutes before noon of a consumption. She was a most lovely child. 18 months & two days old'.

This long-forgotten infant died the best part of two centuries ago. But now she exists once more inside human minds.

The following pages may be a confidence trick. Perhaps they are not for the benefit of the reader but for the benefit of those read about. By a quirk of fate I am the current custodian of their history. It was in my power, and was in the power of many before me, to consign the letters of these men and women – their voices, and in some cases the only records that they once lived – to a bonfire. But instead I provide the conduit that brings their individuality back from the amorphous multitudes of the dead.

My father's father's father was born in Blair Atholl in Perthshire. My other seven great-grandparents each had a family history of their own, some vivid and full of interest, but I know few details. Great characters stand out. One man died on the block at the Tower of London. Another was 'Captain of the good ship, frigate or vessell of war, called the *Grace of Pittenweem*' and carried Charles II to Holland. Yet another was drummed out of town for being a common scold. And, through 'America's most versatile Medium', one, a charismatic divine who died in 1897, still writes books from the 'Great Beyond', where, as he informed me in a recent letter, 'life is far better than life in the world'.

But great-grandfather Alexander inherited and passed on a cache of his ancestors' papers that go back to before 1600. They came to me in a large trunk and a variety of other containers some 15 years ago – at first glance a mildly alarming inheritance. I knew they were old, and Scots, because the fact that our family was Scots was imbibed with mother's milk. They had always been in a corner of the house where I grew up, but nobody really has time for ancestors when young, and the documents looked dull and impenetrable.

I was a writer, then living on Exmoor in Somerset, and looking for a project when I obtained the archive. My first action was to open the nearest container, a small, black, iron deed box with an outsized, keyless lock. Painted on the front in large letters was REVd ALEXR R. IRVINE. On top lay a rough family tree. One name immediately jumped out – David Stewart of Kynachan, killed at Culloden. I knew that Culloden was the last battle in Bonnie Prince Charlie's doomed attempt to win the British throne in 1746 – and the last formal battle fought on British soil. If David Stewart had been involved, and died, there would be the basis of a good story. I could research the campaign and the battle, insert this man into the tale and produce a swashbuckling historical novel. The more I could find out about him and his times, the less I would have to invent and the more authentic it would be.

This began a quest that took me back to live in Perthshire and sent me 1,000 years or more into history, for David Stewart is only one of hundreds of characters that tumbled out of the letters and documents revealing the rise and fall of a dynasty over several generations. Today one can spend hours playing computer games in virtual worlds on the Internet. Here I came across real individuals in real worlds, facing real struggles on their paths through life. With a bit of detective work, it was possible to tease out the facts of their existence and their fates. And in many cases their personalities are made evident through their own words.

If someone thinks about his or her family tree at all, it is usual to imagine a great inverted triangle with the individual at the bottom and parents, grandparents and great-grandparents spreading out above. But, until recently, people rarely travelled and usually found their spouses within their own neighbourhood. This was certainly true of those in the archive. Great-grandfather Alexander married a girl from Kirkcubrightshire in 1873. In the previous three centuries his ancestors all found partners born within a day's ride of their own birthplaces – and most were related to each other. His ancestral 'triangle' was a narrow, knotty affair, with the same names appearing again and again.

They lived in Atholl, the ancient earldom and Pictish kingdom that occupies the very heart of Scotland. Most were Stewarts and Robertsons, members of families that intermarried for centuries, and whose roots often went back into the district before the time of record. The kinds of people they were and the alien, constantly evolving societies of which they were a part can be clearly seen through the papers, as can the past of this remarkable area of Scotland, which was the stage on which they played out their lives.

Atholl is defined by both geography and history. At one time it covered some 450 square miles between Dunkeld and Dalnacardoch, encompassing Lochs Tay, Tummel and Rannoch and the towns and villages of Aberfeldy, Pitlochry, Blair Atholl and Fortingall. To the south it was bounded by the Highland line at Dunkeld and Amulree, where the mountains descend to the lowland plain. To the west and north lie the wastes of Rannoch Moor and Badenoch, where Perthshire and Inverness-shire meet; to the east, Strathardle. By any standards it is a stunningly beautiful part of Scotland, with its heathery hills, lochs, broad fertile straths and steep-sided glens carved by spate burns which meet the rivers Errochty, Lyon, Garry, Tummel and, eventually, the Tay. Grouse and deer populate the hills, wild cats and pine martens the forests, trout and salmon the lochs and rivers.

1

Hunting Davie

It began with David Stewart of Kynachan. Now, the corner of Atholl that he would have called his country is tranquil. Residents there cater for visitors, farm, retire or peer at computer screens. Strangely, the landscape is wilder, emptier and more rugged than it was in his day. The most obvious difference between then and now is the tree cover. Today one can see forests, heather, bracken, scrub pasture and reeds. In the 18th century, the time of his particular drama, there were only a few, carefully preserved, trees; the countryside was dotted with little townships huddled round a good spring or well. Peat smoke leaked through the crude thatch of the tiny stone cottages. The land around them was striped with curved strips of barley, oats and bere, a primitive barley, demarcated by weedy furrows.

Higher up, the slopes were chequered by meadows of grass in various shades of green and rankness. A wall of turf or stone ran along the flanks of the hills, and above this – the head dyke – lay the moors and the mountains. The strongest impression on the traveller would have been human activity, for the land carried a much greater population than today. The little hamlets were intersected by a network of paths; dozens of ferries plied across the rivers; and, higher up, the land swarmed with cattle, ponies, sheep and goats which, in summer, grazed almost to the mountain tops.

These days, torturous tarmac roads link the small towns and villages; farms lie a little back from the highway. Approached by long, winding tracks, mansion houses stud the gentler hillsides, although these buildings are much more imposing than the modest dwellings they replaced. Most still lie in the midst of estates that have carried the same name and had much the same boundaries for over a thousand years, but nowadays they are rich men's baubles, and only one or two are still owned by descendants of the old lairds.

Gone, too, are the great magnates. In the 18th century, three dominated the region. The Campbell earls of Breadalbane finally went in 1949, the chief of Clan Menzies two decades earlier. Even the Duke of Atholl, who used to be virtual dictator of Atholl, is now resident in South Africa, although his kinsfolk still control Blair Castle (to which over 150,000 tourists come each year) as well as a huge tract of the surrounding countryside.

I have already told the story of David Stewart of Kynachan as a novel, but its protagonists deserve more than that. To a remarkable extent their tale was based on historical fact, and as it gradually unfolded it became a detective story. Such rich and interesting biographies are the holy grail for all those who scour the Internet for details of their forebears. This story was just waiting to be uncovered, and, to a faintly eerie extent, the shadows of the characters seemed to help me along the way.

The '45 Rising is a well-ploughed field, smothered in romantic myth, and it is as much a cliché of tourist Scotland now as it was already 200 years ago. To write the book, I would have to strip away all the flummery and try to find and portray its reality from David's point of view. The myth says the Rising was Scots fighting for their freedom against the English. In fact, it was a civil war, with more Scots, and more Highlanders, against the rebellion than for it. Recent times have shown just how unpleasant civil wars can be. This one cannot have been any different.

My starting point for David of Kynachan's story was the family papers. The mother of ALEXR R. IRVINE was born Janet Stewart. She was David's granddaughter, the second youngest of a family of five, but none of her siblings married. Her brother, named David after his grandfather, was the most important figure in the archive. He was a soldier, retiring from active service in 1816 as a much decorated and oft-wounded colonel. All his life an antiquarian and an enthusiast for the Highland culture, he wrote *Sketches of the Character, Manners, and Present State of the Highlanders of Scotland with Details of the Military Service of the Highland Regiments*, which has rarely been out of print since first being published in 1822.

A great-aunt had made a start on sorting out the papers in the 1930s by bundling some together, but it was Colonel David a century earlier who decided what to preserve from the earliest days. Even he found it difficult. To some he pinned the notes 'old and illegible', and the pins are intricate marvels – tiny collars round a piece of wire with their heads hammered flat which, as Adam Smith observed, required 'eighteen distinct operations' to make. Until this David inherited them, the documents had suffered. The outside of the vellum of the earliest charters is dark grey, gritty with dirt. Many papers are torn and fragile; some have been nibbled by despairing mice; still others are discoloured, some by spilled claret; others have more sinister stains.

In a letter of 1822, the colonel made reference to the way the material had been stored: 'If I did not know the careless manner in which family papers were kept in this house, I would be surprised what became of this document – my uncle's will was found dirty and squeezed up under the old book case in the low east room in the house – the girl brought it to me last summer to ask if it was worth anything.'

From my perspective the problem of legibility was paramount. Many of Colonel David's letters had been preserved. Naturally right-handed, a musket ball had smashed his arm and rendered it useless. The wound remained infected all his life, and each time it flared up he went through torment, which was eased only when the abscess burst. In consequence his neat italic handwriting descended into an idiosyncratic script – dashed off at great speed with his left hand – which John Prebble described as 'an Oriental pattern of curves and whorls, heavy strokes for the consonants and a light feather touch for vowels'. Even with practice, it could be impossible to read. Through the ages, handwriting styles had changed from italic and the daunting secretary hand of the 17th and 18th centuries to more familiar lettering. Often it was the hand of the least educated that was most legible. One could follow the agonies of the carefully formed script of an unaccustomed signature. Sometimes the awfulness of the writing was combined with idiosyncratic spelling, producing the most intricate of calligraphic puzzles from which to try to tease a meaning.

The Scottish Record Office, now the National Archives, had cherry-picked the collection during the 1940s, but only a few of the very shiniest fruits were taken. A guess would put the number of individual documents at 1,500, many of them late 19th-century legal papers of stultifying tedium. The oldest stretch back to the mid 1500s.

First I needed to find out how much was known about the real David of the '45. He was described in the family tree as being 'of Kynachan'. Before going any further I needed to understand what that meant. Kynachan turned out to be an estate, just north of Schiehallion (which means the Seat of the Caledonian Fairies), and on the south side of the river Tummel. Blair Atholl, with its wedding-cake castle, lies a few miles north. In David's time, Atholl was a regality within which the duke acted as virtual viceroy. Through the regality court, he could condemn men to death – and reprieve them, supposedly the prerogative of the king.

The meaning of the word Kynachan is obscure; some said 'a mossy place', others 'place of the dogs'. The name likely stretches back more than a millennium. The fact that he was designated 'of Kynachan' meant that David had been the laird or owner of the estate. A quick trawl through the papers revealed some documents that related to it, most of them vellum land charters. The property was not just a tract of land, but a community of some half a dozen little villages.

Soon I moved house to Aberfeldy, only a few miles across the hills from Kynachan. It gave me a chance to look at the land where David Stewart once lived. These days it is whiskery, covered in heather, bracken and conifers, with only a few pasture fields cropped by sheep; ospreys nest on the electricity pylons which carry power from the hydro-electric schemes that now control the tributaries of the river Tay. When the estate was advertised for sale in 1833, it was

> upwards of 5,000 imperial acres of hill pasture, and 283 imperial acres, or thereby, of arable and meadow. The hill pasture is of the best quality, and the wintering of sheep is remarkably safe. It abounds in moor game of all kinds, grouse, black cock, ptarmigan, white hares etc. In the River Tummel, which bounds this property for four miles, is excellent trout and pike fishing.

Not very much has changed. Most is moorland, some covering a substantial hill – Craig Kynachan, with a small loch on its top plateau, where, legend has it, the warriors of Fingal lie, swords and shields by their sides, waiting for the sound of a trump to awaken them to defend Scotland once again – and more stretching to the summit of Schiehallion which dominates the landscape for miles around.

David's home was burnt in the 19th century but the shell remained, and, bar the larger windows and the dormers, it still looks much the same as when he built it in the 1730s. Alongside are the remains of the walled garden that he constructed. The view has changed. Then, the ridge on which the house stands overlooked the river Tummel that used to meander sluggishly past, a few hundred yards from the house. In 1948 it was dammed for electricity generation; this raised the level of Loch Tummel by some 20 feet and overwhelmed the river and pasture in front of the building.

The 1841 census showed 182 souls living at Kynachan, and almost all made their livelihood by farming; on such land, one wonders how they could have possibly survived. Their descendants have scattered across the globe, but the ruins of the old townships where they lived and from where they worked the land in common still remain. A few were supplanted by Victorian farmhouses when the little fermtouns were amalgamated into economic units. Now those units are also unprofitable, and the houses are occupied by the retired or used as holiday homes. The estate now offers half a shepherd's job, a quarter of a gamekeeper's and a tiny proportion of a forestry worker's.

When I began my exploration, Kynachan House was occupied by the MacIntyres. Peter, in his seventies, with a twinkle in his eye and a great respect for whisky, had looked after sheep on the mountain for decades and he knew something of David's story. He proudly showed me a photograph of a rocky outcrop. In the foreground was his craggy self with a deerstalker, a sheep and his cromach. Draped about him were a gaggle of tweed-clad models. The girls wore expressions of professional arrogance and boredom. Peter looked as if he'd just heard news of a lottery win. A fashion photo-shoot team had stumbled across him a few years earlier and exploited the opportunity. He took me behind his house and pointed to the outcrop. 'It's hollow,' he said. 'There's a cave beneath it that was used to store gunpowder during the Rising, but the entrance is lost. I've never been able to find it.' He pointed out two huge boulders left by a retreating glacier. One was called St Mary and the other St Margaret.

'Why?' I asked. He shrugged.

In 1822 Colonel David wrote in his book that each significant rock and tree had its own name and was the trigger for the tale of an event that may have taken place centuries ago, but he lamented that the old way of life was disappearing, with the Gaelic language under threat and the old stories rapidly being lost. The last Perthshire Gaelic speaker died more than 20 years ago. The only old traditions and legends that survive were recorded in the 19th century, but nowhere is there an explanation for St Mary or St Margaret, or any tale of hidden gunpowder.

2

Origins and early rebellions

With an idea of the environment in which David lived, the next step was to try to find out about his social milieu and family. Two great clans have their country in Highland Perthshire, Clans Menzies and Donnachaidh – the Robertsons. There were also powerful Stewart families, most descended from bastards of kings. As Robert Louis Stevenson wrote in *Kidnapped*, Stewarts 'all hing together like bats in a steeple'. This was certainly true in Atholl; the web of kinship bound them together, as it did the whole population. Dominant were the dukes of Atholl, Stewarts in early days, and later Murrays. To the west lay the Campbells in the shape of the ruthless earls of Breadalbane, with their seat at the east end of Loch Tay at Taymouth and a string of castles gripping their land which stretched west to the Atlantic.

But Kynachan and its story seemed virtually unexplored. Local history books have proliferated over the last half-century, but none seemed to have touched this particular corner. Then I came across one of that plethora of Victorian/Edwardian books, most of them privately printed in editions of 100 or 200 copies paid for by their authors, and about their ancestors. This one was a slim volume entitled *Family and Genealogical Sketches*, published by a minister named Thomas Sinton in 1911. He was descended from David's younger daughter, and much of the book was the more-or-less accurate story of the Kynachan Stewarts.

Word had spread by now that I was researching this family and their era. I had met an antiquarian book dealer, Alasdair Steven, who lived in the remains of the mansion house of Ballechin in Strathtay, most of which was pulled down due to rot after the Second World War, leaving only one gloomy wing which was so stuffed with his stock that its capacious rooms had become small grottoes connected by narrow passages amid tottering piles of books. Alasdair had a vast and eclectic knowledge of the byways of Scots history and literature and could unerringly put his hand on a particular volume amid the largely uncatalogued and unorganised thousands amid which he lived. For me, he became an essential lending library. My first loan was his copy of Sinton, but I did not need it for long.

By this stage I was researching in Blair Castle, which holds the documentation of four centuries of Atholl history. And here the first of the slightly eerie, serendipitous coincidences which were a feature of the search for David Stewart's story took place. In the bookshelf of the Charter Room at Blair, I noticed two copies of Sinton's book and coveted them. Surely the castle could spare a copy? I picked up one and on the flyleaf was the original owner's name 'Rev. A Irvine Robertson' – Great-grandfather Alexander. Some honeyed words and a cheque later, I had it in my possession.

David was the second of his line to own Kynachan. His father was a younger son of Patrick Stewart of Ballechin. This property lay a dozen miles southeast, the largest and lushest of the string of estates that face south along the Tay between Ballinluig on the A9 and Aberfeldy. His branch of the family descended from the Stewarts of Stix, and the first of that line was a natural son of James II. They were one of the most powerful and well-connected dynasties in Atholl.

One reason why David was fighting for the rebels at Culloden became clear. His family had fought in rebellions to restore the Stuart kings to their throne for a century beforehand. His honour would have demanded he do no less. They fought with Montrose in 1645. In 1654 the heir of Ballechin was killed at Dunkeld, fighting against Cromwell's troops in Glencairn's attempt to restore Charles II to the throne. In 1689, David's grandfather, Patrick Stewart of Ballechin, held Blair Castle for Viscount Dundee in his Rising to restore King James VII and II.

Patrick was one of the most colourful figures of his generation. His Gaelic nickname translated as Patrick of the Battles. He was the baillie, the chief law enforcer, to the Earl, later Marquess and later still Duke, of Atholl and, on behalf of the government, led the Athollmen against the Campbells in 1685 when the Duke of Argyll was rebelling against King James. Argyll lost his head in Edinburgh and Patrick's troops hanged 17 leading Campbells from the walls of Inveraray. Through the romantic mist of tartan and flashing broadswords, one could see the abominable reality of such civil and inter-clan warfare. Among those hanged was a Major John Campbell. Before he was executed they chopped off his arms.

The duke had one grave problem in his rule of Atholl. The Duke of Argyll was a Campbell and had the clan loyalty of all the Campbells. Atholl's ancestor had married the daughter of the last Stewart earl. His surname was Murray. All but a tiny minority of the lairds to whom he granted charters of estates – ownership of them that could be bequeathed

to their descendants – were Stewarts or Robertsons. Sometimes they felt
they had higher loyalties than to the duke.

James II and VII abandoned his throne to William of Orange in 1688.
The Scots convention supported the new regime, as did the Marquess of
Atholl, who ordered Patrick to ready the Athollmen to counter Dundee's
nascent army. However, Patrick turfed the garrison out of Blair Castle
and held it for the rebels until Dundee and his 2,000 clansmen arrived.
The battle of Killiecrankie took place on 27 July 1689, a few miles south
of the castle. General McKay and some 4,000 government troops came
through the pass, saw the rebels on the hillside above them and drew
themselves up into line of battle. Dundee waited until the sun had gone
down before launching his charge. The conflict was decided in minutes.
The Highlanders endured a volley or two of enemy musketry and crashed
into their lines before the redcoats could fix their bayonets. Under the
broadsword, the soldiers broke and fled back into the heavily wooded
pass. Dundee was dead, along with 800 to 900 of his men. But in the
long summer twilight, the survivors butchered their enemies amongst
the trees and the local people hunted fugitives through the hills. It was
the bloodiest battle in Perthshire history, and perhaps 2,000 government
troops lost their lives.

The Revd Robert Stewart was a nephew of Patrick and the minister of
Balquhidder. He also was given the lands of Tom of Cluny, just up Strathtay
from Ballechin, by his uncle. He took part in the affray, and, after his offer
of quarter was contemptuously refused, he bisected Brigadier Balfour with
his sword. He continued through the woods, hewing down straggler after
straggler. At the end of the day he had to go to the blacksmith for help in
extricating his swollen hand from the basket hilt of his weapon.

Although the rebels won the battle, their charismatic leader Dundee
had been killed. The Robertsons, under their young chief Alexander, who
absconded from his studies at St Andrews University to join the rebellion,
were late for the battle and lost up to 100 men in an ill-advised attack on
government troops near Perth. Then a sullen assault on the Cameronian
Regiment in Dunkeld was repelled and the rebellion fragmented.

Patrick of the Battles continued to fight with a small rump of the most
committed Jacobites. Most of the rebels accepted the indemnity and went
home, save – according to Sir Patrick Moray of Ochtertyre writing to
the Marquis of Atholl on 3 September 1689 – for Patrick 'with his three
sones, who continue as obstinate as before they were treacherous'. During
the Highland unrest which continued until the Massacre of Glencoe in
1692, they stayed with Dundee's successor, Colonel Cannon, as part of a
mounted troop of about 60 men that included Alexander Robertson of

Struan and Dundee's brother. In June 1691, Patrick was Jacobite governor of Eilean Donan Castle. By 1693 he was imprisoned in the Canongate Tollbooth in Edinburgh, where he remained until 1697. One of his 'three sones' was John, who, in 1700, was the first of his family to receive a charter for Kynachan.

The next great Rising in favour of the exiled Stuart kings came in 1715 when many rebelled at the accession of 'German Geordie' – George I. John held a commission of Lieutenant-Colonel in the 1st Battalion of the Atholl Brigade. If the duke had had his way, they would have been fighting for the other side. In one of those mediocre decisions that marked the Earl of Mar's generalship, he ordered Brigadier McIntosh of Borlum to take 2,000 men, including John's battalion, across the Firth of Forth, with the ultimate purpose of joining rebels in the south and attacking the government army from the rear. Most of the contingent crossed the river, although one boat was intercepted and its troops captured, and they took Leith Citadel. The Duke of Argyll marched his men from Edinburgh to demand the rebels surrender – and John emblazoned his name in the history books. The *Annals of King George* states he gave the rebels' response: 'That as to surrender, they laughed at it; and as to bringing cannon and assaulting them, they were ready for him; that they would neither take nor give quarter with him; and if he thought he was able to force them he might try his hand.'

In a curious side-light on this incident, one commentator said that the Hanoverian forces had great need for cloaks on the road between Edinburgh and Leith. It transpired that these were hired by those who wished to preserve decorum when their bowels, loosened by fear, were relieved into the gutter.

On 19 October Borlum decided to head south to join the Jacobites in northern England, with some of whom he linked up at Kelso. From there, after considerable and acrimonious debate, the Highlanders agreed to venture south of the border to meet up with the bulk of their unimpressive English allies, crossing northeast of Gretna on the 31st. On 10 November they reached Preston, where, on Saturday the 12th, they were attacked by a government army. After some fierce fighting, the rebels surrendered on 14 November, the day after the battle of Sheriffmuir, the indecisive encounter between Mar and Argyll near Stirling which virtually marked the end of the rebellion.

The captured Scots officers were initially imprisoned in the inns. To give the prisoner some comfort, John Stewart's friends sent in a well-filled snuff box. He investigated its suspicious weight and found golden guineas, which he used to bribe his gaoler to loosen his chains. The 'Irons with which John Stewart of Kynochan, in Perthshire was loaded' were presented to the Society of Antiquaries of Edinburgh in 1840 – and have since been lost. Along with 200 other officers, John was marched first to Wigan and thence to London and the Tower. On 31 May, he pleaded guilty to the charge of high treason before the Court of Exchequer, and the lands of Kynachan were confiscated.

3

Gentlemen of Atholl

The government's answer to the Rising of 1715 was to send General Wade north to build a network of roads that could carry artillery into the Highlands to deter the clans from making further trouble. Wade's greatest and most enduring achievement was the bridge over the Tay, the only such crossing over the river in its day. On its south bank grew the little town of Aberfeldy. Just north of the bridge is the village of Weem, where Wade made his headquarters. There also lies Castle Menzies, seat of the clan chief and built in the 16th century. While living in a cottage behind the castle, I began to transcribe the Kynachan papers in the archive. History provided a framework of reality for a novel about David. I now needed to know if information existed that would put flesh on the bones.

Hard detail of the estate was cracklingly preserved in parchment and vellum in the form of charters, signed by the Duke of Atholl, which described the boundaries, the farming townships and the size of the estate – 11 merklands, one of several kinds of land measurement in use. Originally a merkland meant the area of land for which one merk or mark's rent was paid.

One dilapidated folder at the bottom of a rotting leather box contained a cache of papers. Many of them needed to be peeled apart. A note in the handwriting of Colonel David showed that they had been unread since 1816. Perhaps 100 pertained to the adjoining Garth and Drumcharry estates, east and north of Fortingall, which were the core properties owned by the colonel's family. A slightly smaller number concerned Kynachan, which was inherited through his mother. A few of the documents were beautifully written by clerks and were easily read; others were not. The Kynachan records began in 1700. Most concerned money, but far from all. I was interested in writing a novel and needed to populate it with characters, and characters aplenty were there.

David's father John had received from his widowed mother his 'Bairn's portion' in 1701 which consisted of all the livestock on two of the estates owned by the Ballechin Stewarts. He was granted a wadset, a long-term lease, on Kynachan, by the Duke of Atholl, for which he paid £17 sterling and one cow annually. (£1 sterling equalled £12 Scots, the currency in general use in Scotland for accounting purposes during the first half of the 18th century.) John married Janet Omey, daughter of a minister and well-connected in her own right. A kinsman was Smyth of Methven. He was part of the Perthshire establishment with a large castle a few miles west of the city.

Letters from John's friends were there. His contemporary, the eccentric chief of the Clan Donnachaidh, Alexander Robertson of Struan, passed on his regards to John's 'good, tho little wife'. He fought alongside John in 1690 and lived three or four miles west of Kynachan. He won lasting fame as the most fanatic supporter of the House of Stuart, losing his estates and spending much of his life in exile in France. One of his soubriquets was the Poet Chief, as he dashed off political squibs, obscene verses and somewhat torrid pastoral poetry in English, French, Greek, Latin and Italian. In 1712, a jocular letter from Smyth refers to a drinking bout between himself, the powerful Laird of Grantully, whose estates John ran for a few years, Struan and another kinsman, Sir Thomas Moncrieffe. Depending on one's point of view, John either starred or disgraced himself and was in danger of being 'put in the Gazette for losseing your plaid, for being guilty of self murder and a hunder worse crimes, which will make you so odious that none but the Laird of Grantully, or his tutor, or suchlike gentlemen who know not how to pass their time, will dare to drink with you, more than you were excommunicated by the General Assembly'.

The year before the Rising of 1715, John was offered a commission in an Independent Company commanded by Colin Campbell. These companies were set up to control cattle theft, the Highlanders' favourite pastime, and were precursors of the Black Watch. John refused; it may have been that he felt he had enough on his plate with an estate, four sons and three daughters to keep in order, or he may have been unwilling to commit himself to an organisation overwhelmingly recruited from clans loyal to the regime and largely and deliberately officered by Campbells. Or it may have been that Campbell realised the inappropriateness of an offer to John with his history and family. Nonetheless it must have been an indication of the regard in which he was held.

Evidence of his troubles after the Rising was there. He signed a document from the Tower of London where, along with the other Perthshire officers captured at Preston, he was awaiting trial:

> Forasmuch as in respect of my absence from Scotland I cannot conveniently manage my affairs there and being sufficiently assured of the care fidelity

and diligence of Janet Omey My Spouse Therefore witt ye me to have made constitute and appoint the said Janet Omey my actrix and factrix.

So I had discovered that Janet was physically small and quite capable of looking after her husband's affairs in his absence. I was also realising that women were considerably more than chattels of their husbands. One indication was the retention of their maiden names. Janet, for example, was not referred to as 'Mrs Stewart'. Usually she was 'Janet Omey', as in the quotation. Sometimes she was 'Janet Omey or Stewart'. A woman's property did not automatically become her husband's, but was retained in her own name, and its disposition after her death was to the 'children of her own body' rather than to her spouse.

Those in the Tower were not left to rot. The good looks of Archibald Butter, one of the captured rebel officers from Atholl, made him the darling of London society. John Stewart managed to buy himself a viola da gamba; the instrument is now played in a London string quartet. When the trials took place, some prisoners were executed, some transported to America; others had their lands confiscated, amongst them, John. The surveyor for the Commissioners for the Annexed Estates produced an abstract of the rents of Kynachan. It was worth £63 19s 8d sterling per annum, of which £8 11s 6d was in cash and the rest in kind – bere, oatmeal, butter, cheese, geese and 42 hens worth 3d each. Kynachan did not revert to the crown; its superior was the Duke of Atholl, and, though he had sons and cousins in the Rising, he had made sure he would retain his power and his dukedom by supporting the government. There is little information about the upshot for the other Atholl officers, but there is no reason to suppose that the outcome for John was exceptional. The Stewarts lost their wadset, but the family stayed in residence. Not until 1718 did matters come to a head. John was served with notice to quit the estate, along with his family, servants and other dependents. The notice was read from the pulpit of the parish church at Dull.

This may have been no more than a ploy, for, within three months, the duke 'for certain onerous reasons' agreed to re-instate John's possession. The onerous reasons are not known. It was likely that the duke had no desire to give more than lip service to London trying to dictate what went on in Atholl. It may be that the reasons were financial, for the duke found it hard to live in the style to which he aspired with much of his wealth based on rough Highland acres, however many he controlled. It may be that he could not afford to lose so many of his lairds, his officer corps, on whom he depended to carry out his wishes and manage the unruly people.

David began to appear in the papers. The family, like most local

Jacobites, were Episcopalians, whose ministers continued to pray for the exiled Stuarts, and their details do not appear in the Presbyterian parish records. His parent's marriage was at Methven in 1702, which means that he can only have been seven years old in 1709 when he seemed to be signing, on behalf of his father, meal tickets. These only exist for that year, which may indicate a particularly poor harvest. There are a dozen, all dated in April, when stores would have been almost empty. John had a stash of meal in Perth and was, for example, instructing the corn merchant to give 'Finlay Fisher & James Fisher two bolls two firlats Meal'. John must have been busy because many of the rest are signed by 'Jannet Omey'. And three are signed by David with a large and not very well formed 'DS': 'Sir, Give the bearer hereof Thomas Stewart in MikleTomban a boll of bear of Kynochins bear. DS.'

Paper was expensive and not to be wasted. Members of the family used the back of documents to practise handwriting. Two examples exist, one a poem which, bizarrely, is a propaganda exercise in favour of King George, copied out in 1717, a matter of months after John was convicted of treason.

In the years after the Rising a handful of letters survive that give a glimpse of the life of a gentleman in Atholl. John took in an orphan, the son of a John Macdonald who had been in the duke's service. A rather embarrassed letter from Clanranald, the chief of the boy's clan, says that he knows he should be taking care of the lad himself but he would be grateful if John would continue looking after him through his education, since his own unsettled state made it impossible for himself to do so. There is a bill for gunpowder and golf clubs from St Andrews, a letter from the duke's baillie telling him to take men into the hills to chase bandits and a bill for a coffin for one of his sons. He and Janet had at least eight children, as well as putting up Master Macdonald. The household must have been anything but peaceful.

The house itself would likely have been a long, single-storey affair, bulging with dogs, children, servants and tenants. Dealings with the latter are the most frequent kind of correspondence – the buying and selling of livestock and extensions of credit, some from landlord to tenant, and some the other way round. A tumble of names of the folk who lived on the estate emerges. John was sending his sons to Perth Grammar School and received a pair of doeskin gloves for settling their boarding expenses so promptly.

In 1724, the lease on Kynachan was converted to a hereditary charter. This ended the need to pay the duke an annual rent, although not the obligation to serve on his juries and parade the estate's fencible men – those between 16 and 60 – with their weapons at wappenshaws, where the strength of his following could be measured. The only direct financial return to the duke from a charter holder came in a kind of capital transfer tax when the estate changed hands from father to son.

Presumably to avoid this, the charter is in the name of both John and David, and they paid 24,000 merks, or £1,300 sterling. In the Highlands there was a notorious lack of ready money, and banking had hardly emerged from the womb, let alone being in its infancy. Capital was usually transferred through promissory notes. An incurred debt could be paid by a note issued by a credit-worthy laird 100 miles away, and such a note could have already served as currency in half a dozen transactions.

In 1730, David and his father were given the contract by General Wade to build a bridge 'easily passable for Wheel Carriage or Canon', that would carry his military road across the Tummel. The payment was £250 sterling, and they undertook to keep the bridge in good repair for a further 20 years. The bridge still stands, dominating the humble steel-girder construction alongside, which replaced it for road traffic in the last century.

Wade was a remarkable man, sent to Scotland by the government with the express purpose of curbing the independence of the Highlands and the power of the chiefs. Yet he made himself very popular amongst them. This was a time when men drank immense quantities. Wade held his own and could even surpass such renowned topers as Struan Robertson and Lord Lovat, who had retainers carry his guests up to bed. On one occasion, the laird of Foss, an estate bordering Kynachan, joined his neighbours for a convivial Saturday evening in a local inn. They only broke up when the church bells sounded – the following weekend.

One of David's officers in the Rising, Allan Stewart of Innerhadden, who was described as a 'coarse satirist',

> sometimes would have Occasion to go to the nearest publick houses, where he met some of his neighbours when they remained perhaps two days at one sederunt drinking strong whisky pure without any water or suggar enjoying themselves composing & singing songs after the manner of the Country, as when he was a little warm flustered with Drink he always composed more freely.

Later in the century an Englishman was a guest at an Edinburgh dinner. He soon realised that he was incapable of matching the amount that others were drinking and decided that he could best survive by pretending to fall asleep at the table. He started up on feeling a hand at his throat. 'Don't fret, sir,' came a reassuring voice. 'I'm just the laddie that loosens the cravats.'

In his book, Colonel David mentions a bet between John, Mr Smyth of Methven, Sir David Threipland, Mr Moray of Abercairney and Sir Thomas Moncrieffe:

The object of the wager was, who could produce a boll of barley of the best quality, my ancestor to take his specimen from his highest farm . . . Marshall Wade was to be the umpire . . . Methven produced the best barley, Sir Thomas Moncrieffe the second, my relation the third . . . The spot which produced the Highland specimen is at the foot of the mountain Sichallain, and is now totally uncultivated.

Remember that John was convicted of high treason, and yet in 1730 Wade signs the equivalent of a firearms certificate, giving Charles Stewart, son of the laird of Inchgarth, a neighbouring estate, permission to carry a 'gun, a sword and a pistol', 'on the recommendation of John Stewart of Kynachan'. Charles's son James was killed at Culloden.

John died in 1733*, by which time David was already acting as laird. Sir Robert Menzies, the clan chief, thanked him for the return of some borrowed books, discussed a duff horse and 'courtships in your neighbourhood'. And a couple of letters survive from his cousin Thomas Moncrieffe, one asking him to train his 'Setting bitch', named Beauty, to the net. Such a dog would point, allowing its master to tiptoe up to a clump of heather, and throw a net over a pack of grouse. In the other letter, Moncrieffe asks for 'three or four black cocks', as well as revealing that Beauty's training took nine months.

There is a kerfuffle over George Cairney. He was the tenant of Pitkerril, a farm at the base of Schiehallion, and had looked after cattle wintering on the mountain for more than 15 years. In 1736, he was fined £1,000 Scots by the regality court for taking 100 of the Duke of Atholl's trees a year for nine years. David lent him the money to pay the fine; this meant that George owed David twice as much as he was worth and was bankrupt. But David, 'for the favour and respect he bears to the said George', gave him lifetime occupation of his farm and guaranteed him protection from his other creditors.

Little information survives about the fates of David's siblings, except for Clementina and Elizabeth; a cryptic reference by Colonel David tells that the latter eloped. A single letter exists from brother John in 1737. He was in South Carolina and asked to be sent £20 sterling. If not forthcoming, 'it will be the ruin of my character and they'll think me a villain', he wrote.

---

* See Appendix 1

4

Prince Charlie arrives

By now I had a good idea of the structure of David's life and knew something of the people around him. I knew of his wife, too, but I was now concentrating on his progress through Prince Charles's attempt to win the throne of Britain. The run of documents broke abruptly in April 1745. For David's exploits during the Rising, I had to turn to the history books, and here I had a great resource, *The Chronicles of the Atholl & Tullibardine Families*, a narrative history compiled in 1908 from documents in the Charter Room of Blair Castle. It gave a detailed account of the Rising in Atholl and, with augmentation from other sources, I could trace David's movements almost day by day. But first a bit of background.

In 1775, Dr Samuel Johnson could still write, 'To the Southern inhabitants of Scotland, the state of the mountains and the islands is equally unknown with that of Borneo or Sumatra; of both they have heard little and guess the rest.' The Highlands of Scotland held what has been described as the last tribal society in Europe, utterly different from the rest of Great Britain, its natives seen as savage barbarians. North of the sharply defined border of the Highland line, people spoke Gaelic instead of English, wore plaids and tartan rather than trousers. Their music, culture, customs and many of their laws were different. In the far northwest, Catholicism had not only held out against the Reformation but also battled against paganism. A mutual contempt was almost all that Lowland and Highland societies had in common.

By 1745 life was beginning to change, but the king's writ still held little force across the trackless moors, bogs and mountains. Control was devolved to the great Highland magnates who wielded absolute power within their domains and who had private armies to support their authority. The dukes of Argyll and Atholl could field 3,000 men each, Breadalbane 1,000, the Mackenzies 2,500, and so on down to lesser clans with a few score followers. If one of these mighty subjects became dangerously dominant, the government would encourage his neighbour to wage war upon him and thus preserve a balance. It was as if Britain, in its northern extremities, contained a failed state, controlled by squabbling warlords with every man armed to the teeth. In fact in 1816 Walter Scott wrote a 'Comparison between the HIGHLAND CLANS and the AFGHAUN TRIBES', in which he concluded there was little difference between them.

Kynachan lay on the southern edge of the Highlands, and there were clear differences between David and his Lowland equivalents. For a start, he was bi-lingual, speaking English and Gaelic, which was the language of his tenants – few of them could speak English. The relationship between landlord and tenant was also distinct from the south. The cement binding society was kinship. Highlanders could recite the names of their ancestors back through the centuries and, certainly in Atholl, could make blood connections with many of their landlords. The lairds had themselves intermarried for generations. Younger sons and daughters married tenants and spread these links throughout society. It meant that the most humble could call his landlord cousin and shake his hand. Social division was not differentiated by wealth and status. Athollmen of whichever class had more in common with each other and mixed more easily with each other than with anyone else. Insiders were from the same estate, the same clan, the same strath or glen. Everyone beyond Atholl was an outsider. Society was not mobile as it is today. There were no white or grey settlers, nor did people move to live in other parts of the country. Usually they were born and died within a mile or two of where their grandparents and great-grandparents had their homes. Highlanders considered themselves aristocrats, descended from kings. Lowlanders were an ill-bred rabble. But the laird still held enormous power over his people, and the duke had capital power over them all.

Unlike the Rising of 1715, which probably had the support of the majority of Scots, only a minority of clans and few Lowlanders were prepared to follow the prince during the '45. Many contemporaries could see that it was doomed from the outset. The rebels had many different motives for joining the rebellion. Some were against the union with England; others were hoping to escape debt; still more wanted adventure; and many, almost certainly the overwhelming majority of the common soldiers, had no choice, because their laird or chieftain called them to arms, and their livelihoods and possibly their lives could have been forfeit if they had disobeyed. But some, and this included David, had ancestors who had fought for the Stuarts for a century, and they felt that their honour demanded they do the same, even if they thought the cause hopeless. The greatest rebel general was Lord George Murray. He wrote to his brother, the Duke of Atholl:

> I own francly, that now I am to ingage, that what I do may & will be
> reccon'd desperate . . . taking a resolution that may very probably end in

my utter ruen. My Life, my fortune, my expectations, the Hapyness of my wife & children, are all at stake (& the chances are against me), yet a principle of what (seems to me) Honour, & my Duty to King & Country, outweighs evry thing.

Prince Charles landed in the west in July 1745 with a handful of supporters. These included the Duke of Atholl's elder brother, who had been disinherited due to his support for the Stuarts. He was known as Duke William to differentiate him from his younger brother, Duke James, who held the estate. Prince Charles appealed to the clans to join him; the Camerons, Stewarts of Appin and Macdonalds did so. With 1,800 men, he marched east. General Cope, in charge of government forces in Scotland, took his troops up Wade's road through Kynachan and across Tummel Bridge to link up with northern clans loyal to the crown, and Charles came down towards Atholl without opposition. Knowing the temper of the Athollmen, the duke retired to Dunkeld, then to Edinburgh and eventually to London, and Charles took possession of Blair Castle. Duke William was now in charge.

One of the characters who emerged from the papers was a kinsman of David, Thomas Bissett, Duke James's chamberlain. He remained in post but fed information to the authorities. He saw his duty to his ousted master, to Atholl and its people, and knew that the Jacobites would bring a disaster that he must strive to ameliorate. He reported to Duke James that David and a fellow laird who lived half a dozen miles north, James Robertson of Blairfetty, were going round Atholl drumming up support for Prince Charles.

The Atholl Brigade was reformed in three battalions. Lord George commanded the second and Duke William the third, with their cousin, Lord Nairne, the commander of the first. The latter was made up of the men west of Loch Tummel. Most of the officers were Stewarts and the men they commanded were their tenants. For the purposes of the novel I was writing, I was sticking to historical detail whenever possible. If history failed to arbitrate between accounts, then I would select whatever was the most dramatically satisfying of the stories preserved. Only when these were wanting would I invent material. So far history seemed to be doing an excellent job, but when it came to the number of tenants in David's personal following I had nothing better than an oral source, and I did not enquire too carefully about the figure of 36 that it came up with. It was roughly right for the population on Kynachan.

David's father was the most senior officer in the 1st Battalion under Lord Nairne during the '15. David held the same position under his son, leading the men who lived between Lochs Tummel and Rannoch. The

Nairnes were cousins of the Atholl family but brought very few men of their own to the prince's flag. Since, notoriously, Highlanders would only follow their own officers and chieftains, one suspects that Lord Nairne's command was little more than titular. David's adjutant was Charles Stewart of Bohally, about whom I knew quite a lot. Bohally was a small estate just across the Tummel from Kynachan. Charles's father had come from Stewart clan country in Appin and acquired a few acres on Loch Tay. David had a charter on Bohally in the 1720s and seems to have surrendered it to Charles.

Ten years younger than David, he was clearly a great friend, wooing and later winning David's youngest sister Clementina. Known as Tearlach Mor (Big Charles), he featured in his great-nephew's book *Sketches of the Highlanders*. Charles, according to this, 'was remarkable for his strength and activity, and one of the best swordsmen of his time, in an age when good swordsmanship was common, and considered an indispensable and graceful accomplishment of a gentleman'. He had bested a son of Rob Roy in a duel. During the 1730s, like many of the Jacobite officers, he had been an ordinary soldier in the Black Watch in the days when most of its men were the sons of lairds. They are described as riding to musters with a ghillie in attendance and with a pony carrying their uniforms and weapons. The descendants of Alexander Stewart, the Wolf of Badenoch, were known as 'Stuibhartaich Ghorm-shuileach' – the Blue-eyed Stewarts. Those immigrated from Appin were 'Stuibhartaich Dhubh-shuileach' – the Black-eyed Stewarts. I imagined Charles to be what, in the English of the day, would have been described as a big, black man.

Prince Charles spent a couple of days in Atholl at the beginning of September, staying in the castle and attending a ball at nearby Lude House. The local gentry and their ladies flocked to see him. It would have been inconceivable for David and his family not to have been present. In spite of this, only about half the lairds would join the rebel army. The prince went on to Perth where Lord George took charge of drilling the Atholl Brigade, and on to Edinburgh. David's contingent marched there during the second week of September. The rebels captured Edinburgh and, on 21 September, trounced Cope's soldiers, who had been shipped south from Inverness, at Prestonpans. The Athollmen were in the second line of the Jacobite army and do not seem to have taken part in the bloodshed.

Prince Charles held court at Holyrood. David's battalion policed the city and he was sent back to Atholl, guarding 150 prisoners taken at the battle who were confined in the jail at Logierait. David's job was to drum up recruits, and I came across a letter dated 12 October from him to Blair Castle, addressed from Castle Menzies, only 100 yards from where I was reading it. Within a day or two, he returned to Edinburgh with a reinforcement of some 300 Menzieses. David's friend Sir Robert Menzies supported the government and would have been an unhappy host. But his wife was a Stewart and a Jacobite; much of his clan joined the Rising and they formed a highly effective unit.

Charles persuaded his council to march south, and, haemorrhaging men through desertion, his army entered England on 8th November. I knew the dates when David was in charge of the day's march. I knew his codename, Carlisle. History was giving me all I could ask of it. For my purposes, David was going to be an excellent officer, but it would be serendipitous if I could find some evidence to this effect. And it turned up.

The rebels reached Derby, 150 miles from London. In an acrimonious council of war, the prince was persuaded to retreat. After the meeting, Lord George returned to his lodgings and discussed the affair with his brother, Duke William, and three others, asking their opinion on the decision reached. They all agreed it to be correct. Those canvassed were, to quote Lord George, 'as three good officers as any in the army'. One was named as David.

Shadowed by vastly superior forces, the rebels retreated back to Scotland. They beat off their pursuers at Clifton in northern England and defeated a redcoat army at Falkirk. In both engagements, the Athollmen distinguished themselves. In the latter, most of the Highlanders chased after beaten formations of the government army in the hunt for plunder. Only the discipline of the Atholl Brigade which held its ground won the field. There had been some grumbling in the rest of the army because Lord George seemed to favour the Athollmen, but he thought them the best of his regiments and was determined not to squander them.

In spite of Falkirk, the retreat continued. The prince led the Highland infantry up Wade's road through Crieff, Amulree and across Tay Bridge and, on 6 February 1746, arrived to spend a few days at Castle Menzies. David went home after a four-month absence, but the correspondence shows he was busy trying to gather in the many men who had deserted before the march into England. On 10 February, the Highlanders continued the retreat north, leaving Atholl open to the Campbell militia and the redcoats on their heels.

The prince ended up in Inverness. Lord George led a hugely successful raid on Atholl the following month, which included the capture of Kynachan house, but David did not join them. He and his men were ordered to take and hold Castle Grant in Strathspey to secure the rear. The Jacobites re-occupied Atholl on 17 March, capturing some 500 to 600 of the government militia with scarcely a shot being fired. They then lay siege to Blair Castle. A fortnight later, they were gone again, ordered north to counter the Duke of Cumberland's army which was approaching Inverness from the east.

The battle of Culloden took place on 16 April. David had been killed in the battle – this was the very first fact about him that I had known. He was going to die gloriously in my account, but, as usual, I checked history, just in case information about his fate was recorded. The Atholl Brigade was positioned on the right of the Jacobite line. David's battalion was on the flank. Charles of Bohally is recorded as being with the Appin Regiment, absent from David's side for the first time. Optimism had long drained from the rebel army and Charles probably chose to fight and likely die with his clan. The day was cold; sleet was driving into the faces of the Highlanders. They were exhausted and hungry, having been marching all night in an attempt to surprise the redcoats at their camp, but this had failed.

After an initial exchange of artillery in which the government had overwhelming superiority, the rebels on the right of the line charged. Their flank was under fire as they closed the 400-yard gap between the two armies, and they smashed into the two redcoat regiments on the government's left, but could not break them. The charge died, and the Athollmen were cut to pieces by grapeshot, cannon fire and musketry. Half were said to have been killed. The defeated rebels retreated and the army disbanded at Ruthven soon afterwards.

After the battle, Cumberland sealed off the field and is said to have ordered the killing of any wounded still remaining. In the *Atholl Chronicles* it mentions 'Major David Stewart of Kynachan, Atholl Brigade; last seen defending himself with a broken sword against two dragoons; believed to have been carried wounded to Old Leanach, and burnt on 17th.' I now had David's rebellion, almost entirely historically accurate and as dramatic and exciting as I could wish. But for a novel I needed more. I needed to know about his wife and family and how they had coped with the disaster that had befallen the men of Kynachan. For only one is said to have survived, a boy of 16 who was captured and imprisoned in Inverness before escaping to come home. But, as with David, before I created a romantic Highland love story that ended in tragedy, I needed to discover what else history had to offer.

5

Bonnie Jeannie Mercer

In 1739, David married Jean Mercer. Once again, I was surprised at what record remained and astonished at its opulence and suitability for my purpose. The first source I turned to was the Kynachan documents. Jean's first appearance was in the couple's marriage contract made in March that described the assets that both brought into the marriage. She was one of the four heirs of 'John Mercer, her father's brother', and the contract listed a couple of estates near Perth, fishing on the Tay, a mansion house in the town itself and large areas of land covered in shops and commercial premises. John Mercer had been a successful lawyer. The family had been in and around Perth for five centuries by his time. His father and grandfather had each been town clerk of Perth and were descendants of the Mercers of Aldie, one of the most powerful families in the county. It was unclear how much of this wealth, if any, Jean actually brought with her; the bequest was disputed by cousins named Wood, and lawyers were still happily working away on the case 60 years later. Jean's father William was an Edinburgh lawyer and a member of the Royal Company of Edinburgh Archers. He married Anna Chalmers and had a string of daughters before dying insolvent in 1728. The girls and his widow were supported by their uncle in Perth. Jean was the eldest, likely born in 1715. Clementina and Helena died young; the others, Charlotte, Barbara and Abigail, all married, but none had children.

Robert Scott Fittis, a Perthshire historian, wrote for the *Perthshire Constitutional and Journal* on the city's history and antiquities. His columns on the Mercers of Perth were collected and published for private circulation in 1879, and these provided me with golden material. In fact, its richness was something I would not have dared to invent.

The pamphlet said that David Stewart had a dream, and in the dream he saw the face of the girl whom he would marry. Soon after, he went to a ball in Perth, and there, through the dancing candlelight, he recognised her and engineered an introduction. By this stage I had begun to write my novel and was researching as I went along. I found that the annual Perth ball, which still continues, was held in the autumn after the last race meeting of the year. It provided a final chance, before the onset of winter and the consequent difficulties of travelling, for the gentry of the county to come together to socialise. I decided that the ball of 1738 would have been the likely occasion of the meeting between David and Jean, or Bonnie Jeannie Mercer as the pamphlet called her. I discovered the Duke of Atholl was at that particular assembly, as was David's cousin Thomas Moncrieffe, who had caused a scandal there by quarrelling with his brother and knocking him out with his gold-topped cane. So I had some sort of narrative for the occasion.

I knew Jean must have been beautiful – bonnie, at least – and must have been at the ball with her sisters, but I needed to dress her in order to describe her when she first met David. Amongst the papers was an inventory of Abigail Mercer's clothes when she died in childbirth in 1740. A poignant document, it lists a considerable quantity of garments, ending up with 'a velvet Cap. Her best diamond ring in a timber box, Her cradle clothes. A Bairne's whistle and a Silver Spoon. Her Common Prayer Book and Whole Duty of Man and Two fans. The above with her mother's mahogany cabinet is set aside for her daughter Charlotte.' Her prayer book showed that the family was Episcopalian, like the Stewarts of Kynachan, and Episcopalians were supporters of the deposed Stuart monarchs. The *Whole Duty of Man* was a religious work, written in 1657 by the royalist Richard Allestree, which is still in print. Of Charlotte there is no further record, which makes it likely that she scarcely outlived her mother, but I latched on to a 'red damask ball gown' in this inventory and decided that this would be worn by Jean at the ball.

I put David and the Highlanders in tartan, the Lowland lairds in knee breeches, and was just dressing Jean in her gown when I received a telephone call. A voice I had never heard introduced itself as belonging to my fourth cousin, once removed. Whilst my brain grappled with this relationship, he told me he lived in Wales, was a retired social anthropologist now studying his own forebears and had heard that I was writing about the Stewarts of Kynachan. We both descended from David and Jean's granddaughter, he said. My ancestor was her eldest son, the minister of Blair Atholl, the REVd ALEXR R. IRVINE of the deed box. His was the parson's brother, a doctor in Pitlochry. We made polite conversation, and then he asked what point I had reached in the story. I told him I was describing the ball at which David and Jean had met. 'Ah, yes,' he said. 'And what is she wearing?' An odd question, I thought, but I explained about the inventory and her sister's red gown. 'No,' he replied. 'That's not right. Her dress was gold and shocking pink silk, and I have it in front of me.' Serendipity again, at the very least.

The garment had been handed down in his family although it had been remodelled in the 19th century. He sent me an offcut and I took it to the National Museum in Edinburgh for an expert's opinion on the material. She dated it to about 1708, originating in either Lyons or Spittalfields. The fact that it was used in a dress some 30 years later was simply due to the length of time it took fashions to reach the provinces and Scotland from London. The pattern on it shows chinoiserie swirls, and this came about because oriental porcelain was being imported into Europe at the end of the 17th century. Meissen and the silk weavers copied the style.

So I changed Jean's dress to the real thing, and I also altered the way she looked. I had imagined her blonde, but in my mind no blonde would have worn a silk gown of this colour and pattern, so she was transmuted into a brunette. This cousin, the delightful Joe Loudon, also had a portrait of John Stewart of Kynachan and bits of silver from the family. The earliest piece is a large spoon celebrating the union between Jean's parents – William Mercer and Anna Chalmers.

According to the documents, virtually the first action by David after his father died was to build himself a house. In the charter of the estate granted to David in 1724, no mansion house is mentioned; instead is the phrase 'mains of Kynachan', which would normally apply to the home farm of an estate, so the building David replaced may have been a comparatively humble dwelling, rubble-stone walls and a thatched roof, very similar to, if longer than the houses of the tenants. No sign or record exists of any more substantial construction. Although David's house was burnt in the 19th century, its interior can be reconstructed.

In the summer of 1733 David was buying quantities of nails for floorboards and doors, the following year for windows, along with shutter bands. An inventory exists for later in the century which describes the furniture in each room, and from this it can be deduced that David built a modest mansion house: four up, four down, with an additional room above the front door and the entrance hall, slate-roofed and built of stone from the estate – in fact, very much what is still there today. He would have utilised the skills that he and his tenants learnt or observed during the building of Wade's bridge. At the back was the kitchen and to the east a walled garden, the building of which is said to have been interrupted by the arrival of Prince Charles and never completed.

The house would have been ready for Jean for the wedding on 3 March 1739. I married them there. Jean then would have taken over as chatelaine of the estate. Laird's wives took on the name of the property and Jean would have been generally known as Lady Kynachan. For my purposes the marriage would have to be successful, a union of high romance, after such a first meeting, but it would have been nice to find some confirmation of this.

And of course it was there. Jean, her sisters and their husbands were listed by Robert Scott Fittis in 1879, although he transposed the spouses of Barbara and Abigail. Curiously all of them married Athollmen. Charlotte married the laird of Fincastle, a Stewart estate at the other end of Loch Tummel from Kynachan. Barbara – Babi – wed Stewart of Kinnaird where the Tummel joins the Tay. Abigail married James Bissett. Above this list in my copy of the pamphlet, someone had written, in pencil, 'an old native of Atholl used to describe them thus: Abi – Bean a choimisteir, Charlotte – Bean an Fincastle, Babi – Bean an phluiteir, Miss Mercer – Bean Daibhidh Choimeachdan'. These were their Gaelic nicknames. Abi's meant 'Wife of the Commissary', for her husband, James Bissett, the nephew of Thomas Bissett, the duke's chamberlain, was an official of the Commissary Court at Dunkeld. Charlotte, conventionally enough, was 'Wife of Fincastle'. Barbara's was harder. 'Phluiteir' means club- or splay-foot. Her husband, Alexander Stewart of Kinnaird, featured considerably in my story, and the soubriquet was puzzling until I found a reference to his profession. He was an Edinburgh music and dancing master. One can imagine the amusement of the locals when this creature minced across the moors with his toes neatly pointed and, perhaps, his arm describing an arabesque.

When it came to Jean, Miss Mercer, I enlisted help. My expert came back with, 'Wife of Davie, who is always in attendance. That's a nice tribute to David Stewart.' I now knew that their marriage was so close that it gave rise to her nickname. I paraphrased it as 'Wife of Doting Davie'. Cousin Joe, who was as interested in what I was finding as I was myself, had a more caustic view. 'It means he was tied to her apron strings, hen-pecked,' he said. 'Women have always ruled in my family. She probably set the pattern. I reckon she was a shrew.' I told him such an opinion was heresy in the context of my novel, but she certainly turned out to be a woman of formidable character.

Others lived at the new house besides the newly-weds. David's mother was there – the 'good, tho little' Janet. Of David's sisters, Clementina, the youngest, was also in residence, being courted by Charlie Stewart of Bohally, a couple of minutes' ferry ride across the river Tummel. I also had a name for their steward, Donald, who featured in an inventory as having care of the household furnishings. I knew the names of most of the estate tenants and of many friends and relations, and I also had a fair idea of the activities and lifestyle of the Stewarts themselves. The bills showed them to be buying spices, wine-glasses, glue, oranges, silk, tea, salt, iron, snuff, ink, tobacco, oil, rope and the ingredients for soap-making.

In the first years of their marriage, nothing much happens in the documentary record. David gave venison to the Threiplands of Fingask, who would be deeply involved in the Rising. Donald Macdonell of Tirnadris thanks David for helping a dependent with a legal action. He took part in the first skirmish of the '45, commanding the guards at Highbridge across the river Spean who captured a redcoat patrol. He was executed in 1746 at Carlisle after being taken at the battle of Falkirk when he mistook some dragoons for his own side.

Otherwise there are the usual financial transactions – borrowings, lendings, bills for the repair of dancing pumps and payment for webs of bleached linen, which was one of the few ways that ready cash could be earned in the Highlands, and by women. David was asked by his brother-in-law, Alexander Stewart, who had just bought half of the estate of Kinnaird near the junctions of the Tay and the Tummel, to march the boundaries with him and his neighbours to ensure no disputes in the future. One document stands out and I used it in my depiction of the honeymoon. David was appointed as one of the commissioners to survey the shielings of Glen Lyon, those hilltop pastures where folk went in summer to graze their livestock and keep them out of the growing crops. The survey must have taken a week or more, travelling the hills on either side of the 30-mile long glen, estimating the amount of livestock each area could carry, the boundaries and who had rights over them. If the weather was good, their honeymoon in such beautiful surroundings would have been a memorable experience.

Their first child, John, was born in May 1740; Janet came along in October 1742, Euphemia in 1744. And then Prince Charles landed.

6

Women at war

I had begun to realise that the most interesting story I was uncovering was not about David. Men go to war with lamentable regularity from generation to generation, and David's swashing and buckling in the cause of the prince met with all my expectations. But those men leave behind their wives and families, who have to cope as best they can. And their tale is much less often heard.

The '45 Rising was a civil war, with friends and relatives on opposing sides, particularly in Atholl where the lairds split almost down the middle between those who supported the rebellion and those that backed the government. These men knew each other well, and, virtually without exception, they were related to each other. To a lesser extent, the same was true of their tenants. As modern history shows, any war and civil war in particular produces depraved manifestations of the human spirit. Bonnie Prince Charlie and his doomed tilt at the British throne is now overlaid by years and exploited by countless whisky brands, shortbread tins and sweet, sad songs of loss and romantic endeavour. But for those involved there would have been more than a whiff of Bosnia. The detail of the record I was finding meant that I could follow the course and consequence of the Rising from Jean's point of view. I knew no happy ending was possible. David and the tenants in his tale never came home and now lie in the mass graves of the Culloden battlefield. But what was it like in Atholl for those left behind?

Kynachan was a tightly knit community. Today's communications give each of us links to the whole world that would seem inconceivable not many years ago. In the Atholl of the mid 18th century, most people would never have left the district. Their furthest venture from home would be to communion, known as the Great Event, which, in summer, rotated round the local parish churches. Otherwise the only folk with whom they passed the time of day were from their own villages on their home estates. News was local gossip. The best news was very local gossip, particularly about the goings-on in the mansion house. National events were broadcast by pedlars who were welcomed as much for the information they brought as for the goods they carried. And yet the modern world was seeping into the district. Wade's roads had brought Lowlands and Highlands closer together and this was particularly so for Atholl, owing to its proximity to the south. Although many of the lairds were still Episcopalian, the parish churches were held by Presbyterian ministers and they preached support for King George, so the idea of joining a rebellion to put Prince Charles on the throne was not generally popular.

The casualties of the 1715 Rising are unknown, but many of its survivors would have still been alive in 1745, not to mention their spouses and children. They cannot have welcomed the news of another uprising. Nor could John's widow Janet, who had run the estate in his absence. She would have known of the rebels' executions and must have dreaded the same fate for her spouse in the Tower of London. And it is scarcely likely that Jean could have welcomed her adored husband going to war. David, though, seems to have had no doubts.

Prince Charles raised his standard at Glenfinnan on 19 August 1745. Cope's army of 2,000 redcoats marched through Kynachan five days later on their way north. It would not have been a cheering sight for the people of the estate. Cope was hoping to pick up local recruits but they were not forthcoming. Almost immediately afterwards, David, his cousin Charles Stewart of Ballechin and Blairfetty were drumming up support amongst the local lairds. Charlie Bohally, across the river, may well have been the one who mustered the Kynachan men. Or it may have been Hugh Reid. He was the tenant of one of the Kynachan farms, Balnarn, and was a *duine uasal* – a gentleman – and an officer in David's battalion. Perhaps some of the young men of the estates actually welcomed the opportunity to be soldiers in the fight to restore the Stuarts, but, for most, evidence is to the contrary.

The correspondence is full of the difficulties the Jacobites faced in recruiting Athollmen for the rebels and the delight from government supporters for the comparative paucity of volunteers. Thomas Bissett, admittedly spinning as hard as he could, wrote to the duke after the battle of Prestonpans, saying that most of the Athollmen 'were pres'd men, deserted before the actione, and I have the satisfactione to tell that none of yr Grace's men were engag'd against the King's troops, the fue that did not desert not being intrusted, and who have all to a man deserted since.' The Macphersons from Badenoch, under their chief, Cluny, had no kinship links in Atholl and were therefore chosen to spearhead the local recruitment drive. They were reported as using harsh measures to force men to join the rebels. David was trying to round up deserters every time he was home. In the *Atholl Chronicles*, there is a petition from Grissel McDonald asking Duke William to order Bohally to release her husband because she had 'a numerous small family of little strength, and very little to maintain them . . . one of my Children is Prodigiously tormented with the Gravel Stone . . . besides my Husband that went abroad had a very unhappy disease, of which he takes fits now and then.'

With a laird of David's convictions to lead them, there would have been little chance of his tenants escaping service. When the Jacobites went south, Kynachan and the neighbouring estates would have been stripped of all their fighting men, leaving the elderly, women and children to farm and fend for themselves. Whatever Jean's feelings, she would have had to support her husband, and she cannot have been popular. David left with his men in mid September. He was back within three weeks, and then he was off again for months. Prince Charles timed his arrival to ensure the Highland harvest was in. The people of Atholl would have hunkered down in their customary manner for the winter. With little daylight and often savage weather, those months did not permit field work and so the men could be spared for fighting.

The Athollmen returned, having marched the best part of 400 miles south, and then all the way back, fighting off redcoats as they came. There is a flurry of correspondence in the *Atholl Chronicles*: on 8 February, Duke William said that between 400 and 500 Campbells of the Argyle Militia had advanced to Dunkeld and this was bringing Athollmen to the standard. The same day, Lieutenant-Colonel Blair of Glasclune unhappily told Duke William that he had to resort to burning tenants' cottages in order to force men to join his ranks. David was supervising the gathering-up of men from Rannoch, Glen Lyon and along the Tummel. On Sunday 9 February, government forces were reported to have crossed Taybridge at Aberfeldy and occupied Castle Menzies.

Colonel O'Sullivan, the prince's adjutant-general who was later responsible for the unfortunate selection of Culloden Moor as the battlefield for the final confrontation, sent a letter from Blair to David at Kynachan ordering him to cut Tummel Bridge to hinder the advance of the redcoats. David wrote back that he had neither tools nor masons and it was thus impossible. O'Sullivan sent these down to do the job. On 10 February, a plaintive letter was sent by the Hon. George Colville to Duke William who had already retreated to Dalnacardoch. 'I have certain intelligence of the bridge of Kynachan being yet entire . . . My informer told me he saw the masons deputed by your Grace beginning to demolish it, and that they were actually stopped by a "Major Vis", so I humbly think the only remedy will be another message from the prince, backed with a sufficient force.'

This seemed a puzzling incident. No Major Vis exists; whoever it was hid his identity. The only major around was David. Could this 'Major Vis' have been him? If so, why did he wish to prevent the bridge being cut? The obvious reason was that it would seriously hamper local communications. But there is an even more compelling motive. In the contract to build the bridge for General Wade in 1730, it states that David must 'uphold the said Bridge at his own Expense for the space of twenty years from the date hereof'. Whatever the outcome of the Rising, David would know he would probably have to put his hand in his own pocket to pay for repairs.

The Athollmen retreated north, leaving the bridge intact. They knew that government forces, particularly the Campbells, were on their heels, and they must have hated to leave their families without protection. Meanwhile, those left behind must have dreaded the immediate future. Robert Scott Fittis wrote down what happened next at Kynachan. Lieutenant-Colonel Leighton and the 27th Regiment occupied both Castle Menzies and Blair. A heavy fall of snow blanketed Highland Perthshire. Over the pass of Glen Goulandie from Strathtay and Castle Menzies, past the ruins of Garth Castle, came a redcoat patrol. I decided to give command of it to Captain Webster, later the senior officer at Castle Menzies. The soldiers must have struggled through the snow, and fear of ambush would further slow them down. Darkness was falling by the time they came down the track to the mansion house of Kynachan and knocked on the door. Inside, Jean and the rest of the household would have known that the enemy would soon arrive. They also knew that any number of people would be telling them which were the rebel families in the neighbourhood.

The officer was polite, explained they were snowbound and asked for accommodation for the night. To quote Scott Fittis,

> They were kindly received and plenteously regaled. The officer in command appeared touched by the lady's lone and unprotected condition, and, pointing out the dangers impending over her head, advised her to pack up all her silver-plate and other valuables, and, as the best precaution in her power, entrust them to his keeping, lest she should be plundered by a succeeding party, as had been done to Jacobite mansions around Perth. The lady was shrewd enough to penetrate his motive, but affected to adopt his counsel, and to repose in him her full confidence. She accordingly bundled up her plate and jewels; and when the night waxed late, she, with the assistance of a trusty servant or two, quietly escaped from the house, with the children and effects, by making egress through a window, and got clear off to a distant place of safety. Next morning, the officer was much chagrined and very indignant on discovering how he had been duped.

Drawing up his men in front of the house preparatory to their departure, he ordered them to fire a volley at the windows, and every casement was accordingly riddled.

Once the initial wave of government troops passed through, the Argyle Militia was ordered to occupy Atholl. Its Highlanders were part of a force of 1,200 men under the command of Sir Andrew Agnew, a foul-mouthed, foul-tempered old warrior, who held Blair Castle with the 21st Regiment, the Royal North British Fusiliers. The Campbells of Argyllshire and the Athollmen had been enemies for generations and had frequently fought each other. The last occasion had been the Rising of 1715. To make matters worse for Jean, David's family had always been in the thick of these confrontations. Tummel Bridge was second only to Blair Castle as the strategic key of Atholl. Kynachan house was the only building of substance near it. Captain Archibald Campbell of Knockbuy, on Loch Fyne, was instructed to quarter himself and 100 men there and to command others at Blairfetty and across the pass into Strathtay. He was told to seize 'all kind of provisions that belong to the rebels', and to give them no quarter. His lieutenant at Blairfetty was Hector McNeill of Ardmeneach, near Oban, to whom I will return later.

William, the Jacobite Duke of Atholl, had gone north with Prince Charles. His brother Duke James was back, rather unhappily, at his mansion in Dunkeld rather than in Blair, which was occupied by the military. He drew up a list of the rebel lairds within Atholl and called a meeting of the loyalists in order to raise their tenants in support of the government. He listed 16 of his vassals with the Jacobites; 17 came to consult with him in Dunkeld, an indication of how evenly Atholl had split for or against the prince. Certainly the duke had no love for those who had gone against his wishes in rebellion. With so many of his lairds and relations against King George, the duke had to be conspicuous in his loyalty to keep his coronet.

Hunger seems to have been the principal price extracted by the militia from the people on the rebel estates. After a month's occupation and with sixty troops in residence, Mrs Robertson of Blairfetty managed to smuggle a letter north to her husband, complaining that they were facing starvation. This was the trigger for Lord George to win permission from the prince to march south with 700 men from his own regiment and the Macphersons to launch a raid on Atholl. Marching 30 miles a day, they left Dalwhinnie at 10 p.m. and split up into small parties at Dalnacardoch. David's battalion was diverted to capture Castle Grant, which would otherwise threaten their rear. In the early hours of 17 March, each laird led the attack on the Campbells occupying his own estate. The raiders achieved complete surprise, capturing every outpost, and the redcoats only just managed to scramble into Blair Castle, to which Lord George laid siege with a couple of small cannon, his only artillery. No more than half a dozen militia were killed; the rebels had not a single casualty.

Mrs Robertson woke up to find her husband below and the militia already prisoners. It may be that Jean and her family were also resident in the house of Kynachan along with the government troops. Colonel David knew those involved in the raid and recorded in his book what happened at Kynachan:

> My grandfather's house was one of those attacked on that night. It was garrisoned by a captain and 100 men of the 21st Regiment, and a detachment of the Argyle Highlanders. The rebels rushed on the picquets and took them prisoners without the least noise. Proceeding to the stables and out-houses, where some of the men slept, they seized upon them in succession. Those in the house knew not what passed till they heard the noise, and saw the court in front of the house full of men, threatening to set it on fire if they did not surrender. After some parley they capitulated without a person being hurt on either side, except an unlucky girl, the daughter of one of the drummers of the 21st Regiment, who slept in the house. When she heard the noise, she ran to one of the windows to look out, and being mistaken in the dark for an enemy, she was killed by a shot from the outside. The party who attacked was commanded by Mr Stewart of Bohallie.

Colonel David was not meticulous about his history. There were no regular troops there; all were Argyle Militia. And Bohally was acting as a guide, since, in the absence of David and his men, this detachment consisted of Cluny's men under the command of John Macpherson of Strathmashie. The papers captured there included a letter that incensed the Jacobites in which Cumberland ordered the militia to give no quarter to rebels in arms. I gave Jean the job of burying the dead child in the graveyard at Foss, and of cleaning up the house. She may not have done that thorough a job, as the girl's bloodstains were said to be visible on the floor for many years afterwards, and her ghost, as attested by Peter MacIntyre in the late 20th century, still walks the house on the anniversary of her death. 'Drummer', incidentally, was the name sometimes given to the piper.

Hundreds of prisoners were herded north to Ruthven and the government had a panicky fortnight while it tried to organise a force to drive the rebels out of Atholl once more. The siege of Blair – the last time a castle was besieged in Britain – contained elements of farce. The Jacobites made their headquarters in McGlashans Inn behind the castle, taking it over from the soldiers who had fled into the stronghold at the rebels' approach. Lord George had only a couple of small cannon and these were set up in the

burial ground of St Bride's kirk in front of the inn. First the garrison had
to be offered a chance to surrender.

Knowing Sir Andrew's cantankerous reputation, none of the Jacobites
were willing to approach within gunshot. The dilemma was solved by
Molly, one of the serving wenches at the inn. She was described by one
government officer as 'rather handsome and very obliging'. She volunteered
to sashay up to one of the ground floor windows of the castle where she
handed in a note asking those inside to surrender. The missive was taken
to Sir Andrew, and his roars of rage made Molly lift her skirts and flee
back to the rebel commanders standing in the churchyard. The redcoat
who wrote a diary of the siege saw Lord George and his lieutenants double
with laughter at her report.

The authorities sent Hessian mercenary troops to Dunkeld and
Taybridge to counter the Jacobite re-invasion, but they were reluctant to
try to cross the passes at Killiecrankie and Glen Goulandie, where they
might be ambushed by the enemy. They contented themselves by parading
on the haugh land on the banks of the Tummel by Pitlochry, hoping to
draw the Highlanders to combat.

For the troops inside the castle, food and water were short. The
besiegers' artillery was too small do to much more than break the slates
on the roof, so the local smith set up braziers to bake the cannon balls and
thus set the building alight. Sir Andrew Agnew's opinion of Lord George
was succinct. 'Is the loon clean daft, knocking down his own brother's
house?' The bombardment was foiled by dowsing the shot from tubs of
urine posted at strategic points. The bored officers inside the castle set up
an effigy dressed as their commander peering through a spy-glass from a
window. The Highlanders enthusiastically blazed away at this tempting
target until Sir Andrew inquired what was going on. The young lieutenant
who set up the dummy had to brave the Highlanders' inaccurate fire and
dismantle it.

Just when matters were becoming critical for the redcoats, Prince
Charles recalled Lord George. The morning patrol of the Hessians found
the Highlanders gone. Those besieged in the castle ventured cautiously
out, finding still alive a horse that had been shut in an outbuilding for
the two weeks of the siege without food and water, and they reclaimed
McGlashans and Molly as their own.

Atholl was re-occupied, this time by Hessian troops brought over from
the Continent to join the 60,000 men already in arms against the rebels.
These mercenary soldiers did their job with fairness and there were no
reports of trouble between them and the local people. Colonel David
reported that their German was incomprehensible to the inhabitants

but sufficient numbers of Athollmen had enough Latin to make this the *lingua franca*.

Culloden took place on Wednesday 16 April, a fortnight later. The following day the rebels disbanded at Ruthven and the prince took to the hills for his three-month scamper round the Highlands before he escaped back to France. In his diary, the Duke of Atholl wrote of hearing rumours of a battle on the following Saturday and confirmation of the victory on Tuesday the 22nd. On Wednesday he reported the first swallow of the summer.

7

After the Rising

The detail of events at Kynachan immediately after Culloden is absent, as are any details of casualties from the men of the Atholl Brigade. The *Atholl Chronicles*, its source Colonel David, lists 22 gentlemen of Atholl – the officers – killed and 8 wounded. Such proportions seem to confirm the reports that the wounded were bayoneted after the battle. Of the fate of the ordinary soldiers very little is known. Duke William's servant wrote an account of the conflict on 24 April. He said that only 12 men of Lord Nairne's battalion, in which David was the major, came off the field. He also counts David amongst the dead.

In the aftermath of a failed rebellion, it was not in the interests of the losers to broadcast that they had relatives or friends who had taken part. In addition, the Highlands were in turmoil. Cumberland had initiated a policy of harsh repression, determined to destroy the culture which could spawn an army that would erupt from the hills once a generation to threaten the security of the state. The king's troops penetrated every glen in the Highlands and Islands in their search for rebels and weapons, looting, raping and killing without discrimination. Plunder flowed into Inverness and Perth for auction. Soldiers were said to have dug up the burial grounds in order to steal the shrouds from corpses, a remarkable indication of the poverty of society in general.

Jean and the folk of Kynachan must have known quite soon that their men were dead. Their bodies would have been thrown, unidentified, into the common graves, but survivors must have filtered back with the information. Atholl was the duke's domain; he had done his best to support the government and he had the admirable Thomas Bissett, his chamberlain, striving with all his might to mitigate the brutality of the redcoats. The prosperity of Atholl was the foundation of the duke's wealth and power and, more charitably, both men had friends and relatives involved in the Rising. Bissett organised the surrender of weapons, as soldiers were shooting some of those who tried to hand them in. He also collected fodder and rations to try to prevent troops seizing what they wanted from the ordinary people. Redcoats on search complained that the tarry deposits from peat smoke impregnating the thatched roofs of the cottages dripped when it rained, leaving black marks on their scarlet coats.

Some estates escaped the worst effects of the reprisals because their lairds supported the government. But the rebel estates were obvious because they were without menfolk. Women, boys and the elderly had to do the heavy farm work, otherwise they would starve. It must have been so on Kynachan. In addition to this, there was the Militia, once again using Kynachan House as a barracks.

Alexander Irvine, missionary in Rannoch 50 years after the Rising, wrote:

> In winter 1746 & spring 1747 all Ranoch was burnt and plundered, and some people were killed by the king's troops. They indeed extended their devastations over all the adjacent vallies without any distinction of friend or foe, the innocent or the guilty. The inhabitants were thus deprived of home & shelter during an inclement season and reduced to wretchedness and despair, and the name of the Duke of Cumberland became associated with every enormity which could excite or deserve the execration of mankind. These facts I had from eye witnesses.

More specifically for Kynachan, Bissett wrote in his journal on 7 August 1746,

> Lieut McNeill, with a party of the Argyleshire Militia carried off all the cows, horse, and sheep, &c, belonging to the Tennents of Foss and Kynichan; this they did in resentment of Kynichan's being with the party of Rebells that seized the party of Argyle Militia that were garrison at Kynichan. The provocation was certainly great, and what they did was justly deserveing, had not a great many innocent widows suffered.

These reports paint a grim picture. Bucolic bliss may be an exaggerated description of life before the Rising, but it had been at least stable and ordered, and there had been men. The word 'skulk' won an honourable meaning in 1746, describing the actions of the fugitives who hid in the hills to avoid the redcoats.

Charlie Bohally survived. His experience was recorded by Charles Stewart, Tyndrum, in 1878.

> In the thick of the fight at Culloden, his sword broke, when coming across a dead or wounded trooper, he snatched his sword and pistol. These are still in the possession of his descendant C.A. McDiarmid of Rockwood, Killin. He was severely wounded and helped from the field of battle by Alexander Stewart, Cashlie, Glenlyon who fortunately got hold of an old white horse amongst the hills, and having mounted Tearlach Mor thereon brought him home. Parties of soldiers were stationed at Tummelbridge on one, and at

Kynachan on the other side of the wood of Kynachan so that it was with great difficulty food could be brought to them and they were saved from frequent want by the tact of the dairymaid at Kynachan, who drove the milk cows daily through the wood, and in their direction.

Another local hiding place was on the estate of Garth to the south. The Keltney burn there forms a deep gorge below the castle that became the habitation of its laird and other rebels.

The circumstances of the marriage between Charlie and Clementina in 1747 were fictionalised in 1925 by D.K. Broster in the novel *The Flight of the Heron*. Charles Stewart wrote it down 50 years earlier:

> Officers were quartered upon [the widow of] David Stewart of Kynachan, to whose sister, Clementina, Charles was engaged in marriage, and it so happened that one evening as she was in the sitting-room spinning her wheel – the useful accomplishment of Highland ladies in those times – and talking to the officers, a servant entered and said she was wanted in the kitchen. Laying aside her wheel, and apologising for her absence, she followed the servant, and found Charles, who had come in by a back window, accompanied by a clergyman, waiting for her. The marriage ceremony was soon over, and Charles having attained his wish of leaving her, in the event of his death, with the position and benefits accruing to his widow, returned by the back window to his hiding-place, whilst Clementina, with a happy yet anxious heart, returned to her entertainment of the officers.

The clergyman was Duncan Cameron, who had been the Episcopal priest in Fortingall before the Rising. He joined the Cameron regiment as its chaplain, survived Culloden, and came home to find his creed illegal and its meeting houses burnt. After the amnesty he continued in his duties and drowned in April 1760 when fording the Tay on his horse.

In David's will is a list of the contents of the mansion house. It includes 'in the Lower east room a broken chest of drawers at £9. IT: anoyr Scretore quite broken in the Midroom at £1-10. IT: a clock in Mrs Stewart's room vallued at £60. IT: a corner cupboard shattered and brock by soldiers valued at £5 Scots. Two large broken Grantellos at £6.' The damage may have been the result of the August raid on Kynachan by the soldiers, or it may just be the wear and tear expected if troops garrisoned a private house.

I wanted to know how Jean reacted to the disaster of the Rising and its aftermath. She could have taken it in two ways; either she would have been embittered by the waste and repudiated the principle for which her husband died, or she would have held to it in his memory. As far as my novel was concerned, Jean would have to remain faithful to the cause. Again, though, it would have been felicitous to know the reality, especially if it fitted with my requirements, and, of course, it did.

Struan Robertson's estate, most of it in Rannoch, had been forfeited by the government in 1690 after the battle of Killiecrankie and, to his irritation, eventually returned to his sister rather than to himself. He marooned her on an island and took possession of the lands, but he never obtained a legal title to them, not that it really mattered. He had plenty of loyal clansmen who gave short shrift to agents of the law, and he deliberately kept roads in bad condition to dissuade official visitors. After the '45, the property was put in the hands of the Commissioners for Annexed Estates, who brought about considerable improvements and did sterling work to alleviate the abject poverty of the people living there. The factor in charge was an ex-soldier, Ensign James Small, and in 1755 he produced a report for his superiors. The Episcopalian church of the Jacobites had been banned because its ministers were non-jurant – they would not swear an oath of loyalty to King George. Small wrote, 'There are no nonjurant clergymen or meetings of that kind on the estate of Strowan, nor in its neighbourhood, except one Cameron, who stays with Mrs Stewart of Kenichan near Tumble Bridge and preaches in the ordinary way, viz. has only four people in the room but perhaps a numerous audience without.'

Another insight into her attitude comes in 1754. As part of a general settling of various legal bills is an entry reading, 'To her half of £52 19 2d sterling as the expense of carrying on and litigating the process at the instance of Duncan Kennedy and others Tenents of Foss and Kynachan before the Lords of Session ag Hector McNeill of Ardmaynish conform to Mr Carmichael their agent his receipt. £26-09-7d.' McNeill was the officer of the Argyle Militia who led the raid on Kynachan and Foss. It seems that Jean and the tenants of the two estates clubbed together to sue him for the damage caused. The laird of Foss, one of David's officers, had escaped after Culloden and must have been absent skulking. But the 'great many innocent widows' on these lands were not rebels; it should have been the duty of the king's soldiers and the law to protect them. Maddeningly, there are no further details. The legal process is recorded in the list of actions coming before the Court of Session in Edinburgh, but there is nothing of the case itself.

Even today such litigation against a soldier carrying out a policy of 'pacification' directly sanctioned by his commander-in-chief, in this case the Duke of Cumberland, would be extremely difficult to follow through. And nowadays the injured party would be able to parade witnesses and video footage in front of the world's press. In the political atmosphere of the Highlands immediately after the Rising, a successful litigation case would surely have been inconceivable. But the process would have forced McNeill to defend himself, and lawyers cost money. Word of his difficulties would have spread throughout the army, and Kynachan would have been recognised as an estate best left alone.

After that first raid, a soldier was killed in a drunken brawl at Kinloch Rannoch and the Militia went on a rampage down Loch Rannoch and Loch Tummel. On that occasion, according to an anonymous author of a manuscript collected by Revd Alexander Irvine, one of David's officers – the 'coarse satirist' Allan Stewart of Innerhadden – 'saw and witnessed from a High Rock above the Farm of Innerhadden his own House and offices set in Fire All in a Blaze with the Kings Troops as also severall other Gentlemens houses in the Country at the same time that was engaged in the same cause'. But they avoided Kynachan and Foss.

8

The Lady of Kynachan

David was dead but his body had not been identified and the authorities believed him to be still alive and on the run. The hills were full of fugitives being fed by the local people and occasionally being caught or killed by the redcoats. The great men were waiting for news of passages abroad; the prince himself had the bounty of £30,000 on his head. The Disarming Act of 1746 banned the holding of arms and the wearing of tartan and Highland clothes, and controlled education and teaching. In February 1747, Revd Adam Fergusson of Moulin wrote to the duke:

> The Gentlemen of Athol who were in the Rebellion, none of them have gone abroad as yet, as I beleev. Shian [Archibald Menzies of Shian headed his clan's contingent. He is said to have died alongside David in the farmhouse of old Leanach] and Kinnachan have not hitherto cast up in the country, and their friends would have it that they are dead, but I much doubt if it is so.

The treatment being meted out by the army in the Highlands was now well known in the rest of the country, and there was a general revulsion which led to the Act of Indemnity in early 1747. Anyone involved in the Rising was pardoned, with the exception of some 80 or so named individuals. Lord George was on this list, as was Struan Robertson and his neighbour Donald Macdonell of Lochgarry, the commander of Glengarry's regiment. Three other Athollmen were exempted from the act – Blairfetty, Robertson of Faskally and David.

Blairfetty and Faskally were abroad. Faskally, who had to cope with a keen Hanoverian for a wife, had a narrow escape, hiding in an oak tree on his own estate whilst his friend and kinsman, Captain John Menzies of the Black Watch, searched for him. Between the lines of the account one can almost hear Menzies yelling, 'Yoo-hoo! Coming to get you! Ready or not!' as he approached. The venerable chief of the Clan Donnachaidh was burnt out of his house at Mount Alexander, then burnt out of his house at Carie, on each occasion being plucked from danger by his clansmen and hidden deep in the wilderness of the Black Wood of Rannoch, a remnant of the primeval Caledonian forest that once covered Scotland. An act abolishing hereditary jurisdictions was passed in 1749. This, at a stroke, took away the judicial authority of the chiefs and brought law in the Highlands into line with the rest of Scotland. Although he was amply compensated, the duke was deprived of the most important aspect of his power over the people of Atholl.

It seemed puzzling that it took so long for David's death to be established. One would have thought it in Jean's interests to put an end to the uncertainty and to call off the search for him, which must have led to many unwanted visits from the redcoats. It could have been that the confirmation of his death might have triggered the confiscation of Kynachan, but there turned out to be a better reason for keeping the authorities guessing as to his fate.

David's heir was his five-year-old son John. Under the law of the time, if a minor should inherit an estate, the rents would revert to the feudal superior, in this case the duke, until he reached his majority. This would leave Jean without an income. Like every landowning family at the time, solvency was based on a complex series of interlocking bonds and debts that required regular servicing. Deprived of the rents because they were being paid to the duke, she would have become bankrupt and would have lost David's estate and his son's heritage. So long as David was not legally dead, she would retain possession of Kynachan and keep its income. She would have had no illusions that the Duke of Atholl would be delighted to see the back of her. Her husband's actions could well have threatened his position, and David was certainly one of the prime movers in bringing so many Atholl vassals into rebellion.

My novel needed a baddie and he was not hard to find. On this occasion, perhaps, I may have coloured him blacker than he deserved, but his actions could well have been interpreted in the way I chose. David's family had held Kynachan for less than half a century by 1745. Their predecessors were another family of Stewarts, descendants, like half of those in Atholl, of Alexander Stewart, the Wolf of Badenoch, who ran into financial difficulties. In the 18th century, the Kirk of Foss, a few hundred yards from Kynachan House, was a ruin, although its burial ground was in use. Three sections are walled off for the interment of the local lairds. One contains the Stewarts of Foss; another is unidentifiable, but I would like to think it was used by David's family. The other is marked with entwined initials 'AS' and announces that it was reserved for the 'Old Stewarts of Kynachan and Kinnaird'. I suspect that this was placed by Alexander Stewart, who would have been laird of Kynachan had his grandfather not lost the estate. I decided this man held a desire to regain his ancestral property.

Alexander was the Edinburgh 'musick' and dancing master, he whom the Gaels mocked by calling the splay-footed man. In 1733, he bought Easter Kinnaird, just south of the confluence of the rivers Tay and Tummel. In 1736, he asked David to join him to walk the marches of the estate. He said he was on his way to visit David and Sir Robert Menzies when the boundary question arose. So he knew David, and probably quite well. In 1739, David married Jean. Almost exactly a year later, Kinnaird wed Barbara Mercer, her younger sister, in Edinburgh. It almost seemed as if he was stalking David.

Barbara was dead by the early 1740s; so was Abigail, who married James Bissett, the nephew of Thomas Bissett, the duke's right-hand man. In 1741, he and David borrowed £200 from Kinnaird, and, in April 1745, further financial transactions took place. Kinnaird clearly had money, and David was in debt to him. Then came the Rising. Kinnaird stayed in Edinburgh and made quite sure he was seen to be on the government side. His elder brother John was living in Atholl on the estate. John had been a subaltern with the Atholl Brigade in the 1715 rebellion and was captured at Preston and transported to the West Indies for seven years. During the '45 he showed little enthusiasm for the cause. He was made a lieutenant governor in Atholl by the Jacobites but, when the rebels came through Atholl on their way north to Inverness, he deserted and so escaped the final battle.

Kinnaird had been buying up more of David's debts and was both his will's executor and its major creditor. Not all the financial details still exist; liabilities could and did continue through the generations; some money was owed to David's cousins the Smyths and the Threiplands; more was due to tenants, but Kinnaird was owed more than £6,000 Scots. At this point in the novel, I had Kinnaird trying to woo Jean. Kinnaird must have thought her game was nearly up. She had to keep up payment of interest on his debts and that depended on receiving the Kynachan rents. But once David was officially dead and John inherited, those rents would go to the Duke of Atholl. However, if Jean should marry Kinnaird, she would not have to pay the interest; he could take over Kynachan with the duke's blessing and, perhaps, make John his heir.

Jean was the daughter of a lawyer and she had many of that profession amongst her friends. What happened next was certainly an unpleasant surprise for the Duke of Atholl and probably the same for Kinnaird. John was the heir to Kynachan. On 29 April 1752, Jean went to the Sheriff Court in Perth and had a busy morning. Her first action was to declare that David was dead. At that instant John inherited the estate. She immediately sued him for debt. She was owed a small sum for 'alimentation' – housekeeping money – under her marriage contract that had never been paid because there was no need for it to be paid. John's guardians, who included Charlie Bohally, now married to Aunt Clementina and thus the boy's uncle, promptly renounced the entire estate to Jean in settlement of the debt. At a stroke, ownership of Kynachan and responsibility for its obligations passed from David through John to his mother. She was no minor, so she could receive the rents and thus pay interest on the debts. And she could hand on the estate to her son in the fullness of time.

The reaction of her enemies and David's enemies can be imagined. They had been on the point of getting rid of this troublesome family from Atholl, and now Jean had cut through the legal and financial chains that seemed insurmountable and appeared to be the unassailable laird in her own right. There was one hurdle still remaining. The transfer of ownership to Jean required the signature of the Duke of Atholl and he refused to sign.

Jean must have hugged herself with glee. The duke had lost his judicial powers in 1749. Now he was subject to the law like anyone else. His endorsement of her ownership had become no more than a formality, and he was bound to obey the decision of the Sheriff Court. He would not, so Jean put him to the horn. This process originally applied only to debt and failure to keep to one's oath to pay. It was extended to cover any failure to abide by the terms of a decision of a court.

However, it was the form such a process took that must have delighted Jean. The messenger at arms went to the Mercat Cross in the High Street in Edinburgh, tooted his horn three times, bellowed 'Oyez' and announced, 'OUR WILL IS THEREFORE and we Charge you strictly and Command the said James, Duke of Atholl . . . to infeft and lease the said complainer & her foresaids heritably in the said lands . . . within 20 days UNDER PAIN OF REBELLION.' This was repeated twice in Leith. The delicious irony of the widow of the rebel David being able to turn the tables on the Duke of Atholl and threaten him with being declared a rebel would not have escaped Jean. And, of course, the duke signed.

9

Effie's tale

One of the decisions that must be made when writing a historical novel is the moment at which to stop. I ended *The Lady of Kynachan* when Jean became the laird, but of course her story and the story of her family continued. I wanted to know what happened next. As well as simple curiosity, I felt as though I was shaking out the rug of history. Real people with real lives were popping into view – and often dying with lamentable suddenness, lamentably young – and I felt a responsibility to tell their story.

Jean had three children, John, Janet and Euphemia. She employed as grieve, or farm manager, a man nicknamed 'the Baillie' to differentiate him from all the other Alexander Stewarts in the neighbourhood. He had been in the Black Watch and fought at the battle of Fontenoy, retiring from the army in 1748. According to Jean's grandson, Colonel David, he earned his soubriquet because he had acted as baillie to Rob Roy before joining the army and was full of anecdotes about the famous cateran.

Clementina moved across the river to live with her husband Charlie. She died in 1765. Charlie outlived her by more than a decade and remained a close friend and advisor to the Kynachan family all his life. They had a couple of daughters, and both had families. He and William Stewart of Garth, another of David's officers in the '45 and Bohally's cousin, were involved in a strange incident in 1751. Only five years after Culloden, it shows how society in Atholl had healed. Another Alexander Stewart, this one living a few miles west on land that had been confiscated from Struan Robertson, was a notorious thief and all round bad character. He was hanged at Kinloch Rannoch that year, but, in an attempt to save himself, he told Bissett that William of Garth and Charles of Bohally had been handling horses stolen by him. Bissett had passed on this information without seeking corroboration. He had told, among others, the Duke of Atholl and Kinnaird, both of whom would have been delighted to receive such reports about these two. But the story was not true.

The apology Bissett wrote could not have been more abject. 'No circumstance in my life', he wrote, 'hath given me greater concern than my folly and rashness of conduct with respect to you two . . .' It may be that Bissett, who appears to have been an excellent and humane administrator of the duke's lands but not a fighting man, feared a challenge from either of the two men.

John, the heir to Kynachan, died in 1752 aged 12, his mother in 1761, leaving Janet and Euphemia. Janet was then 20, Euphemia, who would have liked people to call her Phemie rather than the universal Effie, a few years younger. In 1765, Janet, known as Jessie, married Robert Stewart of Garth. She could not have wed anyone more appropriate. Robert's father was William, Charlie Bohally's cousin. He had been an officer in the Atholl Brigade under David and fought at Culloden. And the young man, as well as already owning the Garth estate, would soon inherit adjoining Drumcharry and Inchgarth. Add in Kynachan and the couple would own land that marched for eight miles between the river Lyon at Fortingall and the Tummel. Their union should have been the foundation of one of the greatest dynasties in Atholl.

There is little to say about Jessie. She was a model wife to an arrogant and somewhat wayward husband with an explosive temper. She left no letters, a signature that seems laboured and one first-class character reference, delivered by a doddery old friend to her son. 'You have the best qualities of your father mixed with your mother's character, and no woman who ever lived I esteemed and respected so much as I did her.'

Thomas Sinton, author of *Family and Genealogical Sketches*, was descended from the younger sister, Effie. He described her elopement and how she was cheated of her inheritance by the 'astute and grasping' Robert. Up to a point, perhaps. I had the advantage over Sinton in owning Effie's letters.

Robert and Jessie were 25 and 23 when they married. They took up residence at Kynachan. Effie was then 20, living at home with the newly-weds. She seems to have been brighter than her sister. Their lawyer, a close friend of the family and Robert's uncle, would ask that she transcribed letters and checked documents. He was obviously very fond of her, and asked for love to be passed to her in every letter to his nephew. One such ends, somewhat enigmatically, 'Tell Effie from me she is a sad lassie. I'll be evens with her yet. My best wishes to her & Miss Rob, and tell them it is a very stupid sort of an operation for them to be hugging each other & if either of them will change for me that I am their hum. Servt.' Jessie had a son and then a daughter, born in November 1767, who died a month later. An aunt of Robert remarked to him the following February that she 'was heart sorry to hear Mrs Stewart being so long distressed'. It must have been a very gloomy household. In March, Effie tiptoed from the house in the middle of the night. She eloped with Mungo Reid, the unsuitable son of a landless widow, whose husband had been one of David's tenants and officers, killed at Culloden. But Effie left a letter. It is addressed 'Mrs Stewart, Kynachan, to be opened by none Else'. In another hand are the solemn words, 'Left by Euphemia Stewart on her Table when she went off'.

My dear, dear Jessie (if I may call you that),

It is impossible for me to excuse the step I have taken so contrary to you and all the rest of my friends but I do not care for all the world so long as you and good, good Robie stay well, and once before I die are reconciled to me. What shall I say, my only dear sister? Do not grieve for me; it is not worth your while tho' I declare not all the world can give me any satisfaction if you are not well and, Jess (since I tell you all), it was only on your account that this did not happen much sooner.

Tho I had on my knees done you all the service in my power, I could never repay the half of what I owe you and your good husband.

For God's sake take care of your self and be not cast down about me. Wherever I go I'll always hear of you, tho I will not pretend to think that you would write to me or acknowledge me in the least. Yet, though it were two hundred miles, I'd come and see you in dead of night tho you should kick me with your foot. Heaven grant you good health and long life.

Your welfare, Jess, but you will not believe me, is nearer me than my own. For me, I'm like one out of the world and there is no great matter what happens to me but I hope my crime is mostly in the eyes of men and will be forgiven by my God.

I dare say you will not have the patience to read this but I beg you'll give it to no other body. There is nobody to blame in this but myself. I had no confidant, neither had he [Mungo] which made it be so well keepd up.

I hope Robie will not follow the foolish custom of the world in going after me. What pleasure could he have in bringing me back to the country to affront himself and make a show of me? For I would neither eat nor drink a bit after such a thing happening in my own Country.

O my blessing, my blessing be forever with you. O take care of your own health.

I left my Perth accounts for Robie to pay. He'll be angry but I could not help it.

Farewell my dear, dear Jess. Let nobody see this. O forgive me Jessy and God, Robie and you forgive. I care no more. 14th March 1768.

If that was Effie's mood as she left the house the actual marriage can hardly have been a cheerful affair. According to Sinton, they 'met by a large tree close to the house, and after going through the form of marriage in the presence of witnesses – one being the old nurse of the bride – they eloped to Edinburgh where they were regularly married'. Soon a new song was heard in Highland Perthshire, the gist of which ran 'Good luck to Mungo Reid who stole the heiress of Kynachan'. Effie had been left £500 by her mother. Robert's lawyer uncle in the city, known universally as Robbie Uncle, made sure that money was made available to the couple, and Mungo set himself up as a merchant, but life was not sweet. Effie wrote to her brother-in-law a couple of months later:

> Edinburgh. May 16th 1768. My dear Robie, I received yours of the 23rd April by your uncle and would have answered it before now had I either the courage to sit down or words to express my thoughts. You need an eye to look into my heart there to see the greatest distress that ever lodged in a human breast tortured with reflections of my past conduct. I may now wish with poor Bonskeid to be rid of memory and reflection. [The laird of Bonskeid was killed in Pitlochry in 1765. The incident is referred to later on.] I'm sure my life is much more unhappy than his was tho I hope in God my crime is not so great.
>
> O, may I be happy in the next world for I find my time in this to be a scene of misery. O, Robie what shall I say? No words can express my situation. O, that I had dropped down dead that fatal night that I left your house and put an end to my own happiness. There is nothing in this world but crosses and misfortune and when it pleases God to keep us from any, we wilfully draw them on ourselves.
>
> I have one favour to ask of you, not to believe or hearken to any malicious thing said of me, for your uncle has told me that there is a great deal said which I'm certain is false. I hear Charles at the bridge is very busy saying a great many things of me to the country people but you may give him my compliments and tell him that ungratefulness is worse than witchcraft and I'm sure he is guilty of it when he would say anything of me.
>
> Betty Dewar, her sister and brother-in-law, are very base telling you a great many lies. Tho I be at a distance I'll maybe be revenged on them yet before they leave this world. They pretend they knew of it before. If they did, why did they not tell you of it then which would be showing their regard for the f-family (as they say) much more than speaking so much of it now when it will not mend? It is not their regard for either you or me but their own private reasons that makes them pay you and Jess so many visits on this occasion. But I, like all other criminals, hold my head low and my hand on my mouth. Nobody need reproach me, Robie. I have enough in my own breast. O Robie. Forgive blunders and nonsense for I do not know what I say. My mind is so full of confusion that I'm many time afeared my reason may leave me altogether. Farewell. If you love me, pray for my having a short life. That God may prosper you and grant you a long and happy life is the sincere prayer of the most miserable of her sex. Effie Stewart

Mungo failed as a merchant but the pair were reconciled with Robert and Jessie, and came home. Mungo took one of the little estate farms,

Pitkerril, high on the side of the mountain. Effie's legacy ensured the farm could be stocked, and she seems to have bought a life tenancy. One wishes for a happy ending, but it was not to be.

Effie had eight children; only two survived to adulthood. This was not particularly exceptional for the times, but one incident was and it struck horror throughout the Highlands. Behind Schiehallion lay the shielings where the people of the estates would take their livestock in summer to graze the sweet mountain pastures and make cheese and butter from the milk. At the end of the season in 1795, Effie took her three youngest children up for a holiday. Everyone else had returned to the villages lower in the strath, so they had the burn and the beautiful Glen Mor to themselves.

Hugh was eight and showed a precocious talent on the violin; Catherine was seven and Clementina six. Mrs Grant, wife of the minister of Laggan, wrote what happened next in her book *Letters from the Mountains*, which was published in 1807.

> The children caught a pestilential fever some poor neighbour had brought up into the glen, and, being very remote from all assistance, and the convenience and attendance that sickness requires, the death of all the children was the consequence at a very early period of the disease. The bard who soothed the sorrows of the parents appears to me to possess native genius. Let him speak for himself.

O children belov'd
Where are you removed?
Have you left us so early.
Who cherished so dearly,
For the dark, silent chambers of death.
The fair sun returning,
Shall light the new morning,
Fresh grass on the mountains,
Fresh flow'rs by the fountains,
Shall wake with the Spring's gentle breath.

But no morning new breaking,
My children shall waken,
'Tis hopeless to number
The days of their slumber,
The long sleep that awakens no more!
Shall the cold earth's dark bosom
Still hide each fair blossom?
Have angels not borne them
Where bright rays adorn them,
Where on wings of new rapture they soar?

On my fancy thus beaming,
My eyes ever streaming,
My breast ever heaving,
Their image relieving,
Shall soothe into pensive repose:
In beauty transcendent
In brightness resplendent
I shall meet them when life has no close.

Effie and Mungo stayed on at Pitkerril for the rest of their lives. He died
in 1825, and Effie a year later, aged 82. They were married for 57 years. They
survived to see one grandson became minister of the parish, a second a
prominent Edinburgh lawyer. A third, David Campbell, became factor
for the Castle Menzies estate. He was killed when he lost control of his
horse and both tumbled off the bridge that carried Wade's road across the
Keltney burn at the bottom of the Pass of Glen Goulandie. Local opinion
held that he brought this fate on his own head when he appropriated two
of the stone crosses marking the bounds of the sanctuary of the ancient
abbey of Dull to use as gateposts.

Robert and Janet lost more than one child whilst they lived at Kynachan.
Colonel David records a story involving one of their sons:

> Late in an autumnal evening in the year 1773, the son of a neighbouring
> gentleman came to my father's house. He and my mother were from home,
> but several friends were in the house. The young gentleman spoke little,
> and seemed absorbed in deep thought. Soon after he arrived he inquired
> for a boy of the family, then about three years of age. When shown into the
> nursery, the nurse was trying on a pair of new shoes, and complaining that
> they did not fit. 'They will fit him before he will have occasion for them,'
> said the young gentleman. This called forth the chidings of the nurse for
> predicting evil to the child, who was stout and healthy. When he returned
> to the party he had left in the sitting-room, who had heard his observations
> on the shoes, they cautioned him to take care that the nurse did not derange
> his new talent of the second sight, with some ironical congratulations on
> his pretended acquirement. This brought on an explanation, when he told
> them, that, as he approached the end of a wooden bridge thrown across a
> stream at a short distance from the house, be was astonished to see a crowd
> of people passing the bridge. Coming nearer, he observed a person carrying
> a small coffin, followed by about twenty gentlemen, all of his acquaintance
> his own father and mine being of the number, with a concourse of the
> country people. He did not attempt to join, but saw them turn off to the
> right in the direction of the church-yard, which they entered. He then
> proceeded on his intended visit, much impressed from what he had seen
> with a feeling of awe, and believing it to have been a representation of the

death and funeral of a child of the family. In this apprehension he was the more confirmed, as he knew my father was at Blair Athole, and that he had left his own father at home an hour before. The whole received perfect confirmation in his mind by the sudden death of the boy the following night, and the consequent funeral, which was exactly similar to that before represented to his imagination.

The story of the Stewarts of Kynachan really ends here, for Robert and Janet moved house across the pass of Glen Goulandie to Fortingall when Robert's uncle, the laird of Drumcharry, died in 1776; Robert was his heir. Drumcharry was the richer estate and also had a mansion house, very similar to that on Kynachan. But, in 1772, Kynachan enjoyed a small flurry of national importance. The astronomer royal, Nevil Maskelyne, turned up. He gave a gold snuff box to Janet, engraved with a message which sums up the visit and its purpose: 'In remembrance of the permission given by Mrs Stewart to erect tents on Schiehallion when making experiments on the density of the earth and for her hospitality in entertaining him and his friend Mr. Woodford from Satdy to Monday each week during his stay in the Highlands.'

10

Drumcharry

About five per cent of the contents of the archive was directly applicable to Kynachan. The papers of the Garth and Drumcharry branch of Stewarts made up perhaps a third of the rest, and were the oldest and least legible. Fortunately, the most difficult-to-read documents were all concerned with money, and fully understanding them was not critical for my purposes. The local schoolmaster and historian Duncan Campbell in his *Book of Garth and Fortingall* (1888), describes the incoming Stewarts to Atholl thus:

> The revenue and estates of the earl of Atholl were not very great, but he had a great many allies, and a pretty numerous company of gentlemen of his own surname to surround his mote hill and fight under his own banner. Some of these Stewarts were cadets of his own house; many were collaterals that had been called in from Lorne. A few were descended from the Walter of Atholl line, and more than a few from the Wolf of Badenoch. To these were added Stewarts who boasted ancient or illegitimate descent from kings and princes who, when hunting the deer, wooed Highland maids in sequestered glens.

The Kynachan Stewarts descended from a natural son of James II and received a charter of Stix, southwest of Taymouth Castle, in 1486. The name Stix comes from *stucis*, stones, referring to the spectacular stone circle of Croft Moraig on the estate. The Drumcharry Stewarts traced their descent back to the lawless and terrible Alexander Stewart, Earl of Buchan and Wolf of Badenoch, son of King Robert II, who was baillie of Atholl in 1402. His son James settled at Garth Castle which controlled the hill pass, Glen Goulandie, between the straths of the Tay and Tummel. Colonel David Stewart organised a census of all the Stewarts in Atholl in 1817, and, with the Gaelic oral tradition and its preoccupation with genealogy still in full blossom, he found 4,000 people who were descended from the Wolf.

Today, one of the props of Scottish tourism comes from descendants of emigrants returning to research their family origins. For the majority, the paper trail ends by the middle of the 18th century. However, every Gael left with the knowledge of generations of forebears in his or her head. This was vital, since kinship knitted the culture together and defined his or her place within it. Ask in Gaelic from where someone comes, and the precise meaning is an enquiry about family origins as much as geography. But in the new countries across the ocean, such links were irrelevant and largely forgotten within a generation. This makes Colonel David's census, along with another he organised for the Stewarts of Balquhidder, unique resources for family historians. Perhaps, given those 4,000 descendants 200 years ago, the Wolf now has some 20,000 successors. My own solitary musings at Garth Castle about my lupine ancestor could instead have been a mass experience filling a football stadium – and that would be the progeny of only one of the Wolf's many cubs.

Fear Ghart, Gentleman of Garth – which was Robert's Gaelic sobriquet – was head of the Drumcharry line, an offshoot of the lairds of Duntanlich on Tummelside. In 1609, the family received a charter to their lands from Thomas Stewart of Grantully. These stretched east from the market place at Fortingall opposite Drummond Hill and curved round the brae face that overlooks the Appin of Dull and Strathtay. The ploughable land amounted to little more than 300 acres. The family burial ground was within the wall which now surrounds the ancient yew tree in the churchyard.

Until the beginning of the 18th century, the lairds are believed to have lived in the little, one-time Menzies castle of Comrie on the river Lyon just upstream from its confluence with the Tay. Then William Stewart chose the site at Drumcharry to build a new mansion house, very similar to what was being built at Kynachan at much the same time. This was to remain the family seat for the next century. William's eldest son Patrick inherited the estate.

From the Duke of Atholl, the second son, Robert, obtained a lease, later converted to a charter, on the smaller estate of Garth whose lands lay adjacent to Drumcharry and ran by the gorge of the Keltney burn up the pass of Glen Goulandie. On its northern boundary sat the castle of Garth which had been torched by Cromwell's soldiers in 1654. This was restored in the 1960s.

In the next generation, the second son of Drumcharry obtained a third estate of Inchgarth, which lay to the north of the castle. Now three closely related Stewart lairds held land from Fortingall, round the corner above Coshieville, and north, almost to the watershed between straths Tay and Tummel. In the event of the failure of a male heir, each agreed to bequeath his estate to his kinsman's son in order to prevent the land leaving the family through the marriage of a daughter.

Down the centuries these lairds had married other Stewarts, Flemings, Menzieses, and Robertsons, thus knitting themselves into the kinship network of the landowning families in Atholl. Younger sons and daughters often married tenants on their fathers' estates, and, by Fear Ghart's time, many of the 600-odd folk on his lands could claim to be his kin, and thus descendant of kings.

Although of royal descent, albeit from the wrong side of the blanket, Fear Ghart's forebears were an uncouth bunch compared to the Kynachan Stewarts. Patrick of Drumcharry was famous for his consumption of whisky. His grandfather in Cromwell's time preferred beer, and a song was written about his awesome capacity – 'He so loved it that he would drink the whole brew without lifting his head.' Other members of the family were in trouble with the law for riot, for stealing a horse from the minister of Elie, for stabbing a Menzies.

The minister of Fortingall in 1699 describes William of Drumcharry, by then blind, and his family creating a disturbance in the kirk during service: 'His wife railed all ye tyme I was saying the blessing. They made such a noise & were in such a fury that I was necessitat to flie for it . . . & Drumcharie's second son [Robert, later of Garth], who was cited to make penance yat day for fornication, lifted up his fist & cryed saying, "Man, tho ye make your escape at this time I'lle make yow smart for it".' A perennial problem for all three estates was the lack of shieling ground where tenants could take their livestock in summer to graze. Rights on the hills were also needed for peat. The adjoining Campbells of Glenlyon whose lands met Drumcharry at Fortingall disputed the mountain pastures used by the tenants. This unfortunate family had lost the major part of their holdings in Glen Lyon thanks to the dissipation and incompetence of Robert Campbell, commander of the company of the Argyll Regiment which perpetrated the Massacre of Glencoe in 1692. He was a cousin of Patrick of Ballechin – Patrick of the Battles. As Campbells, this family looked to the Earl of Breadalbane, with his seat at the east end of Loch Tay, just over Drummond Hill from Fortingall, as their clan chief, but they were vassals of the Duke of Atholl, and they joined the Atholl Brigade in the 18th century Risings. The tenants of the rival estates clashed periodically at the shielings, and for the best part of a century their lairds clashed in the courts. The cost of these actions was a debilitating drain on the Stewart holdings.

In the 1715 Rising, Robert of Garth was captured at Preston and was transported as an indentured labourer to Virginia for seven years. At the time of the '45, Drumcharry was possessed by the elderly, whisky-drinking William Stewart, whose son had no male heir; Inchgarth was held by cousin Charles; Garth by another cousin, Black William, who married Drumcharry's daughter. Drumcharry supported the government; Garth led his tenants to fight for Prince Charles and survived. Inchgarth's only son led his people in the charge of the Atholl Brigade at Culloden and was killed. This left Black William's eldest son, Robert, heir to the three estates.

This Robert, Fear Ghart, inherited Garth in 1760 at the age of 16. His most influential guardian was the Edinburgh lawyer Robbie Uncle, who also earned the nickname The Highland Lairds' Lawyer. A generation earlier, a laird would have received some kind of military training. Now disputes were settled in the courts rather than the battlefield, and Robbie Uncle arranged for his nephew to go to university and then be apprenticed to a legal office in Dunkeld.* He also engineered the marriage to Janet of Kynachan.

Fear Ghart chose to spend his life upon his estates in the style of an old-fashioned Highland chieftain, the patriarch of his people, patron of their traditions and provider of free legal advice to the whole country. As soon as the proscriptions against wearing Highland garb were repealed, he would always wear a kilt when at home. On his wall he placed a portrait of Prince Charles. He housed a couple of simpleton orphans, a brother and sister, in his kitchen. The boy grew up to be known, even as far afield as Edinburgh, as Garth's Fool.

Duncan Campbell relates an anecdote concerning these two from 1804.

> They, one night, rushed into the kitchen of Drumcharry House, shouting, with joy, the unexpected news that Robbie Uncle was coming up the road in his carriage, and would be immediately at the door, for they saw him and passed him in the avenue, and his horses drove up the hill very slow, and they hailed him and saw him, but he did not speak to them. So there was commotion through the house, and young and old rushed to the door to welcome the wished-for guest, but no Robbie Uncle was there, and no carriage and no horses. Duncan and Margaret were not given to lying, but they were rated for telling a falsehood on that occasion. In the course of a few days – so runs this well vouched-for story – a letter came to Fear Ghart announcing the sudden death of his uncle in Edinburgh, on the very night, and nearly at the same moment, at which the fool and his sister had seen his ghost or wraith.

Behind his house, which overlooked the beautiful Vale of Fortingall, Robert supported a piping school whose graduates joined the Highland regiments. He encouraged musicians and Gaelic bards, one of whom left

---

*See Appendix 2.

a glowing panegyric – literally singing for his supper amid the candles and
peat smoke at Drumcharry – of the laird's virtues:

> At balls the best dancer,
> Though skilled in knowledge and lear.
> The ardent moor-hunter,
> Whom hounds and glad gillies surround,
> In whose halls wine, venison, salmon,
> For comers abound.
> Hospitality's prince,
> To guests and relatives kind,
> Good chieftain of tenants,
> Who frowns not when rent is behind.

A Highland chief offered hospitality to all who called, even if he was not at
home; a decade after Fear Ghart's death, the unpretentious house still held
71 chairs – 20 of which, along with two sofas, were in the drawing room.

His son, Colonel David, vividly described the richness of the rewards
to such benevolent autocrats as his father:

> To those who live in the busy world, and are hurried round by its agitations,
> it is difficult to form an idea of the means by which time may be filled up
> and interest excited in families who, through choice or necessity, dwell
> among their own people. The secret lies in the excitement of strong
> attachment. To be in the centre of a social circle where one is beloved and
> useful, to be able to mould the characters and direct the passion by which
> one is surrounded, creates, in those whom the world has not hardened, a
> powerful interest in the most minute circumstances which gives pleasure or
> pain to any individual in that circle where so much affection and good will
> are concentrated. The mind is stimulated by stronger excitements and a
> greater variety of enjoyments than matters of even the highest importance
> can produce in those who are rendered callous by living amongst the selfish
> and the frivolous. It is not the importance of the objects but the value
> at which they are estimated that renders their moral interest permanent
> and salutary.

However, Fear Ghart had another side to his nature. David is again the
informant:

> My father was fierce and violent in his temper – his passions often
> overturned his reason, and he broke loose in his language – he was fierce in
> his temper (from want of proper checks, not being in a society who would
> not bear his violence) – open to flattery – if he was called a kind master to
> tenants and saw his table full, and he was called hospitable, he looked not
> to the consequences for his family.

And they suffered. David would make his way in the army with no financial help from home. His mother was disregarded, and the future of the family was put in jeopardy by Fear Ghart's extravagance and incompetence.

Robbie Uncle had occasion to rebuke his nephew in 1766 when he broke the law by selling an impecunious tenant's livestock. In another questionable example of Fear Ghart's practice, he was sued by other tenants when he broke their lease by stripping their land of all crops just before they moved in. As well as a magistrate and a commissary at the church court at Dunkeld, for a time he was a factor to the 4th Duke of Atholl, but he was sacked.

'I don't intend to say but that you mean well,' wrote His Grace in 1795, 'but I mean to say you have not got that capacity for energy and exertion which is requisite in a person who has the charge of an estate such as mine. I do not want to part with you in anger; on the contrary, I am ready to do anything which can be reasonably asked for yourself and family.'

However, the dismissal may have resulted from disagreements over policy as much as incompetence. The duke, who would live until 1830, complained, 'In Dividing of Farms, in letting of Farms, in maintaining among the Tennantry a satisfaction in these farms, in making stated and regular accounts, I have received no satisfaction from you.' Fear Ghart prided himself in being a friend to the country people; he would be most unwilling to take measures that would oust any of the existing tenants.

When Uncle Inchgarth died in 1765 he had indeed bequeathed his estate to Robert as the agreement between the cousins had stipulated, but his will left the income from rents to his own daughter Ann for her lifetime. Fear Ghart went to law and produced in evidence a dubious document which said that the old man had changed his mind, but Ann had financial support from the Campbells of Glenlyon, who saw a chance to damage their rivals. With his cousin enjoying the fruits of the estate, Fear Ghart chased the case through the courts, losing his final appeal in the House of Lords in 1784, and Ann lived on another dozen years before he gained possession. The consequence of these actions was debts that would later endanger the family's hold on the estates.

11

Spurious offspring

Janet, the heiress of Kynachan, died in 1789. By then she and Robert had five surviving children. Their eldest was William, born 1766, who appears to have been inadequate in some way. He had some legal training, took a minor role in local affairs and seems to have lived at Drumcharry all his life. His brother David states in a letter that his elder sibling would never marry, but does not give a reason. However, if unadventurous, he was not sexually inactive. Mary McGregor in one of the Drumcharry townships bore him a daughter in 1795. His father sired an illegitimate son, by an Elizabeth McGregor in the same place, Tynadalloch, in 1789.

In the words of Colonel David, the birth of this child of his father took place 'when one of the best, most virtuous and affectionate of wives was on her death bed. It was the stain of a deep dye on my father's character and it being his failure it ought to be kept in the background and not ostentatiously brought forward and shocking the feelings of those who knew the circumstance and the mother's character.'

Fear Ghart wrote a few lines of verse, which give an idea of how he regarded his wife – and sexual morality. If he showed it to her, as he surely would have, it would have given her mixed comfort.

How bless'd have my Days been, what good have I known
Since wedlock's soft bondage made Jessie my own.
How Joyfull my heart is, how easy my Chain
Since freedom seems tasteless and roving a pain.

To try her sweet temper how oft have I been
And revelled all day with the nymphs on the green.
Though painfull my absence my Doubts she beguiles
And meets me at night with Complyence and smiles.

What though in her cheeks the rose loses its hue
Her wit and good humour blooms all the year through.
And time as it flys gives increase to the truth
And adds to her mind what is stol'n from her youth.

All you that do court with false words to ensnare
And strive to delude the too credulous fair
In search of true pleasure how vainly you roam
To fix it for life you must find it at home.

In Scotland at this time, sexual morality was not considered particularly important. The extended family tree of the Stewarts of Garth and Drumcharry is littered with illegitimate children. Fear Ghart's natural son became a soldier and married the daughter of a baronet. Simple William had a daughter; Colonel David himself sired a couple of children. Jessie, his sister, raised his son Neil, who, to the despair of his respectable relations, spurned the opportunities offered to him and ended up a gentleman's servant. Of course, amongst the landowning classes, men were the ones who were commonly involved in illicit dalliances, but not exclusively. In 1821 David wrote, 'When I looked to my grandaunts, aunt, and sister I began to fear that elopements were to be hereditary in the family.'

That seems to have been the difference. Fallen men scarcely stumbled. For an earlier generation such sinners would face the cutty stool, on which they would sit to be shamed in the sight of the congregation. Now, however, fire and brimstone within the Presbyterian Church were largely on hold until the Disruption of 1843. A fallen woman, at least the daughter of a landowner, had to marry the man who tripped her. Amongst the humble folk of the Highlands, a child here or there was unremarkable, although a useful indication of fertility. It only attracted attention and disapproval if an attempt was made to elevate such children into equality with legitimate progeny. Colonel David wrote to Jessie in 1821 when she asked if he minded her taking their illegitimate half-brother on holiday with her own family. He replied thus:

> While every justice ought to be done to the young man so far as education and placing him in a suitable station it is a scandal to common decency to introduce him as one of the family – the world feels thus. You would be astonished were I to reflect the many remonstrances I get on the subject and Clementina [David's eldest sister] did him incomparable injury in forcing him forward and calling him her brother. People's feelings were shocked and while they rejected him and would not pay him attention this would not have been so strongly marked had different plans been followed. When the Duke of Gordon used all his influence to introduce his spurious family into Society – settled £10,000 on each of them – gave favours and provided appointments to those who countenanced them – but all in vain – not one respectable person invited them to their houses – no person came to Gordon Castle when they were there – they were refused admittance to public balls and such meetings – all this from principles of

respect for decency of manners and when the Duke of Gordon had totally failed – it would have been better for the young man himself if my father had not introduced him into his family and while my mother's children ought to have shown him the proper friendship and support for I have always exerted myself to promote his welfare.

Fear Ghart was described as 'stout and hearty' in 1816, but soon afterwards he had a stroke and William took over management of the estates. He had already made his faint mark on history. He had taken charge of the Fortingall Parish Registers in 1798 to preserve them from rioters intent on preventing their use in a ballot, which was believed to be imminent, to select recruits for the Militia to preserve the country from an invasion by Napoleon. An old woman threw her plaid over his head and snatched the registers, which were later recovered from a ditch and still show signs of water damage.

After William, Clementina was next in age, then David, born in 1772. He was followed by Janet, or Jessie, who was born in 1776, and John, born in 1777.

David was the great hope of the family. The army and, to a lesser extent, the navy were conventional careers for younger sons of the gentry. Only a couple of generations earlier such men had led their father's tenants in clan armies and now they were recruited en masse into the Highland Regiments to fight the French. Two of Fear Ghart's brothers had already done the same, one in the Black Watch and the other in Montgomery's Highlanders, so David became a soldier.

From his beginnings as a very small, very young, short-sighted ensign, he progressed to become a much loved and much battered major-general and governor of St Lucia. He was truly heroic, taking important roles in battles of the early French Wars, and may well have been instrumental in turning defeat into victory in that first British success on continental Europe, the battle of Maida in 1806, when he is said to have shot his commanding officer, taken over command of his regiment and turned its retreat into an attack. I have already written a dedicated biography of him, *The First Highlander* (Tuckwell Press, 1999), so he requires little further exposition, but he wrote his own memorandum of service* in 1823, in which he summarises his military career – and his own merits.

Brave soldiers were ten a penny at the time. David's fame and his entry in the *Dictionary of National Biography* do not stem from his military career but from the book he wrote after the war ended. In his *Sketches of the Highlanders*, he not only produced a detailed history of the Highland

---

* See Appendix 3.

Regiments, but also an excellent study of the old Highland way of life. This catapulted him to national prominence at a time when Walter Scott was thrilling the nation with best-selling Highland romances. David was Scott's number two in organising the King's visit to Edinburgh in 1822 and became the principal authority on all matters Highland.

As an obituarist put it, he 'was a man covered in golden opinions', for he was immensely popular amongst all classes of society. His soldiers loved him; the rising middle class admired him, and the ordinary people knew him as a champion of their interests in vociferously opposing the Clearances, particularly those in Sutherland.

When he came home in 1820, he found disaster. His father was senile and dying; he and William had failed utterly in the task of running the estates. They kept virtually no records. They had not bothered to collect rents or pay bills or interest for the best part of 20 years, and they tried to conceal the shambles. As David wrote, 'my poor brother has one talent of which he has made too much use – that is the art of concealing his mismanagement'. It took David more than a year to discover that the debts mounted to some £40,000, well above the value of the land. In his book he had written off the horror and shame with which Highlanders regarded bankruptcy. His family faced disgrace.

William was packed off to a remote sheep farm run by a cousin near Glen Coe, where he soon died, and David took over the management, intending to introduce improvements and pay off the debts. He was also determined to use his extensive network of contacts to get himself a well-paid position, preferably in the West Indies where he had wide experience, to help the family finances. The duke was the natural patron for everyone in Atholl, and David asked him to exert his influence, but nothing resulted. The trouble was that he had attacked the duke for the clearances that had taken place in Atholl. So, although ostensibly friendly to David, the duke was actually sabotaging his attempts to obtain a job. David was not unaware of this. 'I believe there are some who would not be sorry though they saw my brothers and myself sink under the difficulties which our father left us,' he wrote, but he curbed his frustration and turned himself into the most efficient farmer in the neighbourhood.

'Col. David Stewart called here yesterday on his way from Athole House,' wrote Mrs Robertson of Kindrochit to her husband in 1821. 'He has become the most successful farmer in all these Countrys, Miss Flemming not excepted, for even this season while other people's crops are scarcely worth cutting his is as heavy as can grow. This is no rhodomontade for the Crop has been sold at an enormous price.' She reported his troubles in a letter two years later. 'Col. David was expected in Edinburgh this week, but I have not been able to learn whether he came or not, his acquaintances say he has been unsuccessful in his suit with Miss Bruce, and also in his application for the Governorship of some of the West India Islands, which Doctor Stewart, Bonskeid told us he was making all the Interest he could find.'

As far as marriage was concerned, David made his position clear to his brother-in-law.

> Why don't you marry and preserve the family? – From Inver to Lochlyon – from Logieraite to Dunan, or Dalnacardoch, if I step into a house whether gentry or tenantry, it is the same – if I speak to an acquaintance on the road, who is intimate with the family, nine times out of ten – in short high and low it is the same cry – your elder brother will never marry – the younger is in the W Indies, why don't you marry and prevent the entrance of strangers in to a family which the whole country is anxious to preserve? – thus I am constantly teased – my only answer is silence as I can't afford to marry.

12

Enter the Irvines

The two girls in Fear Ghart's family need to be introduced. Clementina was a life-long spinster who never left home. She was sweet-natured, of a nervous temperament and something of a hypochondriac. She devoted herself to looking after her family and took a great interest in the well-being of the tenants and their children on her father's estate. When she died in 1829, David wrote of her, 'Of the tenderest and most humane disposition, with a heart that would not injure a fly – always ready to do good – ever anxious to assist the sick and the distressed, and to promote the comfort and happiness of all around – all that came within her circle'. It appears that nearly a dozen of Fear Ghart's tenants named daughters after her.

She did have one recorded suitor who is mentioned in a letter from Mrs Robertson to her future husband in 1811:

> I do very well remember having heard of your predictions regarding one of the fair inhabitants of Drumachary, I believe the Lady is in no danger of being made miserable by such a companion, he has left Drumachary about a month ago and left it I understand in disgrace. After giving too many proofs of incorrigibleness, he chose to decamp without leave aledging that he saw very well Garth was getting tired of him, he afterwards went to Perth, and is now in his father's house altho rather incognito I blieve, being concealed by one half of the family in one of the attics.

Whoever this rackety fellow may have been, he obviously fell foul of Fear Ghart – and so did Jessie, the youngest of the family and David's favourite sibling.

Joseph Mitchell, superintendent of the parliamentary roads, used to stay at Drumcharry when he was working in the district. He produced a reminiscence of his life, in which he wrote:

> The Highlands of Perthshire presented at this time, 1825–8, a picture of great rural happiness . . . almost all the lairds lived on their properties, engaged in improvements, took an interest in their tenants, and promoted by their influence the advancement of clever lads who were born on their estates . . .

To me, an outsider, looking back, this district at that time exhibited a very happy state of society. Each class was contented in its own sphere, and, as far as I could tell, there were few jealousies. The whole people were comfortable, and lived and moved among each other in a genial and kindly atmosphere.

One such 'clever lad' was a life-long friend and confidant of the colonel. He also kept the letters he received from David, which give a clear picture of his concerns about his family and the estates. Alexander Irvine was the son of James Irvine, tenant of the tiny holding of Ringam, high on the hills above Glen Goulandie on the Garth Estate just above the castle. The origins of these Irvines are obscure, but seem to have moved into Strathtay in the early 18th century as tenant farmers at Tulliepowrie and then at Cluny a couple of miles east of Weem.

The first to appear on Garth was James Irvine. He married Janet Menzies. She was the daughter of a prosperous farmer in Weem who was related to Sir Robert Menzies and her aunt married Black William of Garth. This connection seems to have allowed James, a younger son, to approach his father-in-law, one of the curators or guardians of the young Fear Ghart when the latter inherited Garth at the age of 16, and ask for a farm. He is first shown as a tenant on Inchgarth when he married in 1761. Alexander, the youngest of six children, was born in 1773.

The sons of lairds and tenants alike went to school in Fortingall, and Alexander was bright enough for Fear Ghart to take him under his wing and give him a full education. In Scotland, an education has always been important and allowed its possessor a route towards social advancement. Alexander studied theology at St Andrews, was ordained and became a missionary on Mull in 1796, and, in 1799, he took the same position at Rannoch. This had traditionally been bandit country, but the estate of Struan was annexed after the '45, and the Commissioners for Annexed Estates had brought about great social improvements. There were still men around who had fought for Prince Charles, but their sons were now fully integrated into the fabric of the nation. In the wars against Napoleon no less than 29 officers of the British Army, including two full generals, were born on the shores of Loch Rannoch. The estate had been returned in 1784 to the old chief's successors, and Alexander made friends with the pious old Colonel Robertson of Struan, a veteran of continental wars.

Alexander also frequently went over the hill back to Fortingall to the little farm of his parents, round which he had three brothers scratching away at the poor soil. He would also visit Drumcharry, where he was friend and contemporary of the laird's children. David was already a hero by the end of the century, but his propensity for collecting musket balls and sword slashes meant that sick-leave back home took many months out of his military career. His taste for antiquarianism and for the music and poetry of the Gaels, which would lead to his book a couple of decades later, was already developed, and he found a kindred spirit in the young minister. In fact, Alexander at this stage appeared to be predominant in their intellectual partnership.

In 1802 Alexander wrote a book, *An Inquiry into the causes and effects of Emigration from the Highlands and Western Islands of Scotland, with Observations for the Means to be Employed for Preventing it.* Still quoted today, it was based upon his observations on Mull and in Rannoch, on his own knowledge of the folk who were emigrating and, as he acknowledged in his preface, on advice from 'those whose judgment I esteemed better than my own'. His use of vivid footnotes, based on his own experience, and the mildly radical views expressed are a precursor of the much more substantial work produced by David a couple of decades later. Like David, Alexander uses Colonel Robertson of Struan and the Garth and Drumcharry estates to illustrate points. In fact, it seems inconceivable that David was not fully conversant with the work and had input into both its content and style. He was at Drumcharry recuperating from wounds received at the battle of Alexandria in the year leading up to the book's publication.

About this time, Alexander also wrote a flowery account, unpublished: *The Antiquities of Fortingall,* which tried to prove that the medieval homestead southwest of the village was a Roman camp. He also decided that a medieval cooking pot found in the banks of a burn was Roman. He would have no doubt cleared his flattering description of Drumcharry and its policies with the laird.

From Duneaves the eye soon turns to Drumchary (the seat of Mr Stewart of Garth) when the beauties of Fortingall are seen to great advantage. It is adorned by lofty firs covering the ruin of an old circular fort or castle already mentioned and by rows of planes and elms of a most majestic height. When the tempest rages, the noise of these trees is terrible beyond description, and rendered more so by the screams of the owl. Nature has beautifully varied Drumchary and art has not been idle. The lawns are edged with rows of laburnum, willow, ash and other trees in every variety. The banks varied with birch, fir and other forest trees, the streamlets concealed by their shade and the corn fields drawn to the scene, the ground divided, and the cattle grazing to favour the intentions of nature – the overhanging cliffs interspersed with trees, herbs, flowers, and the retiring heath rising on the mountains capped by the clouds presents a group of objects equally remote from the meanness and uniformity where the imagination is allowed to range and colours are admirably controlled, shade lengthening into shade and the sunbeam tingeing the groves, dimpling in the streams, blazing in the cascades, or dazzling in the spangled rocks.

After a visit to Drumcharry in March 1804, Alexander left his watch behind. Jessie, David's 29-year-old youngest sister, sent it after him to Rannoch with a tender note, signing off with, 'I shall allways I trust be able to subscribe myself My Dearest friend your faithful and affectionate, Janet Stewart'. Thanks to the influence of Fear Ghart, Alexander was given his first parish in February 1805 when he was appointed minister of Fortingall. But a romantic friendship had developed between Jessie and Alexander. In what must have been an appalling interview, he asked Fear Ghart for her hand in marriage. It was contemptuously rejected, so, in April that year, he and Jessie married without her father's permission in his kirk at Fortingall.

In what seems otherwise to have been a lifetime without risk or blemish to his reputation and keen cultivation of relationships with the influential, this was remarkable. Duncan Campbell, the 19th-century historian of Fortingall, wrote, 'Caste feelings refused sanction to the marriage. The son of a small tenant, however superior in natural talents and scholarship, was not thought a fit mate for the bonnie daughter of the laird. So, as the straightforward application for her hand was refused, the lovers made an elopement marriage.' It has to be said that Campbell was stretching the truth to call Jessie 'bonnie'. Members of her family were notoriously uncomely.

More detail of the event was supplied by David in a letter to Alexander some 15 years later.

> You mention in your letter that no past circumstances even the most frowning ever diminished your affection etc. etc. – In many letters you have expressed such sentiments – I have never noticed them in return as I did not, nor do not now properly comprehend to what they allude, unless it is my father's opposition to your marriage, and his violence after it took place.
>
> On the subject of your marriage and the manner of it, there is only one universal opinion, no persons have ever spoken or even hinted to me on the subject, but with an expression of regret and surprise – I strongly felt the same myself – but whatever my feelings were when I first heard (and I never had the least hint previously as I always discouraged tale bearers) of the marriage and its manner – my affection for my sister, my personal friendship for you, my respect for your talents and character, made me soon forget every feeling but that of a desire to promote your joint happiness and welfare – but a more universal feeling of disapprobation of your marriage and its manner it was conducted I have seldom seen . . . My father is dead. Long, long before he died all unpleasant feelings towards you and his

daughter were forgotten – With the exception of one month after I heard of the marriage (I did then feel strongly) my feelings have ever been those of the truest affection.

Not everyone was as appalled by the marriage as Jessie's family. Charlie Bohally's grandson, Charles McDiarmid, lived in London and was a fellow enthusiast in collecting poems in Gaelic. He congratulated Alexander on being given a parish, and also on his marriage:

> I may affirm that I felt much pleasure at your having got into port while I continue to be tossed about in the waves. Nor do I look upon the possession of a good living as a greater piece of good fortune that the possession of that without which (I am told) no other worldly enjoyment can make the happiness of man complete. Your marriage with my fair friend I had long anticipated & I sincerely hope that you will derive from it all those pleasures which the connubial station can impart. Pray offer Mrs Irvine my best wishes for her happiness. She has indeed the strongest claim on my remembrance, not only on account of our intimate acquaintance but also on account of many attentions and acts of kindness which I have received at her hands.

It shows the regard in which young Alexander was held by his betters that, within a year, he was given a parish at the other end of Atholl – as far from his father-in-law as possible – at Little Dunkeld and the couple moved the couple of dozen miles towards Perth. A delightfully garbled version of the circumstances of their marriage was recorded by Beatrix Potter in her journal during a visit to Birnam, which adjoins Dunkeld, in 1892.

> There was once a Mr Irvine who was Minister of Little Dunkeld. It must have been a long time ago. This minister 'came of poor folk', in fact he was once employed as a herd-boy by old General Stewart of Garth, who took a fancy to him and sent him to college, which the rascal repaid by running away with his benefactor's daughter. They were married by moonlight under a tree. General Stewart refused to see his daughter but the minister made his own way and was appointed to Little Dunkeld.
>
> One day the General posting through Dunkeld stopped to look at the view and spoke to a lad herding a cow. Whose cow was it? The Minister's, Mr Irvine. Tell Mr Irvine to send to such and such a place and they'll be another cow for him. The Minister sent for the other cow and it was the beginning of a reconciliation. It is said that when General Stewart came to see his daughter, she, in great perturbation, hid away the cradle but it was all made up and they lived happily ever after.

Duncan Campbell wrote of Alexander in 1910:

> He was prominent among the leaders of the Church of Scotland. Because he set his face as hard as steel against the narrow views and intolerance into

which the revivalists plunged headlong, he has been classified among the Moderate leaders of the Church of Scotland; but in his preaching he was as fervently evangelical as any of the men who went out at the Disruption. His memory is still green in Little Dunkeld and Strathbraan as an eloquent preacher in English and Gaelic, and an indefatigable parochial worker . . . The graceful, lively style of General Stewart's History owes much to Dr Irvine's revision and assistance. He was a ready debater, with flights of fancy and touches of humour to set off solid arguments, and impressive preacher, and a whole-hearted Highlander who did much for Gaelic literature and the gathering of Ossianic poetry which has come down orally from generation to generation.

According to David Stewart's *Sketches* in the late 18th century, 'the inhabitants of Strathbraan were considered the most degenerate and worst principled race in the country . . . these people have been blessed with a humane and indulgent landlord, and a conscientious and, able, and zealous clergyman (the late Dr Irvine). The consequences have been striking and instructive.'

Alexander was involved in the controversy about the authenticity of the Ossian poems. These purported to have been discovered by James Macpherson in the 1750s as survivals of epic poetry relating to the heroic days of Fingal. They took Europe by storm, but educated opinion reckoned that Macpherson had made most of them up himself. The Highland Society of Scotland investigated them after Macpherson's death in 1796, and Alexander, who wrote an article on Ossian for the *Edinburgh Encyclopaedia*, was criticised in the *Literary Journal* in London in Sept 1805. He was suspected of fiddling the evidence by substituting a manuscript which he had been given by Captain Morrison, who accompanied Macpherson on his trawling expeditions in search of literary fragments in the Western Isles.

Charles McDiarmid, in a letter of 1805,

anxiously hopes that you will not, like many of your brethren of the Church of Scotland, abandon those pursuits which occupied your attention in an earlier period of life. I cannot recollect the many conversations we have had in regard to the situation & antiquities of our native country, without expecting that you will not desert a subject which you are so well qualified to illustrate.

He also says,

You mentioned an intention some years ago of writing a book on the manners & customs of the Highlanders. Of such a work I have spoken to different persons here, & they all unite with me in thinking that it would be both conferring an obligation on our country, & at the same time prove highly popular. I know of no person better qualified than yourself to do justice to such an undertaking.

This is the subject covered by David Stewart in his *Sketches* nearly 20 years later. Alexander tried other literary works. He laboured long and hard over a *Lives of the Caledonian Bards* and even received sponsorship for it and honorary membership of the Highland Society of London, but the surviving manuscript is of little value. He tried a novel and preserved a comically critical letter from one of his parishioners, Mrs Izett of Kinnaird, the wife of the king's hatter, who had literary friends in Edinburgh. Surely its survival is evidence of both his humility and sense of humour.

> 29 June 1811 . . . At length however I return your interesting manuscript which I have perused with great pleasure. But since you do me the honour to ask my opinion I will candidly confess to you that amidst great beauties I perceive some faults which though of minor importance would greatly obstruct its usefulness.
>
> These I found chiefly in the style which is often so abrupt and obscure as greatly to perplex the reader and make him pause for explanation when he ought to be listening with interest. The episodes too, though in themselves pretty, appear, to me, too frequently introduced. I think likewise that the story would have been infinitely more interesting if the lovers had made greater resistance to their passion and the hero fewer attempts upon his life. His threats of self destruction are so often repeated that at last they lose their power of alarming the reader and are even in danger of exciting his contempt (for we talk not at present of Christian obligation). This is peculiarly the case when he sinks into despondency upon the loss of his castle which affects him in precisely the same way as the loss of his mistress did.

Professionally, Irvine easily coped with the regular demands of his job. Dunkeld was bilingual. Its position on the edge of the Highland line had long made it an interface between English speaker and Gael. To the west of the parish lay Strathbraan, which was still largely Gaelic-speaking. Gaelic was the minister's mother tongue and he preached sermons in both languages. A dozen survive, including his post-Waterloo address, which took as its text Lamentations 5:3. 'We are orphans and fatherless. Our mothers are as widows.' In it he describes the French as 'the most insolent, the most wicked, the most impious people on the face of the earth'. His entry in the *Fasti Ecclesiae Scoticana* states,

> He took a considerable share in managing the business of the Church, was a frequent and ready speaker in the Gen. Assembly, and conscientious, able, and zealous in discharging his parochial duty. Possessing an accurate and critical knowledge of the Gaelic language, he was highly serviceable

in revising and preparing for publication the Quarto edition of the Gaelic Bible.'

His *Inquiry into the Discipline of the Church of Scotland* (Perth, 1811) made one clerical congratulator 'much gratified with the manly independent spirit of the Writer'. The literary testosterone must have sprung from the page as another admired its 'manly tone'. He also produced *Defence of Bible Societies* (Edinburgh, 1815); two single sermons (Edinburgh, 1816 and 1818) and *Substance of a Speech on the Erection of New Churches* (Edinburgh, 1819). He received a Doctorate of Divinity in 1812.

One of his main legacies is his collection of Gaelic verse and prose, which is now in the National Library of Scotland and is an important source for researchers. He wrote 36 letters concerning the Gaelic dictionary and a copy was presented to his son by the Highland Society of Scotland, its promoter, 'in testimony of the value they put on his father's services in compiling the work'. He also collected poetry written by some of the local lairds of the 18th century, including manuscripts by the most famous of the Clan Donnachaidh chiefs, the Jacobite Alexander, who died in 1749. Irvine produced a literary biography of this remarkable character, but it remains unpublished.

From his letters, one can see that the district was still comparatively wild. In 1810 he wrote to his close friend, the Revd James Boyd of Auchinleck, that his successor

the Minister of Fortingall a few weeks ago declared himself married to his kitchen maid in circumstances which have ruined his publick character & I fear his usefulness for ever. It is said that there was a child which was smuggled, nobody knows how – In short the story is the worst of the worst – Tuesday first, we meet & fancy will make some inquiry, know not whether we be all zealous for the law, or let compassion cover a multitude of sins. Within these few days a girl was burnt, I may say, to death & a boy was drowned. This morning another girl about four years old was so scorched that she is despaired of; both by their clothes catching fire. Last night as some of our Highland Whiskymen were going with whisky to Perth; the excise men met them and one of the smugglers was shot dead. I did not hear whether by a dragoon or a gauger – the poor man of the name of Stewart left a widow and children – such the misfortune of contravening the Law – But it is hard if a Gauger can command military force & deprive a subject of life and liberty without trial – Self defence is the only defence of such an action. The girl burnt the day before yesterday died shortly after – daughter of James Dow the excise man – the mother is scorched a little too.

The humble dwellings of the people had their peat fires in the middle of the floor, the smoke being allowed to leak through the roof. The dangers were obvious.

Domestically, the Irvines seem to have been happy. Described by Boyd as 'the sweet little pledges of your love', their children – in Alexander's hand – were 'Alexr Robertson born 30 Jany 1806, Clementina Anne Stewart 29 July 1808, Robt Stewart 22 Feb 1809, David 14 July 1810, William 23 May 1812, James John 26 May 1815, Janet 18 July 1817, – and died 20 January 1819 twelve minutes before noon. She was a most lovely child, 18 months and two days old.' The eldest was 'name son' of Colonel Alexander Robertson of Struan.

Jessie was prone to headaches about which her brother David worried. The manse at Little Dunkeld must have been damp and poky, for David urged the building of a new, healthier home, which was completed in 1816. The children used the ferry across the Tay to go to classes at the grammar school in Dunkeld. This was the main road north, and the substantial chain-hauled barges carried coaches, carts and livestock as well as passengers. The bridge was built in 1819, and it cost the children 3d a week for the toll.

The minister had a large garden and glebe land, both of which were thoroughly cultivated. Bills survive for onions, carrots, cabbages, greens, cauliflowers, gooseberries, apples, pears and peaches. In 1825, 194 yards of the Irvine's linen were bleached. They had a one-horse gig and the full complement of farm livestock.

David suggested that the family boarded the sons of local gentry who might wish to attend the grammar school. This was not primarily intended as a source of income but to allow the Irvine children to make friends of them and secure positions as their social peers. Improving and protecting social status, and making money, come across as the main purposes of life. Perhaps because the alternatives were less comfortable and less forgiving than today, these goals were more overtly stated than they are now. Nevertheless, Alexander had already jumped the social chasm between tenant and gentleman. A minister's income was often greater, and the manse a better building, than that of a laird. The new manse was, and is still, an extremely elegant dwelling.

13

Family obligations

As a result of Alexander's social position, he was now expected to use his influence to the benefit of his brothers and their families, although they clearly anticipated more from him than he could deliver. In 1815, for example, his nephew was in trouble, and the minister wrote to the judge Lord Boyle on his behalf. His lordship returned a rather dusty answer.

> Hawkhill Edinr 27 Oct, Sir, I this day received your letter of the 24th inst on the subject of James Irvine convicted before Lord Succoth & me at last Aberdeen circuit of the Crime of Horse stealing, and sentenced to transportation for 14 years. It is perfectly true that he was recommended to mercy by the Jury; but it is equally well known that there are many instances of a Capital Punishment being awarded for the Theft of a Single Horse, and as the conviction proceeded on what appeared to the Court conclusive Evidence of the Prisoners guilt, he received the benefit of the recommendation of the Jury by the mitigated punishment awarded against him of transportation only for fourteen years. As to what may be the result of any application to the Prince Regent it is not for me at present to give any opinion, it being my duty to report about the case when commanded by His Royal Highness through the Secretary of State; and if I am so in regard to this case, I shall, as I do in all others, lay the whole circumstances of it as they appeared upon the trial before the proper quarters. I remain Sir, your most obedient humble servant, D Boyle.

Much of the correspondence to Irvine that survives came from fellow clerics, and all treat him with warmth and respect. One friend was Ann Grant, widow of the minister of Laggan. She achieved great success with the publication of her *Letters from the Mountains*, which went into several editions, in which she described the way of life of the Highlanders of her husband's parish. She was also a close friend of David and had written up the story of the death of the children of his aunt Euphemia behind Schiehallion in 1796. Dunkeld was on the main road south from the Highlands, and the Irvines received many callers on the way through, many of whom departed with quantities of produce from the manse garden.

A complication in their life was Dunkeld House, which was the southern seat of the Duke of Atholl. His Grace had lost the power to hang malefactors within Atholl, but he still had immense influence. He controlled the livelihood of numerous locals who were his tenants or employees, and his patronage extended to appointing many of the ministers, including Irvine.

In 1819, the duke tried to close down Struan Church which roused outraged opposition from the adjacent lairds, particularly the Robertsons who considered it, and still do today, their clan church. One clansman wrote from Perth on the subject:

> Our worthy Minister, I presume, by the advice and with the consent of His Grace, presented a petition to the Presbytery of Dunkeld, every man of which, I am informed, owes his living to the Duke; of course, due obedience and active diligence was expected from these faithful servants, and certainly they did wade through thick and thin to gain their point. I trust the iniquity of these time serving sycophants will be duly exposed. Chiefs Niven & Irvine.

Alexander had a tricky path to trace with the duke. Socially, the minister was vastly inferior to the Atholls, but Jessie was the daughter of a laird and sister of the famous Colonel David, and this brought her above the duchess's horizon. David presented a case of stuffed birds to the Duchess of Atholl in 1812, sent from Trinidad where he was stationed, and she thanked him, delicately:

> I saw your sister Mrs Irvine the day before yesterday, she is quite well, as are Dr Irvine and the Children – Your Father is quite well – Your sister Mrs Irvine mentioned a great many other Birds you had been so kind as to send to me, but which have never come to hand, it is vexatious after your trouble, and I have to entreat you not to send any more, as we are more than satisfied with the fine specimens you have sent us which have arrived and we all beg to return our sincere thanks for your kind attention in thinking of us, the birds are the surprise and wonder of all that sees them.

David was probably the most famous Athollman of his time. He was a social lion, friends with Walter Scott and most of the Scots aristocracy, and, when down in London, he mixed with the royal dukes who were members of the Highland Society of London.

But David's book made Alexander's life difficult. The Great and the Good, a phrase used by one of the colonel's correspondents, found it dangerous because of its criticism of Highland landlords, and David had to carry off an encounter in London with Lady Stafford who owned the Sutherland estate, about which his remarks were so trenchant that there was talk of legal action against him. However, he wanted the Duke of Atholl's endorsement of his manuscript before publication. David's handwriting was execrable. This meant that Alexander had to trot round to Dunkeld

House and read controversial passages of the manuscript out loud to the duke. His Grace did not approve. The unfortunate minister passed the information back to his brother-in-law, who made changes, but the revised version was no more acceptable to the duke than its predecessor.

Alexander had good reason to be wary of the duke. He would have not been pleased if he had known of the correspondence between the minister and his brother-in-law. David, then in London, wrote in 1823,

> The account you give of the D of Athole's doings is quite deplorable – If all landlords were equally grinding and cruel oppressors as the Duke you would in a few years have your parishioners Irishmen – burning houses, murdering, and giving public orders to pay neither rents nor ministers stipends and denouncing all who offered to pay . . . If you will write a few facts of what is passing in Athole with a few observations – short but pithy and to the point I will get them inserted in the newspapers here – the Duke is considered a great Patriot and most indulgent landlord in this town.

When David took over the management of the family estates, his main confidant and advisor was Alexander. His input was expected on a myriad of details.

> . . . The debts are great. I cannot at present command money to pay off one half. Will you send me a correct list of all debts in your parish and neighbourhood, and say who want their money immediately and who have not had their interest paid – and I will send you a few hundred to pay off the most pressing . . .

> . . . As I intend to propose a new arrangement of my father's land I will be much obliged for your ideas on the subject. I will be most grateful for any information and assistance . . .

> . . . It will be time to look out for another subtenant for Litigan – Have you one in view? – you mention in your last letter about dung and going to law on the subject. I do not understand what dung is meant or what is the subject . . .

But Alexander's loyalties were not always straightforward. He must have already realised that none of his wife's siblings was likely to marry, which left his own children as the presumptive heirs to the Stewart family's estates. But this was a bird well hidden in the bush. Closer to hand were his three brothers, who were farming on these lands.

He was buying tree seedlings for David, advising on how and where to plant them. He did the same for David's oats. But matters became more complex when some of the farm boundaries were being redrawn. He was nobbled by his eldest brother Duncan, patriarch of a brood of twelve children, and, along with another brother, Neil, one of the tenants involved. Duncan told Alexander that the matter was being forced through without consultation, and the minister wrote a less than temperate letter to his brother-in-law. David replied, mentioning Duncan:

> his is the man who was present two and three days when so much pains was taken to please him (not upon his account, but that of my sister and yours) when my line was drawn before his face, himself frequently, if not always, fixing the landmarks and stones on the marches – this is the man who told you on a Sabbath day after hearing the Word of God – that the marches were not pointed out to him.

But Duncan did more nobbling and Alexander wrote again on his behalf to David.

> I cannot comprehend how such glaring inequality should have been attempted against a poor man . . . Your antipathy now in public to these poor men who have been long faithful servants and tenants to your father is to me inexplicable. I cannot believe that their relation to me should be any objection – partiality on this account I did not expect or ask but I expected preference on equal terms.

David was not pleased. He responded from London.

> Your last letter has been long unanswered. The trouble is that I have not been accustomed to receive such letters, consequently not accustomed to the unpleasant task of answering such communications – Being the first of the breed I have received I will now attempt to answer it.
>
> I shall now only say that as the husband of the person for whom I have a stronger affection than any other human being I have always felt towards you, and treated you as such, and would now consider it a misfortune to give up all correspondence with you, and as a continuation of such communication as your last would inevitably lead to that conclusion, I must decline all further correspondence on the subject.

The minister was, one suspects, in awe of the success his brother-in-law had carved for himself in the world. Generations of Irvine forebears, too, would have tugged their forelock at the laird and his family. It is unsurprising that he prickled at a perceived slight upon him and his brothers. David buried the hatchet with a fulsome letter, setting out the circumstances of the boundary dispute in terms that made it obvious that Alexander was being used by his brother. He ended by saying 'my feelings have ever been those of the truest affection, friendship, and the most anxious desire to promote the honour, happiness and prosperity of you and my sister and of your family'.

Alexander was in receipt of many letters about the family estates and the apparently insurmountable problem of trying to meet their obligations. All would depend on the youngest of Fear Ghart's children, John, and his West Indian enterprise.

14

Profit from the Caribbean?

David's driving force was promoting the Highlanders and the Highland way of life, and he was trenchant in his criticism of the injustices meted out to the people by landlords. Thus it seems strange that he seemed blind to the wrongs of slavery and was willing to profit from it. But in the late 18th century, the slave trade was an accepted part of culture, albeit one with increasing numbers of people opposed to it. Slavery was only a degree or two away from the press gang, or from the situation of the Fife miners who were born into their servitude with no legal means of escape. Not until 1779 was it enacted that 'all bound colliers and coalbearers shall be free'. In addition, many Highlanders cleared from their ancestral lands paid for their passages by binding themselves to serve for a number of years to the person who raised their fare. They could then be bought and sold to the highest bidder until the term of indenture was completed.

The Victorians could send their surplus sons to administer the Empire, but this was hardly an option in the 18th and early 19th centuries. The army or navy were favoured occupations for a gentleman, as were the law and medicine, and Scots thought it perfectly respectable to go into trade or the 'manufacturies' of the Lowlands. India could beckon with its promise of riches with the East India Company, and there was always the Caribbean and sugar planting. At least 50 sons of the gentry of Perthshire followed the latter path in the 18th century. John Stewart was one of them and he was not the first of his family to take this route.

After surrendering at Preston with the rest of the Atholl Brigade during the Rising of 1715, Robert Stewart, 1st of Garth, John's great-grandfather, was transported to Yorktown in the *Elizabeth & Anne*, as a bonded labourer for seven years, a virtual slave. James Stewart, this Robert's great-nephew, was the first of the family to go voluntarily to the West Indies to make his living. He disappeared into Jamaica in 1765 and was heard of no more. A letter to the family from the Indies a few years later described what is likely to have been his situation – and his fate:

I found here a great number of my young countrymen respectably employed in the humble capacity of negro-drivers, or assistants in what they term a Store but in fact no better than a Huckster's Shop. Alas, little does many a fond mother at home know the drudgery that her favourite child has to go thro before he can get to anything like a respectable situation. Yet many of them by assiduous attention and patient perseverance realise fortunes but almost always at the expense of a broken constitution.

The next to take this route was Charles Stewart. He was born in 1756. His father was a tenant farmer, Robert of Garth's second son, which made him a first cousin of Fear Ghart. The only evidence of Charles's existence is the paperwork that was sent to Robbie Uncle from Jamaica after his death. However, from this a picture of his life, as well as his death, can be perceived.

He died, aged 31, on 22 October 1787. He had been in poor health for some months and the cause of death was described as 'a putrid fever'. This was probably typhus. He died in the house of Dr Robert Spalding. The good doctor had supplied £6 1s worth of medicines. The coffin cost £20; tea, chocolate and cakes consumed at his funeral cost £1 8s.

So what did Charles own? His will described him as a planter, but he left no house and no land. He did own an astonishing quantity of clothes – 4 coats, 18 jackets, 21 pairs of breeches, 15 shirts, 10 neck cloths, 18 pairs of stockings, 13 canvas trousers and 7 nightcaps – but this was not an indicator of a lavish lifestyle. His stable consisted of 'an old American horse' worth £10 – four times its Scottish value – and the harness for a little carriage, but no carriage. Two old guns, a pair of pistols, an old hat, a pair of boots and a pair of shoes, a few buckles and pins, a silver watch, a shaving case, a small mahogany paper case, and an umbrella, in all worth £45. He also left just short of £180 of cash – and owed £4 17s 7d for Madeira wine.

A couple of letters from the Kingston agent about the winding up of Charles's estate exist. He was no shop assistant, nor a Negro driver. He was a jobber, a slave owner who rented out his slaves to plantations held by others. He possessed 11 slaves at his death. Jack was valued at £90, Bob £85, George £85, Mungo £85, Stephen £85, Sampson £75, Peter £75, John £70, James £75, Amey or Emmy £80 and Will £60. Slaves, it seems, were worth the equivalent price of a modest motorcar today. All, save a boy named Will, were hired out to planters. Will may have been his master's personal servant. He was the first to be sold, raising £60. The others had leases to complete that were not due until February 1788. The cost of their annual rental was £100, which yielded about 11.75 per cent of their capital value.

The hazard of the business is apparent. Any slave could be treated brutally. In law, they were little more than beasts of the field. As John Reeves, author of *An Enquiry into the Nature of Property and Estates as defined by the Laws of England* (1779) stated, 'Negroes were Property and a species of Property that need a rigorous and vigilant *Regulation*'. Common sense should ensure that only the perverse would not seek to preserve the health and thus the working capacity of one's own slaves, but when it came to rented slaves the same constraints need not be applied. When the lease was up, only nine slaves were delivered, who raised £655 at public auction. Two, Peter and James, each valued at £75, had died.

So the first foray of the Stewarts into the Caribbean resulted in the remittance of £937 back to Perthshire. Clementina, Fear Ghart's eldest daughter, received £40 of it, 'in gratitude for the care and attention paid to [Charles] whilst in that family'. An aunt, Elizabeth Menzies, and her daughter received £30; the rest was split between Charles's three sisters, none of whom married, and that branch of the family died out.

One is left with the picture of young Charles Stewart returning to his rented rooms in Kingston from some plantation where he had spent a few rum-soaked hours doing a deal for the rental of his slaves. He would be on his old American horse, an umbrella over his head to keep off the sun or the rain and his pistols in his belt, perhaps singing one of the Gaelic songs of his childhood with young Will ambling alongside. Not quite the lifestyle he grew up with amid the braes of Atholl, but plenty of Highland Scots like him adapted very well.

The evidence about the first venture into the enterprise by the youngest of Fear Ghart's sons, John, comes from his brother David's will. This he wrote in 1801 as he waited aboard ship in Aboukir Bay prior to the British landing against French-held Egypt and the Battle of Alexandria. To his sisters, Clementina and Jessie, he left 'one half of the annual produce or wages of my stock of Negroes in the Island of St Vincent (the other half being already transferred to my Brother John agreeable to the tenor of my letters to him)'.

There is no indication of how David came by his slaves. In 1795, David was fighting with the 42nd Regiment in the West Indies. The enemy on both St Lucia and St Vincent was made up of Caribs, French and slaves freed to fight. With British conquest, some 5,000 Caribs were deported and eventually settled in the Isthmus of Panama. Presumably the slaves were returned to their servitude, and perhaps it was some of these that David acquired as booty of war – and passed on to John who was 'of Parkhill St Vincent continuing in the charge of the property now under his management' and already had some slaves of his own.

David could not bear to be idle. As soon as he left the army, he was canvassing for a job of some sort in the West Indies which he knew from his service there. His last posting was in command of the Royal West India Rangers in Trinidad, and, after he had licked his regiment into shape – his 'military duties coming in the course of time so easy' – he travelled.

> I employed my spare time in visiting and examining not only every quarter of Trinidad both cultivated and uncultivated, but also several of the neighbouring Colonies and mixing much and freely with the people. I required a considerable share of knowledge of the peculiar habits and character of the Inhabitants Black as well as White, with such a proportion of all that is interesting to know of a Country that I have well authenticated accounts and returns of the Produce in number of pounds of sugar, coffee and cotton and Gallons of Rum with the number of Negroes with those born and dead and the quantity of Cattle etc etc for the last five years on the Islands of Trinidad, Grenada, St Vincent and others, and this not only of the Islands in general, but the amount of produce and increase and decrease by Births and deaths among the Negroes of almost every estate, and what I more than anything else attended to, the treatment, comfort, and health of the Negroes on the different plantations and the various changes and improvement in the comfort and happiness of the Negroes, and I also busied myself in suggesting such improvements as would not only lessen the labour for the Negroes.

He also seems to tread a very delicate path when it came to politics. David petitioned the Duke of Atholl whose patronage he sought and showed that he is fully conversant with the politics of slavery and on cordial terms with both the most important figures in the Abolitionist movement and its leading opponents. He seems closest to James Stephen, a man who once said, 'I would rather be on friendly terms with a man who had strangled my infant son than support an administration guilty of slackness in suppressing the Slave Trade.'

In his letter to the duke, David wrote:

> I have every reason to believe I will be supported by men and parties who might be supposed to have opposite principles but each of them have done me the honour to say that as they know no man whom they would have no more pleasure in seeing appointed to a situation of authority in the Colonies such as would afford the means of forwarding the prosperity of the Country, and more particularly the happiness and welfare of the Black Population – these were Mr Stephen the member with his friend and brother-in-law Mr Wilberforce who hearing of me in some manner I know not how, applied to me for information on the State of the Negroes with a number of queries, and at the same time requesting me to suggest such improvements as I thought would tend to ameliorate their condition. On these subjects I have had several conversations with Mr Stephen, and

I believe I may assure myself of his cordial support – the other parties are Mr Marryot the Member, agent for Trinidad and other Colonies, and a great proprietor and West India Merchant with others of the same Body who appear to form the same opinion as Mr Stephen and as they think that a Governor with the inclination has much in his power to promote the happiness and prosperity of those under him, they pay me the compliment to express a desire that I should have such an appointment at the same time offering their support – I have likewise reason to believe that I will be supported by the influence of some others, and in this I have been obliged to a very intelligent excellent man Mr Colquhoun who has exerted himself in my favour thinking himself under obligation to me for much Information I gave him about the Colonies and which he has published in his late Work on the Wealth of the British Dominions.

It is necessary to mention that there is no Lieut Governor of Trinidad but it is thought that Government will be induced to appoint one (the same as is the case in Grenada, Dominique etc etc) in consequence of the increasing importance of the Island and the interest taken in it by Messrs Wilberforce, Stephen and all the members of the African Institution owing to some orders and regulations lately established to check and put a total stop to the admission of new Negroes from Africa to our Colonies.

Did such people know that David was a slave owner? It was hardly a secret.

On 27 April 1812 La Soufrière on St Vincent erupted in a catastrophic explosion that echoed round the Caribbean. The ensuing falls of ash and pyroclastic flows devastated the north of the island and caused many casualties. But John Stewart had left Parkhill, and the island. He was 85 miles away, well within earshot, but on Grenada. David boasts of his support amongst the planters of St Vincent and Grenada. All must have known that John Stewart, the planter at Mount William in the north of the Island, was the colonel's brother, and probably that they were partners in the plantation.

LEFT. Garth Castle

BELOW. Schiehallion from the west

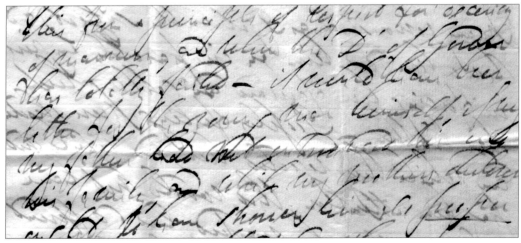

TOP. The mouse-chewed
remains of a power of
attorney dated 1665

ABOVE. 'An Oriental pattern
of curves and whorls.' The
handwriting of Colonel
David Stewart of Garth.

Kindrochit House in the mid 19th century

Kindrochit House, 2008. Beneath the embellishments by Atholl Estates, the original house is still discernable.

Captain Duncan Robertson of Kindrochit

Dr William Robertson of Montreal

James Robertson, 'The Sheriff'

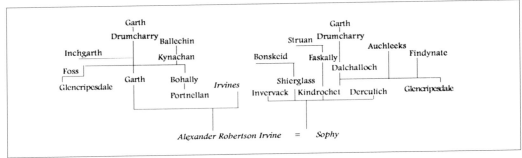

```
                Garth                                    Garth
            Drumcharry  Ballechin           Struan  Drumcharry
    Inchgarth              Kynachan                            Auchleeks      Findynate
                                        Bonskeid   Faskally
    Foss                                                    Dalchalloch
    Glencripesdale    Garth    Bohally         Irvines   Shierglass
                             Portnellan              Invervack  Kindrochet  Derculich  Glencripesdale

            Alexander Robertson Irvine    =    Sophy
```

A simplified diagram of the descent from lairds' families in Atholl of Sandy Irvine and Sophie Robertson

Sophie Irvine *née* Robertson, aged *c.*10

Sophie Irvine a few months before her death in 1856 aged 35

The eldest son of Sophie and Sandy, Alexander Irvine Robertson, as a young man

Revd Alexander Irvine Robertson, great-grandfather Alexander

15

Trinidad

One would have been as likely to survive five years in the trenches of the Western Front as a similar time in the West Indies at this period, though fever rather than shrapnel was the killer. White women were considered more at risk than white men, so few emigrated. This meant that European men found their sexual partners amongst the slaves, or the descendants of slaves, most of whom were of mixed race. Such women were sometimes officially married to their European men, but usually not. These relationships were the norm, so much so that no stigma was attached to them, and these couples mixed at all levels of island societies.

John Stewart's first recorded partner was Charlotte Tobin. Her surname was of high repute in the West Indies. There was a dynasty of planters of the name, and James Tobin, with extensive interests on Nevis a few islands north of Grenada in the Lesser Antilles, was a prominent spokesman for the pro-slavery interest during the Abolition debate. The Abolitionists argued strongly that the black man was in no way inferior to the white. Tobin and other planters found this subject without interest since they did not consider it otherwise. Their support for slavery was economic. Bad luck on those unfortunates who were enslaved, but without them the nation would lose the wealth of the West Indies.

Charlotte is described as a 'free coloured woman'. On 17 January 1810, she bore John Stewart a daughter. The child was baptised Anne at the Mount William estate, Grenada, on 19 March 'according to the rites of the Church of England'. Anne had four godparents, James Grant, William Paterson, Anne Toy and Rennelle Chase. Paterson was son of the laird of Carpow in Fife. Grant likely had a similar background. Could the exotically named women have been their partners, or was their relationship with Charlotte?

John and his family remained on Grenada probably until 1816, for in that year the non-commissioned officer and privates of his company in St John's Regiment of Militia presented him with a gold medal as a 'token of esteem and attachment'. John was a lieutenant. It is the most positive of the indications of his personality that survive.

At that stage, David was just becoming aware of the financial problems faced by his father's estates, and realising that he was the only member of his family capable of sorting them out. He knew that funds from the Caribbean were the most likely salvation. A busy man with a growing national reputation, he had commitments in London and Edinburgh.

In a letter to Alexander Irvine in 1821, David wrote:

> I had a long letter from John yesterday, he is well and doing well, but is now of a stand for want of money – He is now doing that which he ought to have done nineteen years ago and if even a couple of thousand pounds could be sent to him, it would set him completely on his legs – Had he followed the plan I recommended to him twenty two years ago, and I came from the Mediterranean on purpose to set it agoing, and had got money ready (from a kind friend who highly approved of the plan) to send him, he would now be what others are, who did what he ought to have done – that is, with an income of five or six thousand a year – Ask at Mr John Bissett what is the income of Rob Sutherland, J. Cumming, Gilbert Munro, Willm Menzies, and others of St Vincent – John had better opportunities than they had – However his eyes are now opened and if he has health it may not yet be too late.

David already had a share of John's enterprise and now it was appraised. John had left Grenada and moved to Savanna Grande, Trinidad, and it looks as though he had been there for some years. In 1797 the area was surveyed for Sir Ralph Abercromby, the commander-in-chief of the expeditionary force of which David was a part. Then it was described as a 'large tract of drowned Land, part in Savana, although flooded in the rainy seasons. Notwithstanding the center of this Marsh is level with the Sea, yet a considerable portion of it might be successfully drained by making strait Cuts to connect the inflections of the River Caroni; the narrow Channels of which from becoming incumbered at the time of the inundations, overflow all the Lands adjoining thereto.'

In 1816–17, 700 freed American slaves who fought for the British in the war of 1812 settled near Princes Town in the county of Victoria in the south of the island. The black settlers were known as the Merikens and one of their neighbours was John Stewart. He named his estate Garth, which means he probably took on virgin land. Some 350 acres on the flat, hot, featureless plain, it lay on what is now the northern boundary of Princes Town, some three miles down a track from the main road.

By the time it was surveyed in 1821, John was well established, but it was not in any great style. His house was a modest single-storey thatched building, 38 by 20 feet, consisting of a hall and three bedrooms with a gallery of 8 feet all round. It was valued at £300. Close by were the kitchen, storerooms and a stable for six animals, although he owned but a single horse and two mules.

Sugar production was notoriously labour-intensive at all stages of the process. The crop had to be cut the moment the sugar inside reached its peak, and this meant that co-operation between plantations was impossible. Every 150 acres of cane needed its own mill, which carried out a complex industrial process that required a substantial investment of money for skilled labour and equipment. The result was a coarse brown sugar that was packed into barrels – hogsheads – and carted, in Garth's case, to the port of San Fernando, half a dozen miles along clay roads that quickly became impassable when it rained. Then it was shipped to Glasgow and sold.

Garth had a crushing mill with its rollers driven by oxen. It had a boiling and curing house, 60 by 20 feet large, with a gallery to hold three coolers measuring 24 by 10 feet. It had all the iron boilers and plumbing required, and a bagasse house. Bagasse is the biomass of the cane remaining after the juice is extracted. It was stored under cover to dry out and then used to fuel the boilers for the next crop.

That year, 1821, Garth had 30 acres under sugar cane, 15 acres in provision, 36 acres felled and partly cleared, and 239 acres of woodland worth £1,673. To work this were two mules and a horse at £50 apiece and 31 slaves, all neatly listed and valued:

1. Jack, carpenter, – £150
2. John Houston, do & Field – £125
3. John Sharp, do & Field – £125
4. Glasgow, cooper – £100
5. John Brown, do & Field – £80
6. Bob, driver – £150
7. Duncan, boiler – £175
8. Neptune, fireman – £150
9. Robert, carter – £170
10. Joseph, Mule boy & field – £100
11. Moses, do – £100
12. Daniel, do – £80
13. Jackey, do – £40
14. William, do – £20
15. Charles, do – £20
16. Ann, Field – £130
17. Charlotte, do – £110
18. Fatima, do – £80
19. Liddie, do – £130
20. Mary Ann, do – £130

21. Mary Leslie, do – £130
22. Mary Melville, do – £100
23. Jessie, do – £130
24. Polly, do – £130
25. Queen, do – £80
26. Rosette Ker, do – £100
27. Rosette, Mule Girl and Field – £100
28. Eve, do – £75
29. Phebe, do – £60
30. Fran, do – £75
31. Charlotte, do – £50

The buildings were valued at £2,045, the land at £2,983, and the livestock – human and animal – at £3,345.

On the strength of this appraisal, David was prepared to invest in the Trinidad estate, and over the next few years he put in £4,000. John made his only trip back to Scotland in 1823 to sort out the legal niceties. Fear Ghart and William, the eldest of the brothers, were dead. Jessie was the minister's wife in Dunkeld. Looked after by Clementina, David was living at Drumcharry, trying to re-organise the estate to maximize profits, and under pressure from his tenants to find farms for their sons.

David was now famous. He had been chief assistant to Sir Walter Scott in organising the King's visit to Edinburgh the year before. In addition, his book was now in its second edition and third printing after only 18 months and was the bible for the wildly fashionable interest in the Celtic revival. However, he was not a man to use purely economic criteria to exploit his estate. The public champion of Highlanders could not comfortably evict those dependent on him. Even so he received criticism. 'Col David Stewart of Garth after his song of praise upon his selected few for their continued consideration to their highland tenantry,' wrote a sub-factor of the Atholl estate to his superior, 'now begins to play up the other tune. On the estate of Kynachan he is said to have warned his tenantry there (who have no leases) to pay additional Rents or remove at the first term.'

Mrs Robertson of Kindrochit noted John's return from Trinidad. 'John Stewart Garth has come home in bad health poor Man in consequence they say of his disappointment at losing the fair Elenora, the effects of a bad climate is a more likely cause however he means to go out again as soon as he is able, he has brought one of his Black Pets home to leave with his Sister.'

The 'Black Pet' was Anne, the daughter of Charlotte Tobin. The child was now 12 years old. Apparently her mother had died and her father decided that her future would be best served by coming to Scotland.

She became part of Jessie Irvine's family at the manse. Her cousins, the minister's children, ranged from young Alexander (Sandy) who was in his late teens and following in his father's footsteps by studying for the ministry at St Andrews, down to sickly James John, aged eight.

A bill from the Dunkeld haberdasher survives which shows Anne being outfitted. When she first arrived she would, perhaps, have been wearing mourning for her mother, and she had been in that family for no more than a year when Alexander Irvine had a stroke, just after speaking to the pupils at Dunkeld Grammar School, and died. In 1825 she was re-clothed – shoes, wrist cuffs, muslin gloves and a variety of materials including satin, 'Brown Tweed bombazette', cotton, flannel, foundation muslin and calico, as well as thimbles, and hooks and eyes to be sewn into garments. She had a season ticket to walk across Telford's new toll bridge over the Tay each day on her way to school, but she seems to have attended classes for no more than six weeks.

Alexander was 50 when he died. His obituary included the customary panegyric but added, 'He was endeared by a warm generosity of temper, and an unaffected kindness of manner, that are seldom combined, to an equal extent, in the same individual, and the most delightful interchange of cordiality and good deeds.' Jessie had to vacate the manse, which was needed for his successor. She and her family returned to Drumcharry. Anne never married. In fact, no voice for her exists. She spent her life acting as companion to her aunt. There is one reference to her in a letter in the 1850s to Jessie from an old friend. He says that Anne must be a comfort because she had been with Jessie for so long that she knew long-held friends and past times. Anne appears in the census of 1851; she and Jessie were living in Craigatin, a sumptuous residence her son Willie built for himself at the edge of Pitlochry. Jessie would eventually move to a small cottage at the gates of the house for the remaining years of her life. Anne died in 1859 of apoplexy and was buried in Moulin kirkyard. Her name, with that of her cousins and aunt, is on the gravestone.

John and David did their deal in Edinburgh in December 1823. In exchange for his £4,000, David took a third share of the Garth Estate in Trinidad. John went home and proceeded to invest, putting in, for example, a steam engine to take the place of cattle in powering the crushing mill. Meanwhile, David waited for the profits that would save the family lands.

16

The Lieutenant Governor

Sandy Irvine, the eldest of the colonel's nephews, wrote to his uncle John in July 1827. Understandably, the young man made a copy of the letter, in which David is referred to as the 'General'; promotion from colonel to major-general depended on seniority, or survival, and David's turn had come in 1825.

> The General has requested of me to write you that he has received your letter of 20th May here on his way North and will write you when he goes home. The object of my writing in the meantime is to explain his disappointment to find from your letter there is no provision made from the shipment of produce this year for his relief which he had relied on. As he could not at the time write himself he thought it right I should do it and explain the difficulties the disappointment has placed him in. My knowledge of them he considered as a proper reason for doing it. He observed that he has remitted since he had charge of his father's and brother's affairs 4 or £5000, I forget which, under the confident expectation of regular remittances to reimburse him. Of this sum he has only received £500 which was some years ago and nothing since. He trusted particularly to considerable relief this year & you may easily suppose therefore how grievous the disappointment is to him. It would be wrong in me to conceal from you his feelings on the subject and it obliges me tho with no little reluctance to communicate his sentiments. He observed that nothing prevents him from taking strong measures by laying Arrestments in the hands of the house the Sugars are consigned to but that it would injure your credit both here & in the Island. He even went so far as to say he would be under the necessity of sending out a power of Attorney to the West Indies to take steps for him there. These are dreadful alternatives for a brother who has your interest at heart as much as his own and has given proofs of it. Nothing it may be relied on could lead him to contemplate such a thing but the urgent nature of his own affairs here. At this moment it consists with my knowledge that he does not know how to meet the demands upon him. The properties are already mortgaged to the full extent they will bear and it is not to be supposed he can raise money on personal security. Even the Interests at present he is not prepared for. With the bad crops of last year and the losses sustained by the tenants he cannot

get his rents as usual. It is therefore matter of no small regret that on receiving his letters of 22nd January and 12th March you had not allotted part of the produce afterwards shipped for his relief but I hope you will do it still. Indeed it is for your own interest because by not relieving him at this time it puts it out of his power to assist you afterwards and you know how well disposed he is at all times to accommodate you but he cannot do miracles. I am sure I need say nothing more on the subject to engage your earnest consideration of it. Your plans he observed are commendable and so far are what he recommended but then the first thing was to consider your ability without distressing him in withholding the relief he expected. I must now apologise to you for dwelling so long on this painful subject but believe me nothing could induce me to do it but from good intention & under a conviction that it is for the interest of the one as well as the other that your Brother should not be disappointed of the supply he expected and trusted to.

Without help from John, David was able to make little impression on the massive debts that had been bequeathed to him. He also found himself responsible for Jessie's family – patronage again. They were the next generation of his family and could not be allowed to slip back into the social obscurity from which their father had emerged.

In November 1827, he wrote to a Glasgow merchant, asking a favour. 'I had a sister of mine married about 20 years ago, a man with more learning in his head than money in his pocket, and when he died left four sons with little means for their education & support. I therefore have taken them in charge but with a family estate overwhelmed with debt, I cannot do what I wish and must in consequence encroach on the indulgences of friends.' He was soliciting a job for David Irvine, then 17, 'well educated and decent', and the young man found a position in Glasgow with the established mercantile firm of Eccles & Co., run by the brothers William, Robert and James, with sugar interests in the West Indies.

Alexander, known as Sandy, was the eldest and destined for the church. In 1824 he was 18, too young to take over his late father's position, but it did not prevent a faction of the congregation with Jessie in its midst trying to delay a replacement until Sandy was old enough. This was the comfortable pre-Disruption moderate Presbyterian Church. Be the incumbent of a parish and you had the income of a gentleman. The universities churned out ministers, but there were insufficient parishes to go round. It was up to Uncle David to keep him from a life in teaching or the colonies. Fortunately, he could. At this time the Church of Scotland decided to create quoad sacra parishes, in effect building new churches in outlying parts of some of the more unwieldy parishes for the convenience of both clergy and congregations. The new churches were known as parliamentary churches, since they were funded by an Act of Parliament, or Telford churches, since Thomas Telford created and almost standardised the design.

Uncle David had busied himself in promoting new churches at Innerwick and Kinloch Rannoch in the northern part of the great parish of Fortingall, of which, as laird of Garth and Drumcharry, he was a heritor with influence in appointing minister and schoolmaster, as well as being financially responsible for the upkeep of the buildings. David was also laird of Kynachan, inherited through his mother, and this made him a heritor in Dull Parish. Here a new church was to replace the long-ruined establishment at Foss on the border of the estate. David donated the land for the manse and the glebe; the unwritten condition was that Sandy would be its first minister. And in 1830 he was appointed to it.

The two younger boys, William and Robert Irvine, were also found careers. The youngest, James John, was delicate and was still at home with his mother. William went to join David Irvine in Glasgow to study medicine. Robert sailed to Trinidad to train in managing a sugar plantation; he was being groomed to take over Garth from Uncle John. And the new general himself finally landed a job that might repair the family finances. In 1828 he was appointed Lieutenant Governor of St Lucia. Custom – these days it might be called corruption – allowed a doubling of the substantial salary through fees received for licenses etc. His two predecessors on St Lucia each made £5,000 selling manumissions for slaves.

This was a time of hope. It looked as though there might be a change of surname from Stewart to Irvine for the lairds of Kynachan, Inchgarth, Garth and Drumcharry, but the family would continue there. David Stewart, a supreme networker, discussed his intentions with the man who, on the death of his brother George IV, would become William IV, and wrote to Jessie about it.

> The Duke of Clarence kept me from 1 o'clock till near 3 the last day I called at Bushy Park – he was most gracious – paid me marked attention and talked on very confidential subjects – He takes a warm interest in the West Indies and is a good friend to the Planters. He asked about my brothers and sisters – I told him what had been done and what was intended to be done for your boys – He approves highly of the West Indies plans – one part of his words was "You have acted like a man of judgment and independent mind – you will place your orphan nephews in situations where they will have the power of making themselves independent and this you have done without asking favours or depending on others." Thus you see, my dear Jessie, how feelingly he speaks of familiar and family subjects . . . When his Royal Highness is King, I think he will be my friend.

David landed in St Lucia on 17 January 1829. In September he sent a report on the comfort of the slaves. Granted, he had a professional interest, but the report showed in some degree how he felt about slavery, and it is likely that his sister and nephews took on his view – and they were heirs to Garth in Trinidad as well as Garth in Perthshire.

David rode over the whole island and examined every plantation with 30 slaves and more. They were generally contented, he reported to the Colonial Office, well nourished with their own allotments, and they could sell what they grew. The women were well clothed and it was a fine sight to see 'forty, fifty or a greater number of women working in the fields with hoes or other implements and dressed in white or printed calico jackets and Petticoats'. They worked proper hours, and the aged and sick were cared for in hospitals. Some estates were very poor because the owner had much debt, but, as in Scotland, the first sale of produce paid and fed those who worked the land. 'Some of these people would sell their own father or child for a cask of rum,' David reported. Those born in Africa had a higher mortality than island-born slaves. There were only three schools for black children on the island and grossly inadequate religious education. Punishment of slaves was so restricted as to be a hindrance to efficiency. Overseers were forbidden to carry whips and the lash banned.

> So revolting to the feelings as a practice must be of keeping people to their work by compulsion and fear of punishment, it cannot be too soon removed. But in so doing great caution is requested, as with the fiery stubborn dispositions of many Negroes, the fear of immediate punishment is as necessary as I found it with my culprit soldiers. A fortnight ago on a dilapidated estate the slaves complained of cruelty, working the negroes beyond their strength, refusing the usual interval of rest, and the time for cultivating their own lots of land.

The owner was fined $400 and removed from estate. He appealed and sentence was changed to a fine of $450, and an order to supply sufficient clothing, but he was allowed to stay on the estate. David said that he would have banished the planter from the island, and it was he who sent the protector of slaves to the plantation immediately and supplied the slaves with clothes and comforts on his credit. 'By what authority?' asked a grumpy London marginal note.

Pragmatism seems to have been the keynote of his attitude. He described the use of the lash as 'revolting', but he shows little outrage, although the tone of his report seems to show that he knew he was discussing an institution in transition. However, he was the lieutenant governor; his duty was to uphold the law, and slavery was within the law. Even if he wanted to, he could not condemn it and remain in charge of the island.

David Irvine wrote him a letter from Glasgow at the end of November

1829. In a previous communication, the young man had remarked on the economic 'bad times' in the country. His uncle took exception. He lived by Wellington's dictum; look on the positive side of things, avoid 'croaking'. Gloomy and indolent Uncle John, he said, likely influenced his nephew. John was again in his elder brother's bad books since he had taken out another mortgage of £6,500 on the Garth Estate. This time the money came from Eccles & Co., David Irvine's employers. The young man regretted the impression given and resolved to 'instigate greater exertions' to 'be contented with one half the popularity and respect paid you at home and abroad'. He passed on local gossip. Sandy had yet to move into the new manse although he was preaching in the kirk and was popular. His mother was at Drumcharry, as was Neil, his uncle's illegitimate son. Some whisky was on its way to the Caribbean, and a barrel of sugar was gratefully received and of high quality. 'We have you dead several times since you went out. On going home I found the report very general and I need not tell you the joy and satisfaction of the Highlanders on my stating to them that you were in good health, and their anticipation of the protection and support they have experienced, and they fondly look to your return to your native country. I hear now from home that you are married tho I question much if this report be not of a piece with its predecessors.'

Alas, by the time the letter reached St Lucia, the lieutenant governor had succumbed to fever. He died on 18 December, 11 months after landing on the Island, aged 57. His 21-year-old nephew Robert followed him to the grave three months later in Trinidad. Uncle John was dead before midsummer 1830. Jessie, the sole survivor of the children of Fear Ghart, relinquished her interest in the debt-ridden estates. Garth, Drumcharry, Inchgarth and Kynachan were put up for sale. Kynachan was bought by Sir Neil Menzies of Castle Menzies; Drumcharry and Garth by Sir Archibald Campbell of Ava, representative of the Campbells of Glenlyon, a distinguished soldier and a fellow pupil of David in the little school at Fortingall. The sum realised only paid 15 shillings in the pound to creditors. Neither Jessie nor her children had any liability. The general's medals, his uniforms and swords, and his canteen of silver cutlery were shipped back from St Lucia through 'those sharks at the Customs House', but the principal part of the inheritance was Garth in Trinidad.

17

Clementina

Clementina Irvine, Jessie's only surviving daughter, received her first mention at the age of five in 1813, when Uncle David wrote to Jessie, 'Sorry to hear of the accident to your Clementina, but I am more anxious about the Fever which I hope will end in nothing, I beg you will write me how she is by the first opportunity'.

She was 12 when she went to Edinburgh to become a lady by attending classes in such subjects as French and Drawing. She lived with other girls in the household of Mrs Grant of Laggan on Princes Street, directly opposite the castle. The latter was a gratifyingly loquacious correspondent, particularly about her own ailments. She took her charges to see

> all the harassing bustle of the Festival Week. I was at one Oratorio & concert a little cold & by my going up with the young people to see a Balloon rise over the Calton Hill got as much more which has confined me for the most part ever since . . . Now your Clementina who should by rights hold the first place in the letter comes in at last. I can only say of her what you might with much reason anticipate. That she is the best of good girls and a very general favourite in the family. I hope her letters to you & her mother indicate the satisfaction which persons of all ages feel when conscious of being liked & approved of spending time to good purpose. Her health is perfect & her industry about her lessons most commendable. That young lady who is sitting on a stool behind me warming herself & reading the newspaper sends her duty & love to you both & to your brothers. I fancy she is looking for terrible stories about the Radicals who now supply the place of Specters and Goblins to young imaginations.

Mrs Grant was mapping out Clementina's fate six months later:

> Clementina is a creature of so much steadiness & composure of mind, has such good principles and such a good understanding that I hope these advantages will peculiarly fit her at an earlier age than ordinary to be a companion and assistant to her mother & relieve her of some of that burden the weight of which I can so well understand.

She was back at Drumcharry when Mrs Grant next wrote in February

1821. Jessie had been suffering from one of her bouts of headaches and likely went back there to be nursed by her sister.

> I am now convinced I was right in bringing Clemmie when I did, I had a kind of presentiment that she might be worse spared afterwards. With her steadiness & capacity how much she may do to save her Mother's anxiety & care. Give my love to her & tell her I hope & trust to hear that she is not taken up with any one pursuit or object but that of being useful in the Family & that she would earnestly supplicate the Father of Mercies to vouchsafe that spirit of warm affection which will induce her to devote every thought & every action to those family cares which affliction has hurried on prematurely but which are of vital importance to all that are dear to her. Much even at her age may she do to relieve her Mother's cares & add to her comfort. One rule she should lay never to tell her mother of any of the pretty vexations of daily occurrence in every large family. You will advise her on such occasions but her Mother's tranquility must be held secured.

She stayed with her mother for the next decade.

In 1830, Clementina was mentioned in a letter from David Irvine to his brother Sandy, by then ensconced in the manse at Foss with their mother, Clementina and youngest brother James John. Clementina had been given a pony by a neighbour. Furthermore, David wrote, 'I heard of Clementina's attempt to found a sect of Baptists in your burn. It was certainly a burning shame to do the like so near to an Established minister's house.' This strange episode has no follow-up. Another correspondent about this time wondered whether she had 'gone to see the races at Perth with [Stewart Menzies of] Culdares and family – unless indeed the rest of her five dresses have been equally unfortunate with frill or flounce in which I took so much interest to have repaired for her.'

Letters survive from at least one good friend of Clementina. Sophy Robertson was the daughter of Captain Duncan Robertson of Kindrochit whose little estate lay across the river Errochty from Struan Kirk a few miles from Foss. She called Clementina 'Missie'. As Jessie's only daughter she would have been known as Miss Irvine. Sophie reports that Missie, aged 31 in 1839, had become engaged to be married. Sophie was to be a bridesmaid.

The groom was Charles McDiarmid. Four years younger than Clemmie, he was brought up at Bohally across the river Tummel from Foss. He was descended from Charles Stewart of Bohally, and so he was related to his future wife, sharing a set of great-grandparents in the Stewarts of Kynachan. This was not surprising, since virtually every family in Atholl had intermarried with every other family many times over the generations.

But Clemmie's brothers did not approve. David Irvine, by then a Glasgow merchant responsible for supplying and marketing the produce from the Garth plantation in Trinidad, wrote to Sandy.

> If the imprudent engagement my sister has formed should be consummated by her marriage, I auger little happiness for her, but, altho we cannot help this, it must be our duty to make her independent of a surly Boor who could possibly alone countenance the thing from the prospect that my sister's pittance might relieve him & his from his difficulties.

According to David, Charles's father, the 'Bohally Glowerourorum may come down with £300', but the brothers prevailed upon Jessie to make Clemmie a settlement of £200 that would give her some independence.

Charles had trained to be a doctor, but had never got his act together. David said, 'He is a miserable businessman & seems to me to have been fiddling away his time.' Charles decided to emigrate with his bride to Australia and try his hand at sheep farming. If that went wrong, he would practice medicine there. A couple of local lads from Garth, Stewart and McRostie, were joining him as servants.

The couple were married in July 1839, and in October they went to Glasgow to stay with David until their ship the *Tomatin* sailed, in which Charlie had got passage as the ship's doctor. From Glasgow, David dutifully reported the arrangements to reassure his mother. Now aged 63, she must have known that she was unlikely ever to see her only daughter again. On 17 October he wrote:

> Clemy & Charlie got safely to Edinr where they dined with old James [James Robertson was an Edinburgh lawyer, who was soon to become Sheriff of Mull in Tobermory] on Tuesday and never was there such a sensation in any dwelling as in No 66 Great King St on that, the first occasion in which a Lady had dined under their roof. They arrived here yesterday afternoon. Clemy looks remarkably well, I think, and last night we were all exceedingly cheerful. She seems quite contented and what I am more glad to see really intelligent on the ways of the new world and the struggles she will have to undergo & endure at first. Tomorrow we all go down to Greenock at 8am to see the ship and the captain, & see what is to be done and known and everything else.
>
> The passengers for the steerage are all nearly Highlanders – 125 from Tobermory out of 146 in number. That will be of great consequence to Charlie, he and his two assistants speaking Gaelic & they will both obey and respect him more than they would a sassenach. He has however been recommended to lay in an extra supply of sulphur for the Highlanders & a few pairs of hair mitts would save some trouble to the afflicted [in soothing the itch of scabies].

David wrote to Sandy a week later.

> I am going down tomorrow and will see them off. The cabin Charlie &
> Clementina have is not the 'Dr's berth' but one of the two large cabins
> holding two beds, a chest of drawers, a trunk and two boxes with plenty of
> room for dressing, two stern windows. It is the after cabin, a stern cabin,
> and a window in the side, so that they have plenty of room and plenty
> of air.

On 13 November David wrote to his younger brother William, who
was establishing himself as a doctor in Pitlochry. 'I only returned from
Campbeltown last evening very late. Clementina wrote my mother when
they were ready for starting, and I saw her away on Sunday afternoon
last at one o'clock. The wind was not very fair. It was what sailors call a
working wind, but Wingate will be clear of all land before now; besides
that the weather was very moderate. Clementina was pretty well when
the *Tomatin* sailed. She met with great attention & kindness from some
friends there, and so did I too.' And to his mother on 25th November,

> We have heard nothing from the *Tomatin* nor, very likely, will we hear of
> her for 4 months and perhaps 6 months to come. There is a chance that
> some vessel may speak her, but that is but a chance & I rather think the
> first news we will hear will be from the cape where she will probably touch
> for water etc. It depends much however upon their wants as the captain
> wants to make Adelaide in 100 days if he can and if he has no need for
> touching at the cape he will carry on, in that case we may hear of or from
> Clemy & Charlie after they have reached terra firma once more.

The following summer a letter from Charles arrived at the manse of
Foss.

> Melbourne, Port Phillip, April 14th 1840.
>
> My Dear Alexr, I know not how I am to acquaint you of the melancholy
> loss which I have sustained since I came on board. It is with feelings of
> heartfelt pain and deep loss that I have to inform you that God has seen
> proper to take my beloved Clementina to himself. She died on the 23rd
> of January after an illness of five weeks & 4 days about 1,000 miles to the
> westward of the Cape of Good Hope. The immediate cause of her death
> was Cramps in the stomach. She suffered a good deal from sea sickness
> during the first fortnight we were at sea, the weather being exceedingly
> stormy and the wind contrary in the Irish Channel.
>
> After then we got into fine weather and she recovered her health. She
> continued in excellent health till the 14th Dec when she was suddenly
> seized with a vicious diarrhoea which was accompanied with symptoms of
> a slight inflammation of the stomach. About the end of Decr her appetite
> became good and she felt herself improving really fast, on 11th January she

was so well that she said she would be quite strong in a few days but alas this happy state of things did not continue long. She tasted nothing but liquor for four days after, then she commenced to take a little solid food once or twice a day. On the 21st she asked for some porridge to breakfast which she relished very much and felt very comfortable having taken this. She then went to the Cabin and was able to read and join in conversation. She retired about half past nine & was well during the night. In the morning she expressed a wish to have some Porridge. I got this for her & she told me that she relished it more than she did the day before. She no sooner finished than she requested me bring her a Pill which she should have taken before breakfast & at the same time to tell the Steward what to get for her dinner. I went to the cabin for the Pill & was not absent above two or three minutes at most & on re-entering our Cabin I to my horror found her whom I left three minutes before apparently so comfortable now breathing her last. She gasped only twice after I entered . . .

It distressed me beyond measure that I was not with her when she was seized but it is a consolation to me to me that I left at her own request. I scarcely think that I could have done anything to relieve her even tho I had been present but still it would have been a satisfaction to be near her. God only knows what I have suffered since & I fear my trials are not yet over but I scarcely think that I can suffer more that I have suffered already. I am quite overwhelmed with grief & there are no words when I have lost one whom I valued more than life itself. I know not how you are to broach the subject to your mother. I do regret that I was the means of taking her from her.

There was a great deal of sickness amongst the passengers. They brought both smallpox and measles on board the both of which broke out about 12 days after we left Campbeltown. They got the smallpox at Greenock and the measles at Fort William. 8 children & 4 adults died of both diseases & 4 children who died got over the enraptured stages very well but were either carried off by secondary fever or dysentery. Were it not that the diseases were brought on board we would not have had more than 4 deaths among the passengers & these 4 were children who were sickly when they came on board. There were no births. It is a sad thing to treat infectious diseases on board, especially under the line . . .

18

David

David Irvine, the third of Alexander and Jessie's sons, was born in 1810. His only legacies are a Glasgow-made silver buckle for a kilt belt to which is riveted the Irvine crest of a sprig of holly, and a run of letters, most dating from the late 1830s and written to his brother Sandy. David managed the Scottish end of the Garth Estate in Trinidad, and much of every letter was taken up with business. Unlike most of the archive, David's letters provide a complete picture, in this case, of an industry which has both parallels today and, at the same time, is completely alien, owing to its exploitation of slaves. David mixed his letters with humour and gossip as well as business, and one of his anecdotes from 1837 seems a light introduction to him and his more stressful preoccupations.

> Old McLeod [Dr John McLeod 1757–1841] is a droll chap. He tells a story of 'Archy McNiccol, Kilfinan' (the Minister of the Parish to wit) who was a corpulent gutsy chap, at a sacrament. The Dr and Archy slept in the same room – the latter painfully afflicted with flatulence emitted an occasional and most triumphant report. McLeod's patience & sleep were done for at length, he said 'Lord man Archy, ye hae been ill used when they didna make ye Minister of the Kirk O'Shotts.' Archy in getting out of bed for something to relieve him put by mistake McLeod's breeches on. They were too tight by half a mile & thinking that he had swelled unnaturally he threw himself on the floor & roared that he was gone. McLeod, on lighting a candle, found the gone man in his breath & laying on his back.

When his mother Jessie inherited the West Indian plantation in 1830, David had already spent two years clerking in Glasgow to learn the sugar trade with Eccles & Co. The partners seem to have permitted him to act independently when it came to dealing with the Garth estate and marketing its sugar, whilst continuing to employ him as one of their clerks. From the manse at Foss, Sandy kept a close eye on the estate's management, and it is likely he had the final say on any strategic decisions. David reported regularly to his brother and took the tactical decisions.

The correspondence comes in the years leading up to and beyond the freeing of slaves in the British colonies in the West Indies. As can be imagined, this subject features frequently in the letters. David seems generally in favour of the development for economic reasons, but does not give opinions on the ethical aspect. He had no need to, since the decision to free slaves had already been taken. Manumission seems little more than one of the many considerations, and a minor one, that would have a bearing on his profits.

After his brother Robert's death, David wanted to go to Trinidad, find a job and exercise some direct supervision over Garth. He wrote to the governor, General Lewis Grant, asking his advice on obtaining a salaried post on the island. Grant wrote back, 'I can with safety assure you that I see no opening for several years to come for any person. I had a true regard for both General Stewart and John Stewart and in consequence, as well as from a natural wish not to lose property averted from its right channel, I was anxious that the friends of that gentleman should know all. Property in the WIs deteriorate in more ways than one if no person is present to take a right charge of it. I strongly suspect this will be the fate of Garth unless some active steps are taken to prevent it.'

In the event, oversight of the estate was entrusted to a firm of lawyers and agents in Port of Spain, Gray Losh & Co., and, under the direct charge of John Losh, a series of managers seemed to have done their best under adverse conditions before fever killed them and required their replacement. From Glasgow, David juggled the impossible demands of money brokers, the sugar market and the enormous cost and complexity of supplying the plantation. For example, the 1837 supplies included four different sorts of nails, '4 dozen cutlasses', '6 padlocks', '2 dozen hammers', 'engine oil', 'lamp oil', 'neatsfoot oil', 'white paint', 'red paint', 'black paint', 'blue paint'; 'Negro hats – boys', men's and tradesmen's', '2 dozen Scotch Bonnets', '6 gross black horn buttons', '500 assorted needles', hundreds of fathoms of rope of various dimensions, soap, candles, blotting paper, pasteboard, coal, empty barrels and full barrels – of oats, butter, biscuits, beef, herrings, Newfoundland cod and salt.

David also received requests from Trinidad to pay the legacies of £100 apiece left to John's three illegitimate sons on the island: one, at least, had a mother named Susanna Stewart who was also in receipt of a small – very small – pension, but the priority for David was setting the estate on a solid footing and servicing debts to suppliers and money-lenders. In a good year, the crop could be sold for £10,000, but it was never enough, and the good years never came. His overriding problem was that virtually all the factors that affected profitability were outwith his control.

One difficulty was communication. It could easily take a couple of months between the dispatch of a letter to the West Indies and a reply, so it was almost impossible for either end of the business to react to circumstances. And for a manager, perhaps a day's ride from Port of Spain, advice from the Counting House in Glasgow must have felt as though it came from another planet.

The weather could often be inclement. In 1838, for example, David told his brother, 'So very bad are the accounts of the weather that whether I import two thirds of my Crop is questionable. The rains were so incessant that not only was Cartage suspended, but grinding also,' and, 'The roads there are made of clay hauled out of ditches formed on each side. Branches of trees are placed in the ruts when they become very deep but such a road as this in wet weather is impassable.'

A ship was at the mercy of the wind and could be delayed or even wrecked; this happened in 1837, as David reported:

The Brig *Mail* which sailed a week ago has had a consummation to her voyage which I neither wished nor anticipated. On Thursday morning I learned that she had struck on the south point of the Island of Arran on the day before. Thursday night blew great guns from the south & I was quite sure that the *Mail* from her exposed situation could never stand the lea and the blast with which she had to contend. I was right. Today, this afternoon, we had an express intimating that her bottom was out & the Cargo at sea. The wind blowing south would blow any part of the cargo which would float to sea, but Hogsheads of Coals and Casks of meat are not overly buoyant & these must have plumbed out of the *Mail's* bottom to the bottom of the sea. The Captain made every exertion but the severe weather experienced when on the rocks left him without the shadow of a hope for his ship & the concluding catastrophe was the only one which in the circumstances would have been natural. I am amply insured but then my supplies for the Xmas holiday were on board & we cannot for a month send stores to replace those now at the bottom of the frith. The *Mail* was very valuable & will cost the underwriters £5,000 while I do not think they will save £100 worth from the Ship or the Cargo. My Chaps will have but a meagre Xmas I fear on Garth but I hope Losh will attend to my recommendations conveyed to him most fortunately about 6 weeks ago to furnish the manager with meat to be retained out of my future shipments. This will check the Snowdrops from grumbling as they are often apt to do when 'Massa Buckra him dem shabby'.

Prices could go awry and David was operating in a ferocious commodity market. Sugar was shipped over in barrels – hogsheads – that could weigh nearly three quarters of a ton. In a good year Garth should produce 200, which were sold by the hundredweight. In 1837 he gave Sandy graphic accounts of how prices fluctuated. In March, David reported:

The Colonial markets are dead. The blow being given by Rice the Chancellor of the Exchequer. I was as usual fortunate eno to have sold out & off before the Market fell, got laughed at then, but now the laugh, as I told a friend, don't come so free, he being expectant of higher prices. Such things happen. Matters are at a stand in our Sugar sale room. There is no material falling off in price as there is no pressing on the part of the holders. As little unfortunately is there demand on the part of Rollers or Grocers. The Sugar market is a perfect Lottery just now. Eccles (Wm) made a speculation by which he will lose £1200 & maybe £2000. Others hold largely of Sugars purchased when the Market was near the highest and were they now to bring their stocks into the Sample Room they would sacrifice at least 10/- per cwt. The stocks held by speculators are not large eno to affect our market subsequently.

In May things were no better.

Our Sugar market is exceedingly dull. Dealers are living from hand to mouth and there is not a pound taken on speculation. Every man in the trade is husbanding his means. The Sugar Roller who has the Country dealers, refiners and grocers largely in his books does not know how soon they may be declared bankrupt & therefore he requires to be prepared to meet his engagements out of his own capital. Britain never has been as ill supplied with Sugar as at this moment, and yet the purchasers parade our sample rooms with their hands in their pockets. What under all the circumstances is best to be done I feel it quite impossible to say. I never can get on at these prices. Of course you heard of Oswald's failure (MP for City). His debts are variously stated. £250,000 is probably near the mark. This is one brush. We had another yesterday, Leslie Reid & Co but they are very small, only £80,000. Two more are whispered today & there we are. It will not be too much to say that we shall see the fruits of the above failures some 6 weeks hence in a number of small houses being gazetted. Times here set at defiance the most intelligent and experienced amongst us.

Business was perking up in June when David wrote that 'prices are now 2/6 better than they were on the 6th inst. That is to say I could get 54/6 for the Sugar I sold on the 6th June at 52/-. The Market is still rising, and I am out of deep water.' By October, buyers were

playing a tricky game. They were themselves heavy holders till the middle of this month & it was their interest that prices should be upheld. Now that they are getting out of stock, if they went on buying they would require to give advances at advancing prices. They hold off. Sugar becomes unsaleable & in a little while the Merchant whose sugars are exposed is glad to get clear at the prices at which his Sugar was valued when they were laid down. Then the Roller buys perhaps a shilling below the market price. This policy will not outlive Thursday and then I will have the satisfaction of making whoever buys from me dance to my fiddle.

In December, 'The Sugar market is up again but it has not regained what it lost. The sellers are at their old game – holding hard. Gilkison and Brown made a speculation in Sugar by which they could now nett 8/- per cwt & yet they are not sellers. They are waiting for 10/- or 15/-.'

Another of David's difficulties came from dealing with his employers. Just prior to his death, Uncle John mortgaged one quarter of the plantation in order to buy another 47 slaves. Eccles & Co. were the money lenders, and they dominated the trade between Trinidad and Glasgow. Their ships – *Calypso, Arethusa, Gleniffer, Louisa, Spence, Hamilton, William* – thrashed their way to and fro between San Fernando, Port of Spain and Greenock, or the Broomielaw in Glasgow, bringing barrels – hogsheads and puncheons – of sugar and molasses, and returning with myriad supplies for the plantations. The owners, William, Robert and James, were of John Stewart's generation and old friends of the family. As well as controlling the ships plying across the Atlantic, they were big fish in the sugar market where David was a tiddler. In 1838, when David imported less than 200 hogsheads, Eccles & Co. brought in 3,600 from Trinidad alone. Ronald was the senior factotum in the firm and David's regular contact. The progression in their relationship over the years is simply demonstrated.

The first mention of Ronald comes in 1830. 'I was a little amused lately with a petty specimen of the reserve in our affairs,' wrote David.

> I wanted a cask of Sugar for my mother and told Mr James so. He said nothing. I then told Ronald. He answered he could do nothing without orders, and yet all this fuss about a cask if which they lost would only be 25/-. 'Oh Moses!' William Eccles I did not speak to. He has too much matter of fact severity and does not deal his favours much like a gentleman tho he may mean well. On the contrary he carries his 'scoundrel maxim' even to the sacrificing of his private friends if he don't look out.

Matters were little better six months later:

> Ronald is undermining me. I shall give him a bit of my mind. My excellent associate and fellow clerk Lamont is precisely in the same predicament and feels as uncomfortable as I do. Ronald's interest is strong and I do not give him foul play when I attributed his anxiety to have me, in the first instance, out to Trinidad to a wish to have me out of the way, and in the other to dispose of Garth at a sacrifice too humiliating to think of. He is going to marry. "A modest lover makes a jealous husband" they say, and I never can conceive how he managed to pop the question. He marries in three weeks a London Milliner and brings her to Glasgow. I know nothing of her except that in dress she is rather furious. £300 a year will not go far for a wife and family, but Ronald is playing a deep game. The Eccles are old men.

Andrew the representative a fool. You understand why Ronald continues our clerk now. How I would like to thwart him if I had funds.

By May 1837, things were on the up. 'I am on the very best terms with the Eccles & Ronald. Mr William Eccles has done me much good by his attention to me in the sample room & whenever and whoever we meet in public. I am gradually working my way into useful acquaintance.' Over the following months, the relationship continued to improve. By November 1837, David could report that he was 'getting on very agreeably with the Eccles and Ronald. He sees that I will be of use & I never put anything past him when he can accommodate me.' By June 1838, the sun had broken through. 'You will wonder when I tell you that my best & most liberal friend among the entire house of Eccles & Co is Ronald. Yet such is the case.' And, in October the same year, David 'was embraced by Ronald in the Exchange. He is given to impulses & this was one. I may turn these to good account.' A couple of months later, David told Sandy that he had 'the confidence of my seniors & have done well I think in conciliating Ronald who has I verily believe a very sincere friendship for me'.

Like all his family, David was an enthusiastic Tory who worked hard for the party of Wellington and Peel in both national and municipal elections in Glasgow. This was a stirring decade. In the 1830s, the Reform Bill and the Catholic Emancipation Acts were passed, as well as the Slavery Bill, and the Corn Laws would be abolished in 1841. Opinion was polarised, and so David's political ferocity was, one hopes, not exceptional. For example, in 1838, David told the Revd Sandy:

> There is to be a demonstration in favor of Vote by Ballot and Universal suffrage on the 21st May. The time is well chosen. We have all the necessary elements at hand for such a demonstration – plenty of idle mechanics and plenty of poverty. The poor wretches who are victims of the Trades Unions have all of them had their wages arrested for the next 6 months. Others are being [laid off] as Trade gets duller and duller & hence they concoct demonstrations as if the people had the sovereignty of a Republic, which makes all the difference in life as to the fruits of their demonstration. They are mad, & to expend upon it sulphur & Gunpowder would cure more evils that the itch.

The Whigs under Lord Melbourne won the election of 1835 and remained in power, through Queen Victoria's accession to throne – she was a 'stupid lassie' in David's opinion – until 1841. David was acerbic in his views. 'The whole conduct of Government is abominable & Government when it has the power is the most arbitrary in the Universe.' His main ire was reserved for the Chancellor of the Exchequer, a 'superficial jackanapes' who put a 45 per cent tax on imported sugar. 'One consequence of the ill-timed Legislation of our present most incompetent Exchequer Chancellor (who by the way spells Chancellor with one l) is a total suspension of all business.' And, 'to operate upon the good sense or business talent of the Right Hon. Thomas Spring Rice, is just to take the Breeks off a Heilandman, the which we are credibly assured is at all times difficult and sometimes dangerous'. In 1839, David decided that 'we are politically, commercially & atmospherically rotten. Money matters have not been in the same state since 1825, if so bad then, & you will see that Spring Rice has ridden out of the scrape on the back of a Peerage.'

19

Emancipation

Viewed from today's perspective, the oddest aspect of this family enterprise is its reliance on slaves, particularly when Sandy Irvine, a minister of the Church of Scotland, was so closely involved. A bill to bring about the abolition of the slave trade received the royal assent in 1807, before David was born, and the surprise is that the institution still existed within the British West Indies until 1838. The Abolition of Slavery Act was actually passed in 1833, but there was a transitional 'apprenticeship' status set until 1840, which was much the same as slavery itself. House slaves were to be given their freedom in 1838, field slaves in 1840. Not surprisingly, the latter took a dim view of the difference, and, in the event, 1 August 1838 was the date when they all received manumission.

David never comments directly on the morality of slavery, nor is this a subject which interests his brother. The younger man mentions his labour problems often, but his attitude to Abolition is little different from the way his successors would regard any other development which would protect the rights of workers, be it trade union power, a shorter working week, safety legislation or minimum wages. Their importance lies only in their potential impact on profits. And, of course, political correctness was yet to be invented.

The 'Slavery people' are a nuisance, he warned Losh in Trinidad. 'They will send you, there is no doubt, a plethora of bibles and tracts, and other more learned cogitations and recreations for your great and glorious free. These you will acknowledge with all becoming gravity of face and diction, so that we shall realise what Buxton and others aim at, the converting of Trinidad into a moral and spiritual Lazaretto.' He described the anti-slavery activists as 'good dames who swallow tea and masticate sponge cake for the cause of humanity'.

In 1837, he reassured his brother about the future. 'One of the cleverest planters in Demerara writes to Eccles "that the Slave Emancipation Act has been our salvation". He is not frightened by the year 1840 at any rate. In Trinidad the old Niggers are in the horror when they think of 1840. At present they have comforts in abundance but they do not know what they may expect when the law declares them free and independent. We must hope for good results from this feeling.'

And there was the happy thought that the food and clothing he dispatched across the Atlantic to Garth would now have to be bought by the freed slaves rather than doled out for nothing. 'When I send out an invoice of stores for sale, I charge freight and other charges which will be repaid by the free labourers. In this way I will save £150 a year when we now buy labour only when we require it. Formerly we had a constant expense all the year round, and one third part of that term the slaves were unproductive. Add to that we have no children & no old people – no doctor's bills, and these are always formidable. And as far as I can see, always supposing that labour can be had at a fair price, we shall have cause to rejoice at the change. If we can get labour for 1/6 for Garth or even 2/- per day, I see that we shall be richer than we have been.'

But there were concerns.

> The slaves were many of them asking higher wages. That will not do at all and must be got over. Others were moving away to the Crown lands & evincing a disposition to [idleness], but on several estates again there was no change but all hands working away happily and industriously. I know nothing of Garth not having heard from Losh. No news you know is good news. I will not be surprised to hear that some of our people are working badly because under the old regime they were not stretched, but if I can get labour, and that I ought to get, if the indisposition to work is confined to a few estates & the general remains true & uncontaminated. On the whole I have no great fear till we have more of certainty.

David 'never feared the ultimate success of the Manumission Act':

> I felt assured that individuals must be sacrificed and my dread was that we might be numbered among the things that perish. A great part of Hooper's gang is gone. This I told you I expected. They were from example a moral nuisance, and the influx will more than recompense for the great part gone, most likely the most worthless part, but I really think it premature to dogmatise after only 5 weeks experience upon the disposition of an animal the most liable to ridiculous influences and the most untutored of God's creatures. I look upon the state of matters in Trinidad as a progressive one, and am quite assured that gang after gang will return to their huts and their comforts when they have experienced the discomforts of the woods and the hostility of the Indians who are very chary of their territory and of whom there are 600 in Trinidad. Sambo is no match for him.

The purpose of David's letters to Sandy was, of course, business but he usually ended them with gossip or family news, and this is often entertaining or informative – and adds a more sympathetic dimension to his character. For example, he 'paid a visit to the Botanic Gardens last night where there was a promenade of ladies and gentlemen. It was a salamagundi turn out but there were a few respectables. Just imagine one Glasgow merchant of 'high degree' walking about with his hand in the flap of his inexpressibles and among the ladies too; another again was strutting with his hands in his Coat pockets displaying the extent of his 'honor', and this was necessary for he got into a duel and was said to have shown the white feather.'

And he kept an eye open for other business opportunities. The Excise Act of 1823 licensed whisky distillation, but connoisseurs, then as now, wanted the most interesting malts and David could provide them.

> Can you send me a box next week? With a cheese in particular – ask Bruce to let me have two Bottles of Sandy Duff's whiskey made in Balnacraig and Faskally. The one marked Duff F and the other Duff B. I think I can sell almost any quantity from the scarcity of real good whiskey felt here. The older these samples can be sent the better as whiskey is conditionally bespoke already, and I want a good excuse for asking a high price. Put two bottles of your Strathtummel Smuggler's whiskey into it. Such a thing is greatly appreciated here. I dined with Burnley yesterday to meet old respectable merchants. I find the General had a number of friends here and that is a good feather in my cap. My sister speaks of a Davie Alston being in the Country. Did you hear that there was anything wrong there? Don't say so on my authority but an officer of the 79th now stationed here told me that Master Davie got so doubtful that the Colonel hauled him up. That after that he fell on the drawing room floor of a private house and was carried out mortal. George Robertson Strowan my sister says is to be married to the eldest daughter of Major Menzies. Nothing more likely. He is a foolish chap. I know that he is constantly with them.

Davie Alston was a sprig of the laird of Urrard near Pitlochry. George would be chief of the Clan Donnachaidh.

As a matter of course, David attended church on Sunday and reported that he had

> a free seat in St Georges Church during summer and autumn for which I am very grateful. We have a very abominably organised band but most unfortunately for me there is a foreman and a parcel of young girls at my back who disturb my enjoyment of it. If you could conceive a bonnet full of asthmatic Bumbees led by a Peacock you will be very near the exhibition they make.
>
> Have you kept in mind the Terrier I want for Port-of-Spain? When you write say if you have got him, so that I may make my arrangements for his passage . . . The Terrier arrived safely yesterday & to appearance he is quite

the thing. I thank you for so handsome a specimen & I think he should be as good as he is handsome . . . The Terrier is shipped & will I trust push his fortune successfully among the Port of Spain rats. Your plan of rearing two young ones is a good one. Try Charlie Stewart's breed. I have a notion that the wiry haired chaps would suit the Climate better than longer haired dogs. Pitnacree's Callum is a trump.

I can buy beautiful calicos here at 3/3 the Gown piece. I bought 24 Gown pieces in Campbells the other day for Trinidad. I have a dozen rather bilious looking woollen socks for you. I bought them at 7d a pair, strong purpose-like stockings of a bad colour. I think but you might like them well eno. The fame of the last Terrier you sent me has spread. Do you think you could find me two youngish dogs for the East Indies? I think Shoon the Fox Hunter might do well if he would rear young hardy pups. I would take 3 or 4 couples a year from him at 30/- to £2 a pair as they might be bred. The weather is very beautiful today & the potatoes are nearly up. Every drill is lifted with the Grape hereabouts. We had a deal of rain on Tuesday. I got wet thro while out after stores & caught a severe cold and rheumatism from writing afterwards in my wet clothes. My left arm is positively powerless. It is as well it isn't the right.

Sir Neil Menzies of Castle Menzies was a keen Tory, and David kept him informed about Glasgow politics. Here David extracted a recipe – which cannot be recommended – from Mrs James Eccles for Lady Menzies, and had great difficulty in providing the barrel of limes it needed. 'For making Shrub. To every gallon lime juice as 20lbs brown or 24lbs lump Sugar. Put them together on the fire & boil them to a syrup. Skim till perfectly clear. When quite cold add the spirit, the proportion being about 5 gallons rum to every gallon lime juice. Keeping out a proportion of rum, say one gallon in five, & adding it in the brandy, will be found a very great improvement. Tho the Shrub appear quite thick it will soon clear in the bottles.'

In another letter, he reported,

George Eccles, Mr William's son had an ugly spill while hunting Saturday last. His horse got away with him, ran him into a tree & finally threw him at the bottom of a hill. He is sadly wounded about the head & face, but there is nothing dangerous in the accident. He would need to hunt a female kangaroo with a pouch into which he might creep in an emergency. The creature can no more ride that his friend Plug. By the way the latter is not unmanageable. You can manage most men thro their fears or interests.

The weather often featured in David's letters. Ice could halt trade, and flooding could beach ships on the quay of the Broomielaw.

Our thermometers are at 8. Water pipes frozen & worse than that the pipes on our water closets. The Glasgow Green is one sheet of ice & carriages are fairly off the road. A Doctor's carriage came down a hill yesterday with the carriage first. It turned fairly round. All communication between here & Greenock by water is closed & railway shares will I have no doubt rise in consequence. Such cold has never been experienced here & I pity you if you have it as intense. They are worse in Paris than we are. Typhus fever is among us west the Town. There were 4 deaths last week, all of folks moving in the first Circles. The Clyde above & below town is shut. Above the river is swarming with mortals of all sizes and ranks. A poor man was rescued by an acquaintance of mine in a funny way two days ago. The man had fallen in & was bobbing up and down, waxing weaker and weaker every dip. Some children standing by were enjoying the thing marvellously. 'Hurra. There he is again' every time he appeared. This most providentially attracted my friend's notice & he flew at the man & lugged him out just as he appeared for the fourth time & very likely when death had given the last tap & was pronouncing the 'going gone'.

I quite forgot to beg what I often meant to have asked – your Bass [This was probably the instrument bought by John Stewart of Kynachan in 1715]. You can have the little one at Cluny, which I will have repaired for you. I would take it, but to learn on it would spoil my stepping on any other. I want recreation for my evening & one can't always read. I hope you will send me the instrument. It will confer a real favour on me & I will take every care of it. I am anxious about this because it will relieve me when tired, really I cannot always read profitable after a fagging days work at my desk.

Lamont is sick, but I cured him yesterday in spite of himself, with a steak, some brandy toddy and a tune on the Bass . . . The weather has been stormy beyond all example. Houses and chimneys, trees & stacks and all whirling about as if they had become animated and were competing for the best dances of the reel of Tulloch.

Glasgow is in a most extraordinary state. No water except the little to be got here and there among the wells. Something went wrong with the Water Company's works on Friday past. We shan't have a drop from them till tomorrow afternoon. I wish they were as dry in Trinidad . . . Our air is all manufactured air & when we are lucky and have water it is also manufactured and filtered & so bedabbled & bedevilled that the natural green filth of a quagmire is more natural.

Sometimes David moved in surprisingly exalted social circles. He mentions in a letter of 1838 James Hunter of Hafton, a prosperous merchant and shipowner, who bought his estate at Dunoon in 1816.

I have been at Oban and elsewhere for a week & saw an infinitude of Lions. My companion on voyage was Hunter of Hafton. I met Islay. [Walter-Frederick Campbell of Islay, deputy lieutenant of Argyll and MP until 1832] He is a conglomerated idiot. His kilt keeps him on his legs. Monzie [Alexander Campbell of Monzie, MP for Argyll] was also at Oban. At a public dinner Monzie disgusted me, a mile & a half too much Oil & ostentation about him and if he intends to rise in the House he must have more subtlety. The Attorney General Plain John [John Campbell, 1st Baron Campbell of St Andrews] was also of the party. His speech was stupid and egotistical. The Whig aristocracy of Argyleshire are a rotten set.

And, in the same year, he was out soon after the Glorious Twelfth. 'I saw Hunter of Hafton last week, I had a shot at the end of the week, was out at 9am and in at 3pm with 8 brace. I proposed 8 brace & came in when I shot them.' The following year: 'Great returns from the Moors. Burnley & Eccles in Ayrshire 22 brace on the 12th. Wm Eccles Jnr 11 at Hafton. For my own part I put a piece of heath in my coat & "covered" every crow what passed me in the railway coming in, so as to get up a sham 12th.'

20

Hard times

David moved out of Glasgow in April 1839 to commute to work on the
new railway from Garnkirk, where he rented a cottage. His younger
brother William was training to be a doctor at the university, and he
encouraged David to volunteer for the Committee of the Asylum, which
gave shelter to the poor and sick of the city. That summer he was visited
by Sandy and his late wife's younger sister Amelia. She kept a journal of
their trip.

Wednesday 12th September. A most beautiful day. Immediately after
breakfast Alex went out to see his brother David who joined us by 11 o'clock,
when we sallied out to lionize Glasgow, I being quite a stranger there. We
went through the Cathedral which is very handsome and inspires one with
deep regret that so many were so ruthlessly destroyed in Scotland. We
then went through the Metropolis which will in a few years be a very great
ornament when the different slopes and terraces are finished. We thence
went to the Green, and wandered about all the different parts of the New
Town, when we met with Captain David Campbell, Inverness who with D
Irvine joined our dinner party at 5 o'clock. We were very merry recalling
the doings of last year when we three had such a pleasant day's excursion
from Inverness to Strathglass & having parted the end of last Sept at the
door of the Royal Hotel Inverness. After dinner we all went out to take a
survey of the Exchange Rooms and the principal parts of the Town by Gas
light. Some of the shops here are fitted up in a style of elegance not at all to
be expected in a town dedicated more to commercial improvements than
to the fine arts. When we were satisfied with this amusement we finally
adjourned to the House of Refuge or Night Asylum for the destitute, a
most benevolent institution. A great many wooden platters with oatmeal
porridge and a suitable supply of milk were ready for the inmates' supper.
The Committee had just arrived to examine the several candidates craving
admission for the night and allowed us to be present, David Irvine being one
of the 'judges'. Most of them were women deserted by their husbands and
sufficiently melancholy, till the last one, whose account of herself though
not worthy of admission here, was much too amusing to be forgotten by

any of us. It was now verging towards 9 o'clock, so we returned to our hotel, partook of some refreshment and said Good bye.

Friday 13th. Another beautiful day. David joined us early in the day and we agreed to dedicate this day to lionizing the manufacturing wonders of Glasgow. First of all we visited him in his Counting House and thence to a Cotton Spinning Mill where we were much astonished with the rapidity of their movements, all kept moving by the power of a steam engine of 60 horse power. We were taken to the top of the mill first where the cotton is in its raw state, and then saw it in all its different stages of carding, rolling & spinning & weaving till we found it in a finished web ready for the Salesman. There was nothing else of particular note this day excepting the Botanical Gardens, but I must first mention the handsome shop of Duncan & Laing, into which we now for the second time in our sojourn here went to rest ourselves and refresh our wearied persons after the fatigues of the cotton mill, after which we started for the Botanical Gardens, which are at some little distance from town out the Sauchiehall road. On the way there we had the good fortune to meet some old acquaintances, a very agreeable variety was it not? We were on the whole rather disappointed with the garden expecting, according to hearsay, to find it much superior to the Edinr one. However there are some very rare and beautiful plants there and a new garden is about to be made out by 'Kelvin' about 3 miles from Town. We returned home by the Dumbarton Road, dined en trio at our hotel, and spent the evening quietly.

Saturday 14th. A most terrible day of wind and rain which continued without intermission all the day. Notwithstanding we started at 12 for the Iron Foundry with which we were inexpressibly astonished, especially the Bellows working and the working of Bar Iron. It belongs, I believe, to Captain Macdonald from Perthshire who shewed us every attention. At 1 o'clock we left by the Garnkirk railway train for David's cottage, a neat and tidy little place 8 miles from town. The surrounding country is very bleak and sterile. We were prevented by weather from getting to any distance but enjoyed ourselves most companionably within, having the best of cheer, seasoned with plenty of fun, a good cook and attendance, the best mutton chops & sherry I remember tasting. After dinner & tea, having taken an affectionate farewell of Dido, we left for town again, having a tight race from the Cottage to the Station thinking we saw the train at our heels but on our arrival we found to our amusement that it was only one Coal Wagon, with a Stationman, with his lighted lamp coming in her. He was a very extraordinary character with a world of humour, so it ended in our closing ourselves from the rain in his Wooden shed, till the train a propria persona came up. He made us laugh so heartily that we did not regret either our race or the being too early. Neither Alexr or I had till today travelled by a Steam railway. We did not go above 25 miles an hour (At that rate I mean) and liked it very much. The Train was very much crowded, thirty carriages crammed.

In 1839 when the family was preparing for Clementina's departure for Australia, Alexander Stewart, the illegitimate son of their grandfather, Fear Ghart, turned up. This was the man whom Colonel David had been so horrified to see fully acknowledged by his father. In spite of this, the colonel had used his influence to obtain him a commission, and he had also been the legal witness when the colonel put money into the sugar estate in 1823. He was now 50, retired from the army, married to the daughter of a baronet and living in Canada. At the wind-up of the Perthshire estates in 1834, he had lodged a claim from Gibraltar but the trustees rejected it. Now the Irvines were concerned that he was seeking some nugget from the financial debris left by the collapse.

'Captain Sandy breakfasted with me this morning,' wrote David from Glasgow.

> He called yesterday afternoon when I was much engaged & I had him up this morning. He is old, fat & very like the general. He is off to Edin and will see you. He talked a little of the Garth affairs & I, of course, knew nothing at all about them & referred if he wanted information to you.
>
> I really know nothing of Captain Sandy. I asked no questions that could lead into any explanation of his intention in coming to Scotland. Neither did I ask after his wife and family. In short our intercourse was confined to very commonplace attentions on my part which on his part he seemed to feel – to take with a 'koindly feeling' as the Dr would say. I must be even with him. He has many friends here I find, and some correspondence he seemed to say with parties abroad. That is reason eno' for me. He may have it in his power to be troublesome, and you know that he has little principle to restrain him if he feels the inclination to be so. He is not in the 94th I have ascertained. Find you out where he is & what his intentions are. I dare say Rattray [a lawyer] and he have been raising the cinders & we would all need to be on our guard.

The captain went to Foss, where Jessie, by then well into her sixties, was living with her son the minister. 'I am glad on every account that the Captain bold & the old woman foregathered pleasantly. He is a polite, plausible clever chap. I wish him success.' A few months later, he was away again, having found the cupboard bare. 'Captain Sandy is going I fancy. He needed little to confirm him in his intention & that little he must have found in the lawyer's representations.'

The year 1839 was a ghastly one for David. The resident manager on Garth, William Taylor, was an ocean and a culture away from Glasgow, and such men liked to keep it that way. David had remarked to a predecessor, killed by fever, that the lids on the hogsheads he sent home did not fit that well. A response came from Losh: 'managers will not bear to have their conduct reviewed', to which David plaintively replied – to Sandy, not to Losh – 'I will never subscribe to the doctrine that we on this side have no voice in the management of our own property.' Nonetheless, an incentive was needed to prevent the manager from ignoring the interests of the Irvines in favour of the traditional consolations of the West Indies of rum and women. Taylor was sold one quarter of the plantation on a mortgage to Jessie which would be paid out of the profits.

'Taylor will do famously I think on Garth,' was David's expectation. 'I calculate upon 200 Hhds, or at least 180 from Garth this year.' But alas, by August, he noted, 'My Crop will be 160 Hhds at the outside. That is very well if my engagements were paid off, but with £1800 to pay before and on 1 July 1840, I will need to look elsewhere for some aid.' In fact the crop was 150 hogsheads.

The £1,800 was due in two payments to Eccles & Co. As well as their mortgage on Garth, David had inherited a debt of more than £15,000 that had built up over the years with them by Uncle John. David needed to borrow money but none was available, indeed, as he told Sandy, usual credit was no longer being extended.

> Gray has withdrawn his former accommodation. 'The Times' are his excuse & the excuse I am sorry to say is too valid. You can't raise the money by a cash account in Glasgow just now because of "The Times" and with my produce at sea I am most uneasy. A good harvest would make money very much more plenty & I trust we may soon see weather to induce a conviction that Harvest may be secured. Every little however assists, and I beg that you would consider whether you have the means of raising any money till we see if matters mend. I can afford 6% for money, and with so much done in times past & so little comparatively speaking to do for the future, I would make every present sacrifice to go on & meet my engagements. In the meantime I am taking every precaution & tho I have never been so hard up, I have had severe rubs before now too & got over them. I am now after two and a half years toil and after having paid off £6700 besides all the contingent expenses obliged to tie my hands, and live for 6 months on salt and potatoes.'

Sandy's reply to this does not survive, but it provoked bitter words from his brother.

> You say you did not tell my mother of my misappropriation of the funds of the property to my private use. You have done well for you would have made her miserable without cause. The same may be said of your very plain insinuation as to the £300 from Willie. If you will just wait till all the

accounts are before you, you will be in a state to judge for yourself, besides which it will save me much annoyance and save you from yielding, as I fear you did when you wrote the letter from the Manse, to an angry impulse. Your exertions are great and so are your difficulties, but be calm under them & do not I beg you repeat the ferocious insinuations so lavishly bestowed. If any other man had repeated the same expressions and hinted the same insinuation, I would have kicked him from one end of Glasgow to the other and feeling this as the only answer I could make to a stranger. I pass them by in your case, only by requesting you will treat me like a gentleman. That I am prepared to make any sacrifices I have already told – that I have often had to spend more money than I should have also told Willie & you. When I was elected into the Western & Gaelic Clubs, honours which others usually covet which I get from my rank from those who were ignorant of my circumstances, and that this year from Clementina being here, her wants in some cases supplied, her marriage, James's funeral etc I have been more expensive than I hope to be . . . I feel more vexed by your last letter than I do at the loss of friend or sweetheart . . . I shall do nothing in any case without your knowledge and concurrence. You will be careful where & when you speak of any thing we are doing, things cannot on every account be kept too quiet - at least till we have them in a train to hear being talked of.

Did David protest too much? Perhaps. He claimed at one point that he was living on £150 a year. Yet his clothier's bill – Anderson & Son, 33 Buchanan Street – survives for March to December of 1839: his trousers – 2 pairs wool tweed, 2 pair striped corduroy, 1 pair tartan, 1 pair large black & white check, 2 pairs shooting, 1 pair best blue cloth, 1 pair claret doeskin, 1 pair mixed doeskin, 1 pair black dress, 1 pair superior check buckskin; his gloves – Light-coloured kid, 2 pairs French kid, 2 pairs yellow doeskin, buff leather; his waistcoats – black cloth, fancy chaly, Victoria tartan, superior black figured wool, wool velvet, brocaded satin; his coats or jackets – black cloth riding, drab lama, Atholl shooting, superior black dress, superior blue dress, fancy green tartan morning. The account does include a black coat and a black cashmere waistcoat for Sandy and a guinea's worth of stuff for John Gray, working on Garth in Trinidad, but it all comes to just short of £60, which is the equivalent of roughly £3,000 in 2008.

David, in December 1839, reported to his brother:

Warm, southerly, showery, windy & a great deal of sickness the consequence. I am almost terrified to do duty at the Asylum. I have a head and a half of cold, and the usual quantity of stupidity indeed thereby, but today the frost is white on the tops of the houses and you have some inducement to walk into the Country. I propose all well & things being convenient to go home on this day three weeks to spend Xmas & New Year day with you, and I only hope the weather will be good. I have knocked a good deal about of late and have had more than my own share of anxiety, so that to escape from the shop and be quiet at home is a pleasure which I shall relish most excessively.

But he never made it home. James John, the youngest of the brothers died of some 'constitutional malady', probably consumption, at the age of 24, shortly before Clementina sailed to Australia. She of course, died on the voyage.

David's great niece left a note amongst his correspondence in the 1930s: 'This David died of cholera during an epidemic in Glasgow in January 1840 when he helped a doctor friend in work among the slums. My father told me this.' Jessie had lost four children in their twenties, three within six months of each other. The last time the Garth estate is mentioned is 1847, when the Trinidad agents report that the estate had gone £1,500 further into debt the previous year. Presumably its liabilities by then equalled or exceeded its value, and it was relinquished.

21

Willie and Sandy

Willie Irvine qualified in medicine at Glasgow University and survived to a ripe old age as the much respected doctor in Pitlochry. He was probably the most distinguished of Jessie's children, but the few of his letters that exist are uninteresting. Inevitably, the archive only contains papers that came into the hands of great-grandfather Alexander. Those in his family tree who survived and had children would pass their histories down their own families who may, or may not, have preserved them. This was the case with Willie. He was kept informed about the tribulations of the Trinidad Estate and David sometimes wrote to him. He was a student when his brother David was first in Glasgow, and he is mentioned occasionally in letters from David to his mother or Sandy.

In 1834, for instance, he was working in the fever asylum.

Willie is in excellent good health. He has taken the shine out of the other clerks. The Lord Provost sent for answers to certain queries about fever. The no of patients, referrals, causes, treatment etc, And the dismissals for want of room were so very numerous that he has taken 4 flats of a cotton mill for the poor wretches. The Clerk who made out the report had the thanks of the Lord Provost with a further list, but Willie took good care the second time to let his Ldship know that it was the Assistant Fever Clerk who had drawn up the report and not the senior clerk of the establishment. The other day a fellow came to the Infirmary with a sick relation & insisted on leaving his relation there – room or no room. He got very impertinent & Willie sent off a note to Graham, Captain of Police, insisting upon an officer being sent to take the fellow to the office. Graham was at dinner when he got the note & luckily he had two of the most influential directors dining with him. Willie was sent for, explained and was commended, and the cause of the uproar was put in the Police Office. Graham asked Willie to stay which he did. One of the Directors – Lumsden – a furious bombast of a man – began telling W that he had settled that the Fever Clerks were to pay no board. 'But' remarked the other manager, 'This gentleman of course does pay board.' Replied Lumsden, 'this is Mr Irvine of the Fever Home don't you know. Mr Irvine, sir. Allow me the pleasure of introducing him, one of our most assiduous & meritorious Clerks and we will drink Mr Irvine's very good health in return!' Since then he has been asked to send any improvements or suggestions he may see to the managers who will feel much obliged to him.

A biographical pamphlet was published for local consumption in 1896 shortly after Willie's death, when money was being raised for a tribute to him. This became the Irvine Memorial Hospital, which still exists in Pitlochry. The writer of the pamphlet was Edith Molyneux, who added to an article she had already written for the Church of Scotland's *Life and Work*. It gives an idea of his local importance, but, compared with the immediacy of the contemporary correspondence earlier in the century, it is interesting to discover how quickly myth and romance coloured the past.*

Sandy Irvine was the eldest of the family, born at Drumcharry in 1806 when his father was still the minister of Fortingall. Like the other children, he was educated at the grammar school at Dunkeld and went on to St Andrews University with a foundation scholarship in 1819. He had no clear idea of a career initially, but, aged 19 in 1824, on his father's death he became the head of the family.

Sandy eventually plumped for the church, but one has the feeling that this vocation was chosen as much for the influence that Uncle David might have brought to bear in his support as from a calling. His father kept correspondence from fellow clerics in which they discussed theological and spiritual matters. Nothing like this survives from his son. Foss was earmarked for him. He took his time about completing his examinations, but his uncle wrote 'When I heard the probable delay in his Trials, I got the settlement of the minister of Foss postponed for another year – he must be ready then – it is no small matter to get two ministers and stipends when great men have been refused.'

In a later letter to Jessie, the colonel asked her to 'remind Alex that he should have testimonials ready for the Presbytery of Dunkeld – from the professors whose classes he attended – from Principals Baird and Haldane incidentally – all testifying to his qualifications for a church in the Highlands – with consequently a full knowledge of the Gaelic language.' He went on:

> The fact is they are in no ways necessary in your son's case, for Mr Peel will pay as much attention to my own certificate as that of any professor in St Andrews. I will enclose them along with a letter of application and recommendation to the Secretary of State for the Church of Foss which I suppose will be ready next summer ... I am in good favour with the Commissioners at present and as I have given two and a half acres of good land to the minister and have otherwise pleased them with my manner of proceeding, I have reason to hope that they will pay all the expense of the Church repairs, but this cannot be settled for some time and I must

---

* See Appendix 4.

act as if I think I will have to pay all – The Commissioners pay me the compliment to say that if it were not for me, they would not grant a church a stipend in Perthshire, so Foss, Glenlyon, Rannoch may thank me for their being parishes.

Sandy was ordained in 1828. He moved into the new manse even before he was inducted as the minister, and started preaching. 'The church was yesterday almost full,' he wrote, '& it contains 350–400 . . . The general condition of the inhabitants reflects equal honour on their honesty, intelligence & on the proprietors by whose encouragement & example & under whose management they are stimulated to useful exertion & live so comfortably.'

With a job, Sandy could now support a wife. He found one next door. Margaret Stewart Menzies was the second daughter of Joseph Stewart of Foss and Elizabeth Menzies, daughter and heiress of Alexander Menzies of Chesthill, Glen Lyon. Like so many others in Atholl, she was kin to the minister through his mother. They married in 1833 and soon had a daughter, Elizabeth. They also looked after Neil, Colonel David's natural son, and Sandy recommended to the trustees of the Garth Estate that the youngster should be set up in the world with £100, provided he made no further claim against the estate. Sandy added, 'It is a supposition of such a sum being apportioned to him that I charge £5 in my accounts thinking it enough that I should have furnished him with bed & board etc without also being burdened with the sums I was obliged to advance from my own funds on his behalf.'

But the marriage was only three years old when Margaret died, leaving Sandy an infant and £3,000. Amelia Stewart Menzies, known as Emily, was a younger unmarried sister of the late Mrs Irvine, and she moved in to the manse to look after her niece Elizabeth. Sandy was ten years older than his sister-in-law and fitted easily into the role of elder brother. They seem to have had an excellent relationship. The two of them went off together on jaunts round Scotland. Sandy kept a journal of one trip up to Inverness when they travelled in their own gig, and Amelia covered two – one to Loch Sunart where she and Clementina Irvine stayed with a rather louche cousin, Alexander Stewart, the laird of Glencripesdale, and one in 1839 when she and her brother-in-law went to Glasgow, its environs and Inveraray.

At Inveraray, wrote Amelia,

We were disappointed in the shops. We intended to purchase some nice present for Elizabeth but could find nothing but a few carvies [sugar-coated carraway seeds] & barley sugar lozenges, the latter did not at all meet with Alexr's approbation. We started for the third time to the romantic Glen of Essachossen. It is about 2 miles distant. The way is by a magnificent avenue of beeches. I may remark en passant that there is a beautifully wooded drive along by the lake in this of 8 miles extent. At the end of this avenue we came to a curiously shaped Linden named the marriage tree which is covered with innumerable initials. The glen put us in raptures. Although twilight warned us, we could scarcely turn it is so romantic, rendered more so from being the scene in Scott's Legend of Montrose, of Dalgetty's escape from the Castle. There are an uncommon number of springs, the water of which is very good. We partook very freely at a few of them being much heated. We at last did turn at the tree. We kept to our left and continued along another avenue of very fine trees which brought us back towards the Castle. We got to the Inn about 8, having wandered over about 10 miles of ground. We took tea with great pleasure, felt very much delighted with our numerous adventures since leaving Glasgow in the morng. We felt fatigued and went to bed early. I was much delighted with the comfort of sea water to bathe in & slept soundly.

This seems a faintly steamy passage but any question about the innocence of their relationship was surely resolved when Amelia met Captain David Campbell. Born in Fortingall and nicknamed 'Old Schiehallion', he lived in St Andrews where he was a stalwart of the Royal and Ancient Golf Club and a winner of the Gold Medal. He was also 27 years her senior. She mentioned him for the first time in June 1838 at Fortingall when she was en route to Loch Sunart.

I walked to Garth to call for Captain Campbell who returned with us to Glen Lyon House. He is one of the most amusing and agreeable old gentlemen I have ever met with, much as I regret that the delicacy of his health prevented his mixing with Society in Fortingall which he is so much calculated to adorn. He left us immediately almost.

They encountered each other in both Inverness the following year and in Glasgow. Campbell was also a friend of David Irvine, although of his parents' generation, and he wrote to Sandy in September 1839, informing him,

Captain Campbell has been at this [Eglinton] Tournament – back to Greenock where he encountered some stray friend with whom he stopped some days. He then set away for Ayr where he is at the Hunt. He called here on Tuesday evening at 1/2 past 10pm to see me & left his card & apology that he had not found me in! He returns again tomorrow when I may chance to see him. The Perthshire Highlanders made a capital figure at Eglinton. I took extreme pleasure in drilling them. They were a decided hit.

David also revealed that Campbell visited Foss.

My friend Captain Campbell who has been here for 4 days is off today for home which he will reach on Thurs afternoon at 4. I suppose in that case he will catch Clemy & James. He has formed all manner of plans for them during their stay, and many of these plans are so eccentric and unreasonable that I regret much I miss the fun of hearing them mooted and overruled.

Amelia's parents were dead. Her elder brother who inherited Chesthill in Glen Lyon did not approve of the *tendresse* that formed between Campbell and Amelia. His opinion was not valued. He has carved a small corner in local history as, in the words of Alexandra Stewart in *Daughters of the Glen* (1986), 'a notorious lecher', a man who cleared his tenants, installing his mistress in one of their houses, and importuning every servant girl who came his way. He is now a ghost, still groping women in the mansion house.

Campbell and Amelia did not rush things, but they eventually decided to marry. Sandy felt his obligations keenly, particularly as Amelia met Campbell for the first time at Foss manse, and wrote to him in 1842.

From Chesthill's refusal to even acknowledge this sad affair of yours, or to have anything to do with it, there is much responsibility thrown on my shoulders. I must take care to act in such a way as to be able to hold my face and my share in it, for you must be very well aware that it will excite no small surprise & create no small sensation when it comes to be known. You have nothing to offer Emily but the price of your commission, amounting I understand to £3000 stg which is entire as you told me & of which you will of course be prepared to satisfy me when called on. In point of fortune then as in many other respects there are very serious obstacles in the way. Pardon me for saying that I don't think you would succeed in such a scheme as cattle farming or being merchant. Why you would have nothing in a few years on which to live but her patrimony & what comfort could either of you have if reduced to that alternative? Next you are well advanced in life, considerably further I see from the register than I was aware of, or, to pay you a compliment, than you look like – It is not to be supposed that you could for many years prosecute any calling requiring labour & application of mind & body, should you now intend it. As I said before such a situation as a barrack mastership which with no great labour & requiring the risking of no capital would afford a moderate income & perhaps a retiring allowance when the infirmities of age come on is the only one for which I can see that you are qualified & to that I think you should restrict your whole attention. There may be others of the like description usually bestowed on retired militaires which you know about more than I can do but whatever it may be I recommend you look out for a vacancy in such a place & when it occurs put your influence in operation for that . . . In the meantime it is best to write no more on this or any other subject as country post offices are proverbially inquisitive & prying – I will let you know when we go that you may take a lodging for us at St Andrews where I fancy you will be at any rate at your golfing. We are all well I am etc

They were wed on 31 January 1843 in St Andrews and lived on Bell Street with only a single servant. She was 31, he 58. They had no children.

22

Buscar

Very little has been recorded about Sandy's interests outside the church. Colonel David wrote to Dr Alexander Irvine in 1821, 'I have given license to John to shoot game for the family as it is needless to allow others to take it and as a gamekeeper must be a servant a game certificate as such will not do for your son but he may shoot without a license.' The son was Sandy and he retained an interest in such pastimes, particularly dogs. He supplied David with terriers for Trinidad but he also appears to have bred deerhounds of outstanding quality, and the robust story of Buscar does survive and is worth telling. A contemporary was James Robertson, the young Edinburgh lawyer who was the recipient of David's last letter concerning borrowing against his life insurance, and son of the tenant of Invervack. One of his Edinburgh partners was Archie McNeill, and Sandy gave him a puppy.

> Edin 28th Sept 1833. My dear Sir, I should, I fear, subject myself to the misconstruction of being totally incapable of appreciating the value of the fine dog you lately presented me with. Or of a want of courtesy in not acknowledging the amount of the favor conferred, were I to remain silent on the subject of his late exploits. As I am aware that you are not wholly indifferent to those sports I shall offer no apology for laying before you a full, true, and particular account of this interesting occurrence which took place on the 16th Sept 1833. On the above day, being about to visit the Island of Jura, it occurred to me that an opportunity might be afforded me of entering Buscar, so I resolved to take him along with me. During the passage from Colonsay Buscar was very sick & as he was in no training & as far as I know never having previously seen even a hare, I conceived his sickness to have been greatly in his favor, tho' no doubt it must have caused considerable weakness particularly as he received no food previously that day & as the sickness continued for several days.
>
> As I believed him never to have seen either deer or hare I deemed it prudent to take along with me a lurcher who had been bred to rabbit hunting & shore shooting & was thought very swift of his kind. After landing we had not walked above a couple of miles into the Island when a herd of a

dozen hinds were descried at a short distance. The dogs were immediately secured and by creeping for a considerable distance we at length arrived within 200 yards of the herd, when it was found there was no possibility of getting nearer them unobserved, in fact they had even then exhibited symptoms of uneasiness & alarm.

No time was therefore to be lost, a shot of powder was fired to encourage the dogs and they were slipped. The ground on which we were sloped on the one hand with a rather gentle descent to the sea & on the other rose at nearly the same angle to the base of some rugged mountains at no great distance off. Towards these mountains the herd made. The dogs when slipped ran forward together for the distance a hundred yards or so, when Buscar, who seemed totally ignorant of the meaning of all the hollowing & noise turned round and stood for a few seconds but almost immediately catching a glance of the other dog in pursuit he instantly joined and owing to the ground rising in front both were soon out of sight.

The party followed as the best could & after having run with all the speed they were possessed for a few minutes, Buscar was observed at a short distance on our left returning down the hill preceded by two of the herd about 50 yards ahead of him but nothing was seen of the lurcher or the rest of the herd.

Buscar made quick work of it; he had run but a very short way when he was up with the hind nearest him, & immediately took hold of the hock with such strength of grasp as seemed in great measure to paralyse the limb. Notwithstanding the roughness & declivity of the ground down which he was dragged for the space of nearly two miles & which in many places was steep, he never once let go his hold. The Deer at length from exhaustion & laceration fell when Buscar quitting his hold made for the throat, the animal however recovering its legs he again resumed his former hold. This ceremony was gone through six times in my sight till finally the deer received its last fall. On coming up I found it still alive and moaning but more unable to struggle than any I have brought down by bullet, while Buscar who was literally so covered with blood from head to foot as to render it totally impossible to have discovered his real colour was tearing at his prostrate victim tooth and nail, & so excited that he would not permit anyone to approach him. More than once he vented his fury on the unfortunate lurcher who during the latter part of the case had joined us and followed at our heels.

To close this interesting occurrence the throat of the deer was cut & from that instant Buscar took no further notice of it. On examination it was found that the unfortunate animal had suffered severely from Buscar's jaws. Its tail was torn out and with it part of the back bone, the hocks were without hair & much lacerated, the throat much bruised & perforated as also the great gut.

Considering the youth of the Dog, the length of the chase, the steepness and ruggedness of the ground over which he ran, the tenacity and courage which he displayed in preserving his hold & above all his total inexperience unassisted or encouraged, I consider this feat to be unrivalled in the annals of the chase – for a more critical and philosophical essay I would beg to refer you to the sporting magazine. It was strange to observe the deportment of the different individuals of the party during the period of excitement. Some were waving their hats, others shouting, some throwing aside part of their dress, while others quite exhausted lay stretched on the ground.

David Irvine mentioned Buscar a few years later, in September 1837:

> I saw Archy McNeill yesterday. He is particularly important and it was with some difficulty that I could make him abbrowgawt (vide Plug) his jaw on dogs. He was only a few days on Colonsay & then killed 4 stags of these two in one day. Bran killed one single handed after being tossed and severely punished. Buscar is stiff and about done. So says Archie. This must be premature for a 5 year-old dog but they have clogged him into a nonentity & then the occasion of clogging. 'Bless you Sir he took to sheep & they had them home in cartfulls. 20 in a cart, Sir.' Scrope's work with Archy's article will be published immediately, I believe. Caermarthen dogs are not pure, nor nothing like it, and no other man pretending to purity. Archy now says that his kennel is the only one of the pure deerhound in Scotland.

More of Buscar's exploits are indeed related in *Days of Deer-stalking in the Forest of Atholl: with some account of the nature and habits of the Red Deer*, by William Scrope, who writes,

> The finest, I believe, and apparently the purest specimens of the deerhound now to be met with, are those in the possession of Captain McNeill the younger, of Colonsay, of which he has in particular two dogs, Busker and Bran, and two bitches, Runa and Cavack.

James Robertson reported Buscar's demise to Sandy the following month.

> Our friend Archy McNeill is in great distress and dolour. He came over here on Sunday with a most portentous face and his hair standing on end and cried 'I have shocking news'. Bless us, says I, what is the matter – nothing has happened to the Laird? 'No – but Buscar is dead.' If it had been one of his little nephews or nieces I am sure he would bear the loss with resignation but Buscar! Buscar strangled! 'If Alexander does not dismiss that d---d rascal Doherty' Here he paused ominously, bent his awful brows and gave the nod. Seriously the thing is very provoking – the dog was tied up by the unlucky Docherty, and struggled so hard to get free that he broke his chain – but he injured his neck so much that he died a day or two thereafter. Bran killed four stags this season almost single handed; and Forbes got a splendid and proved dog in Sutherland, but there never was and there never will be a deer hound to match Buscar.

Sandy was no sooner established at Foss than he was lobbying the heritors, the landowners who appointed ministers, for a larger, richer, parish.

> Manse of Foss, Jan 24th 1831. My dear Mother, It was not my intention to intimate to you the information I am now to communicate, till I myself knew more of the matter of which I am now to speak. But of course Fame or rather Scandals will carry all over the world whatever she hears the least surmise of. Therefore I will tell you all I know of the matter to ensure accuracy of intelligence. I have applied for the parish of Moulin vacant by Mr Duff's acceptance of Kenmore. My application was made by letter to Lord Glenlyon, to Mr Butter [the laird of Faskally] who I believe will have most to say in the matter, thro Sir Niel Menzies & Foss. I met Butter at Castle Menzies where I first heard of the vacancy at Moulin. I was not then resolved what to do, but asked Mr B to remain disengaged till he heard from me which he promised to do. I then wrote him, and on the understanding the report of which I am afraid was well founded that Lord Glenlyon was to give the presentation to the man of his choice. I asked Foss & Sir N to write him on my favour both of whom did in the handsomest manner at once comply with my request. I should think B will not refuse his own uncle when I am the person recommended & if he applies to Lord G for me & shows the letters of Foss & Sir N you may consider the thing as settled. However there's many a slip twixt the cup & the lip & I may not get it.

He didn't, and was trying for other parishes a few years later. His mother wrote to the Duchess of Atholl in 1838 to plead his cause: 'It was a rule I believe with the late lamented Duke of Athole to prefer the sons of Clergymen whom he had patronised to the livings in his gift, I hope your Grace may be disposed on this occasion to do my son in that account the kindness I now solicit.' But to no avail. David commented:

> What Foss [Stewart Menzies] told me was that he had had a conversation with his Lordship about Blair & that it was promised to you all right. You can credit this or no just as you please, but I would have you depend more upon your own character, claims and exertions than on the promises and exertions of some of your friends who, as in the case of Moulin, give you *a vox et peteria nihil*. I agree with you that you have been questionably used with regard to Clunie. With Dunkeld I trust you may be more & entirely successful. You have in all conscience plenty promises, but if every Patron in the belief that his neighbour is to bestow a living on you giving that in his gift away you may have the crooked stick in the long run. Better a present promotion than a prospective one & God speed you in your legitimate ambition.

But Sandy remained at Foss and his frustration began to show. David wrote to him in December 1838:

I have thought a great deal over your idea & one thing is perfectly plain & that is that if you have mentioned it to any person but to me, you have done yourself an injury. Your friends, if they ever learn, that you entertained an idea of migrating, will consider that a sufficient apology for lukewarmness in your cause, & that their influence and intentions have been under-rated, besides which I do not think there is one of them who would advise you to take the step you seem to meditate. I think the period has arrived when men like you are most needed at home. The present extraordinary position of the Church, the necessity of the popular party being met with vigour & talent & ability by the Moderates, the almost certain promotion that waits you in a very short time now, all these and many more considerations indicate that your leaving Scotland just now for any temporary, or secular consideration, look like a betrayal of that Church in which you are an officer & which may soon need you & such as you to stand between her and her pretended friends. [The Disruption of the Church of Scotland would take place in 1843.] Recollect too how short the time is since you have become urgent for promotion. I remember the time when Foss seemed to bound all your wishes – and if you must not & should not cant & profess to friends merely *ad captandrum* ways. You should 'make a fuss about yourself', or nobody else will & I am sure no man ever makes a fuss with more credit to himself or usefulness to the Church than you – I will hope to hear from you, not what impression anything I write has, but what the issue of your own reflection is, when you have considered all the outs and ins & have heard from me what the Principal says.

The matter was still on the go a year later when David wrote again. It seems that Sandy was again considering emigrating:

I know not what to say at what occupies the last page of your letter. I may however say that nothing has so unsettled one as your intimation of a thought of going abroad. That you were not successful in your application for Dunkeld or Clunie is a loss to a man anxious to arise in his profession, but certain of your friends looking to Blair were perhaps not very urgent on your behalf, nor very caring for your success in either application. Blair is to come & you still have a chance there. The interest of your friends will be concentrated upon you for it & if Robertson becomes Lord Glenlyon's Edin Agent, you could not desire a more anxious friend than him. Then there's Dull. That you are sure of when the present incumbent dies. He has one foot in the grave, & totters on its brink & he can't last long. That your present living is surely disproportionate to your position in the Church your friends admit & admitting lament, but wait a little. You have just now enough to gratify your ambition if you have failed in getting preferment, your standing among your Brethren in the Church Courts is evidence enough to you. How soon you may become a leader, and much as I am attached to you, & desiring more than anything in life your advancement, I will oppose your plan with all the energy & ability & affectionate solicitude I can.

Why leave us to go where none but young men of no family, fortune or patronage seek what they can't find at home? What will you make of Elizabeth? Do you do her justice in taking her out & by leaving her at home, you leave us, & to go out a solitary wanderer, to beg in the world, where Popery is now getting into the ascendant & where you will find little to recompense you for what you leave behind. Let me hope that you have dismissed going to Australia, from your want of success at Clunie & Dunkeld & that you will come to think differently soon.

After 14 years at Foss, the logjam in Sandy's career broke. Sir Neil Menzies, the patron of the parish, appointed him minister of Fortingall on 28 June 1842. He hardly had time to settle when, on 24 August 1843, an even more lucrative opportunity came his way when the trustees of the Duke of Atholl presented him to Blair Atholl, and he lived there in the magnificent manse for the rest of his days. In the census of 1851 his household had a housekeeper, a headwaiter, a general server, a cook, a housemaid, a nurse, a nursery maid, a ploughman for the glebe land and a dairymaid. He preached to Queen Victoria when she visited Blair in 1844. Her Majesty let it be known that the service should last no more than one and a half hours and the sermon a maximum of 25 minutes. He chose as his text 'Ye are the salt of the earth'. According to the *Glasgow Citizen*, 'He gave a plain, lucid and earnest exposition of his subject and that Her Majesty could not have had a better illustration of the Presbyterian Worship, as it is celebrated today.' Lady Charlotte Canning, a lady in waiting, reported in her journal that the queen did not enjoy the service.

Ten days after delivering this sermon, Sandy was married for the second time. Like his mother, his new wife was the heiress to an ancient family of Atholl lairds, the Robertsons of Kindrochit, but, unlike his mother, she still had the estate.

23

The Robertsons of Kindrochit

The Robertsons of Kindrochit were minor Atholl gentry, their founding forebear having been a younger son of Alexander, chief of the Clan Donnachaidh, who died in 1505. It has recently been proved that the family descends in the male line from the old Celtic earls of Atholl and probably from the ancient Pictish kings who ruled before that. Thus Alexander inherited most of the land in Atholl, and this was not to the taste of the Stewart earl, a half-brother of King James II. Alexander married twice, the second time to the earl's daughter. His eldest son, who died before his father, had married another of these daughters, and their child, William, would succeed Alexander as chief.

A couple of months before he died, the chief handed the richest portions of his lands, Faskally, to his fifth son, his eldest by the earl's daughter, by crown charter, which made its owner a vassal of the king and not of future heads of the clan. This son was a minor, so the earl, his grandfather, had control of his estate. William, the new chief, was also the earl's grandson and a minor, so the earl was his guardian as well and thus administered all the clan lands. When the young chief reached his majority he found his grandfather had appropriated much of his patrimony, leaving him no alternative but to raise the clan and resort to arms to try to regain his inheritance. The new earl, his uncle, captured him and chopped off his head in 1516. This left another minor as the chief, and the Stewart earls were able to consolidate their hold on much of the old clan territory.

So there was a distinct chill between the Robertson laird of Faskally and his clan chief, and this seemed to have lasted a couple of centuries. A younger son of Faskally received a charter from his father to the little estate of Kindrochit – meaning head of the bridge – in 1613. It lay across the river Errochty from Struan kirk, which is five miles upriver from Blair Atholl. The laird at the end of the 18th century was James Robertson. His father was in his prime at the time of the '45, but nowhere appears in the record. He probably kept his head well below the parapet. James married Jean Stewart, daughter of the prosperous tenant of Dalchalloch, just up the glen, who also had a tack on the mill at Blair Atholl. This family was an offshoot of the Stewarts of Garth and Drumcharry, and thus linked again to the kinship network of the landowning families of the district. James farmed much of his land and rented more from the Duke of Atholl at Grenich on the hillside north of Loch Tummel; this was where he lived and raised his family until he built himself a new mansion house on Kindrochit in 1823.

James Robertson had three sons. Duncan, his eldest, was born in 1779. He would inherit the estate, but in the meantime he joined the army. A second son died in young adulthood. The third, William, became a doctor in Canada and one of the founders of McGill University in Montreal. He wrote home for 20 years, between 1802 and 1822. James also had four daughters. The three younger ones, Helen, Elizabeth and Anne, never wed, but the eldest, Margaret, married a near neighbour, another Duncan Robertson, tenant of Invervack, with a distinguished clan lineage. One son of her marriage was also named James after his grandfather; he was the lawyer in Edinburgh and later Sheriff on Mull, and, later still, on Orkney. Since James Robertsons were as numerous as Alexander Stewarts in Atholl, I shall call him the Sheriff to avoid undue confusion. He was a close friend of the Kindrochit Robertsons and was also a friend and correspondent of Colonel David of Garth and of the Irvines. He had decided views on Sandy Irvine's second marriage and decided views on Sandy himself. And these he put down in his daily journal.

As might be expected, one clear difference between the Robertson and the Irvine correspondences is the frequency of mentions of and gossip about the lairds' families of Atholl. Alexander Irvine and his sons were carving their mark amid the professional classes of Scotland. Colonel David was chasing a national reputation, but the Robertsons were long-established members of the country gentry and socialised amongst the same families as their parents and grandparents.

James Robertson of Kindrochit, like his contemporary Fear Ghart, seems to have acted as an advisor to those around about. He was a justice of the peace and a heritor. He helped distribute meal in 1782, when the weather produced the worst harvest of the century and the last time that mass starvation seriously threatened. He also, for example, made out a petition to the duke on behalf of a Mrs Moon who reported that she was 'Beadfast with the pallsye for ten years past' and was seeking the equivalent of sheltered accommodation. By 1813, James had lived long enough to become the local sage. In the words of Colonel David, 'Old Kindrochit could himself fill a volume of Athole anecdotes alone'.

William, his third son, is probably the best documented. Twenty-five of his letters home survive, as well as considerable material amassed in Canada, where he made his career as a doctor, but little of this will be considered, except that which refers to the family in Atholl. He left Scotland in 1804 and returned for a last visit in 1842 when he was nearly 60 with his family. During the voyage from New York, he wrote a short description of his childhood. He showed this to his nephew, the Sheriff, and asked about having it published, but the latter 'Wrote to Dr Robertson, about publishing his memoirs; dissuading him from it.' The Sheriff thought the old doctor's mind was going, but the account, in part, does give a picture of what it was like to be young in Atholl in the late 18th century.

> I was born in the year 1784 in the Highlands of Scotland, the son of a laird, went to school at an early period under the tuition of a country Dominie, and got on as well as Highland laddies usually do. Being always smart and active, I used to run and frolic about the hills, dales and glens, but would very seldom walk and was always surprised at how people could walk constantly and sit so long at their meals. Children's meals are short, with porridge and milk for breakfast, except on Sundays when tea, bread and butter, cheese or eggs were given . . . Barley-broth, fish, fowl, grouse (in season) and beef or mutton for dinner, potatoes, milk, or sowens [porridge made from oat bran or husks that have been soaked in water, slightly fermented, and then boiled] for supper. In former days only the gentry drank tea every day and kept very early hours; they breakfasted at 8, dined at 2 and all supped between 9 and 10 pm. During the summer holidays, like other children, we used to be occupied in fishing for trout, perch, pike etc., and when old enough, shooting, snaring and catching singing birds. At Christmas-time, playing shinney [shinty], foot-ball, leaping, running races, throwing pudding stones, tumbling, dancing and singing, and eating all kinds of good things, of course.
>
> It is surprising how many of the old superstitions and customs there were and even now a few of them are kept up and believed in. For example, on Good Friday it was the invariable custom or practice for every farmer to have a pot of sowens prepared into which a buss (made of the slender twigs of the Rowan tree or Mountain Ash) were dipped and put over the barn, byre and stable and was stuck into every manure heap and plough to keep the fairies and witches away. The reason the rowan tree is used is a belief that this was the tree they tried to nail our Saviour to on the cross, but from its pliability it bent and therefore it is looked on as a sacred tree. The cursed Black Thorn, as it is called, was the wand employed.
>
> On Hallowe'en, so well described by the celebrated Burns, a bonfire is made with withered branches of trees and heather fern, and is placed far from the hamlets so not to endanger homes or stacks of corn. A torch was fastened on a Rowan stick, which was given to one of the fellows in the village, and then off he ran with it round the houses and farm-yards,

the rest following him and the Lord have pity on him if he was touched before concluding his course – no wife that year. Otherwise, the witches and fairies had free access to the farm-yards on their look-out for Tam O'Shanter. Dancing, singing and frolicking finished the sports part of the day. Harvest Home afforded a good deal of fun and frolicking. The last holiday or feast to mention is the 1st of May, or Beltane day, when a great egg feast took place – the eggs generally being boiled, but more frequently roasted in the ashes like potatoes, at a particular favoured spot outside the village . . . At the age of twelve, I was sent to school in the southern part of our country with the family of a relation and remained there six months. I then went to Perth with some of my sisters and brothers, took lodgings and remained there until the spring of 1797. Mr Scott, the English master, to whose school I was sent was the first to introduce the change of pronouncing the vowels 'A, E, & I' from Scottish to the English pronunciation, which is now generally used. At this school, as boys usually do, we used to fight pitch battles, run, caper and frolic like other wild boys. During the spring of 1797, I went to the Highlands and was at school when the Militia mobs broke out . . .

At the time Britain was at war with revolutionary France. An invasion by the French of Ireland had been narrowly averted; another was being planned from Holland and the government passed an act authorising the raising of county militias, its members to be selected by ballot from the parish registers, in order to counter any enemy landings. News of the ensuing riots of 1797 was probably the only occasion that the goings-on in Highland Perthshire reached national attention in the century following Culloden. It was the end of August. The harvest was safely in. People had time on their hands. Masked men took the parish registers. Mobs formed in the straths to demand that the lairds signed petitions stating that they disagreed with the Militia Act and would not enforce it. After achieving this, the angry people did not quite know how to proceed. Fifteen thousand were believed to be milling around Strathtay, an army without officers.

The rioters made the outraged Sir Robert Menzies add his name to their protest and then decided to cross over to Blair and force the duke to sign. The duke did what he had always done when trouble threatened. He raised his tenantry, and, with scythes and cudgels, they mustered to defend him. Women armed with long stockings, the feet filled with broken bottles and stones, preceded the mob. It was thought that the castle's defenders would not attack the fair sex. William, aged 13, described what happened to him:

I was in bed at a relative's home when suddenly a dozen men rushed into the room in a most enraged state and insisted I get up and join them. They explained that we youngsters could throw stones with a string as David did to Goliath. However my friend came in and told them I was an officer in His Majesty's Service and, wild as they were, they scurried away . . . My father soon came across the mountain, forded the river on horseback, took a private road to Atholl castle and upon earnest request went and spoke to the country people, and, having always resided in the country, soon calmed the people by offering a proper and friendly explanation.

Charges were brought against prominent agitators – the school teacher in Strathtummel had died of his injuries at the hands of a rioter – but the worst punishment meted out was a year's imprisonment, commuted when the prisoners agreed to join His Majesty's Forces. Everyone in Atholl went back to work, probably spending a few days wondering what on earth they had thought they were doing, and the matter was never raised again.

William was now an officer in the 'Clandonachie Fencibles or Volunteers'. He was shipped to Ireland to join the regiment. This was the year after a force of 15,000 French had attempted a landing in Bantry Bay in support of Wolfe Tone's rebellion, so there was the potential for some serious soldiering.

> My father, James Robertson, went to Greenock with us but as there was no vessel available for Ireland at that time, we proceeded to Saltcoats where there was one waiting for the tide to sail for Belfast.

Big brother Duncan was already in the regiment as adjutant and

> he drew my pay and allowed me sixpence a day for pocket money, which like other boys was spent on fruits, gingerbread, comfits, sweeties (as called then) and licorice – our favourite sweetmeats.

The boy nearly saw some action, calling out the guard when some rebels were sculling up the river to attack and scared them off.

Later, William studied medicine at Edinburgh, writing to his father in 1804:

> I attended four or five classes yesterday and today, the classes which I intend to attend this session are Monro's Anatomy, Hope's Chemistry and the Infirmary which I think sufficient this winter. When we went in to Dr Monro's today he had a subject before him with the intrails of it all spread and put in order and different parts of other subjects cut out in order, they had a smell that would serve to suffocate bees, there has been no great operation in the Infirmary this some days past but there are some sores there that would make your flesh creep to look at.

By 1804 William's elder brother Duncan was a lieutenant in the 88th and he lobbied hard to have his sibling taken on as surgeon in the same regiment, petitioning, amongst others, the Duke of York who was the commander-in-chief of the army. But in 1805 William was appointed hospital mate on a troop transport to North America where he was to join the 49th Regiment as Assistant Surgeon. His ship was wrecked on Cape Breton Island on 22 October. Duncan wrote to his father, 'His escape was wonderful. It was effected by a rope tied to a stone on shore. An officer of the 41st Regt and a soldier that attempted to save themselves by the same conveyance were drowned.'

William was taken in by the family of William Campbell, Attorney-General of Cape Breton Island, where he met and later married Elizabeth, a daughter of the house; they had 12 children. William served for ten years as Assistant Surgeon and Surgeon in the British Army in North America. He saw fighting, and, a dutiful son, he reported back to his father.

> 5th June 1813. My Dear Father . . . I intended writing two days ago but that very morning two of the Enemy's vessels from Lake Champlain appeared in Sight of this Garrison. There were but Three Boats each carrying one Gun. The Commanding officer and I went in a Row Boat with Two flat Bottomed Boats full of men to act according to circumstances, the firing commenced Two miles from the Island, parties were directly landed on each side of the River to fire with Small arms at the vessels and shelter themselves behind trees, the wind was down the River, the Yankees beating against it & the Tide trying to get away. But after Three hours and a half hard fighting they were both obliged to strike. They carried Eleven Guns each & 50 men. One of them was obliged to run aground to prevent her sinking but has since been got off. They are both now at anchor before our little Garrison. There were ten wounded & one killed of the Americans, only two of our own men wounded. Being the only medical officer on the Island I had my hands full for half an hour on their arrival. This is the first affair ever the 100th were engaged in and a braver set of men never pulled triggers. It is to me unaccountable how we escaped so well, for Round, Grape & Canister were falling like hail all around. It is one of the most gallant little affairs that has taken place this war – Twenty Two Guns to be Captured by Three & these in Boats exposed to every annoyance. I have got one of their flags. All winter I had charge of a General Hospital at St Johns and for the last two months have been the only medical man at this post where there ought to be three. I have given over complaining you for not writing as it is now four years since I had a letter from you.

William was present at the storming of Fort Niagara and retired from the army in 1815 to set up as a medical practitioner in Montreal. Big brother Duncan's regiment had spent time in Canada to which William refers in a letter to his father.

> 20th July 1815 Elizth is very well, she was uncommonly low spirited for several weeks after Duncan left us, he is really so good and warm hearted that every body must like him. I trust in God that he will soon be able to

get home & leave the Army to render my mother's and your latter days cheerful & happy, no one is better calculated to do so. Try to prevail upon him to marry some of the Athole young Ladies. It will be the surest way to get him to settle at home because it is now really time for him to think seriously about it. Let him get a woman equally good as himself & they must be happy. When the peace was concluded I was in hope that such a reduction in the army would take place as would provide husbands for a number of Athole's bonny lasses, I cannot tell you how much it distresses me never receiving any letters from home, it is now several years since I have had one.

Duncan too would complain that their father was a decidedly idle correspondent. No writing by their mother survives. It may well have been that she was illiterate, or nearly so.

The practice flourished, as his wife reported back.

Montreal Feby 4th 1816. It will afford you much satisfaction to learn that Doctor Robertson is succeeding remarkably well in practice indeed much beyond his expectations for the first twelve months, and we are not without hopes of being enabled in a few years to return to old Scotland and settle near you and the rest of our valued relatives in that Country.

And to Duncan from William:

12th Feby 1817, My Dear Brother, Last mail I was delighted to get a letter from you date Decr but judge of my surprise and mortification on looking at the date & finding it to be 1815. It was marked from Paris. How it was so long on the way is to me inexplicable, about the same time a letter came from my Father wrote last summer, from the post mark it was put into the office at Halifax. Donald Robertson from Invervack was the bearer that far. He most probably has settled in Nova Scotia. I am happy to find that a new house was to be built at Croftdan & hope you have planned it & will see to its building for my Father will perhaps from economy spoil it, as you will yourself enjoy it much longer than in the course of nature can be expected.

The laird's modest new mansion house would not be completed for another seven years.

27th Sept 1819 . . . John Stewart Findynate wrote me last winter he gave the latest accounts from Athole previous to your letter, what you mention respecting my Father's affairs grieves me much. Our uncle John & family [the Dalchalloch Stewarts] have been a burden to him since he was married in one way or another, it is too bad now when his own children are in a way to assist him. It strikes me that it would be as well for you to take the difference & retire on half pay, the interest of what you would receive together with the half pay would certainly be better at home than full pay & allowances following a regiment & now particularly when your presence is so requisite at home, do think of it seriously. I think Mrs R will be of my opinion. My Father would surely be delighted to give the whole management into your hands.

Findynate's father had married James's sister-in-law, a Dalchalloch Stewart. This family lived five miles up Glen Errochty from Kindrochit and squabbled amongst themselves and looked to James to arbitrate on their differences, but John of Findynate was a doctor and was closely involved in the lives of his cousins' families. The Stewarts of Findynate had been in place on their little Strathtay estate since 1575 and sold it towards the end of the 19th century. It changed hands in 2007 for £7 million.*

When the Montreal General Hospital opened in 1822, William was the senior member of the medical staff and performed the first operation, an amputation at the thigh. In 1829, he was appointed the head of the medical faculty of the new McGill University and held successively the chair of Midwifery and Disease of Women and Children, and the Theory and Practice of Medicine. Aside from medicine, he was a magistrate and read the Riot Act following an election in 1832. Troops fired into the crowd, killing three people. Some accused him of murder, and William challenged one critic, Louis Joseph Papineau, to a duel, which was refused on the grounds that the offence was a public matter. William retired in 1842, owing to ill health.

This was this year that he and his family travelled to Scotland for the first time. The visit was recorded by his nephew, the Sheriff, who visited them in April 1843 in Edinburgh, where they rented Gorgie House. The visit gives a picture of this Canadian branch of the family.

> I dined at Gorgie. When we arrived Sir George Ballingall was in seeing poor Uncle, who in driving through the Town yesterday was overset with his son William at the head of the Mound, and both considerably injured. Went in to the dining room, and when Sir George left, to the Drawing room.
>
> Saw Caroline first. Then my Aunt came in. At the first glance she looked older than I had expected. She is tall, dark and extremely Lady like, and I think sweet tempered. Sophia came next, and I mistook her for her sister Kate, she looked so much less in her mournings. Kate is a little creature, but very pretty and with a high nose and longer chin than any of the rest of the family. They say she is like her brother James, tho' I cannot see it. Sophia is liker James than any of the rest. She also resembles her mother, as does Georgie who will by and bye be the finest woman of them all. Sophia is rather undersized, and very pretty though not so handsome as Mrs Robertson. Duncan the second son is extremely like the Kindrochit

---

* See Appendix 5

family, and a fine boy. George the youngest again is like his mother, and a
still finer little fellow. William, the eldest, who is confined to bed with his
bruises, resembles no one that I have seen, and tho' seemingly a good lad
he is the plainest and least promising of the family.

Saw poor Uncle in bed before dinner. He reminded me very strongly
of Kindrochit, and still more of old Dalchalloch. Alas his mind seems
entirely gone but even under the distressing eclipse it is easily observed
that he was a man of very considerable powers. He talked wildly of various
impracticable plans and speculations.

The Sheriff said his farewells the following Sunday. 'Took leave of my
Uncle, Aunt and Cousins. They are a very fine family; and Mrs Robertson
is a remarkably agreeable woman. I have never met a person that I liked so
well on so short an acquaintance.'

24

Captain Duncan

Duncan, the eldest son of the laird of Kindrochit, would have enjoyed the same idyllic childhood as described by his brother William. Duncan was already in the militia when his brother joined as an ensign, and, in 1803, he was appointed adjutant. Like his brother William, he was a tall, good-looking man. In 1804, he was appointed to the 88th Foot, the Connaught Rangers, an Irish regiment with a fierce but rackety reputation, and posted to camp at Eastbourne. The Colonel of the 88th was an Athollman, General Reid of Straloch, and it was likely his influence that persuaded some of the locals to join. Duncan was as assiduous a correspondent as William to his father, and his father was as dilatory in his replies to him as he was to his younger brother.

A friend, Patrick Robertson of Trinafour, an estate a few miles up the glen from Kindrochit, who afterwards became innkeeper at Dalnacardoch, wrote when Duncan joined the 88th. His letter demonstrates how a commission was regarded at the time: 'I assure you it gives me a great deal of pleasure to hear of your being so comfortably provided for at last.' The war against the French gave a marvellous career for tens of thousands of Highlanders. The sons of the lairds became officers, and the young on their estates joined the ranks. Colonel David wrote to the same Patrick Robertson in 1814 about a fellow officer when Napoleon was in exile on Elba. 'This peace for which we have been praying and fighting for so many years is a severe check to him no doubt as many others.' It sometimes seemed that the main function of the enemy was to cull superior officers to give opportunities for promotion to their juniors, and the end of the war meant stagnant careers. In 1809, Duncan, then in Portugal, felt that his advancement was in jeopardy and wrote to Wellington.

> I hope you will pardon the liberty I take in addressing you upon a subject that materially concerns the whole of the junior officers of the Regt and most particularly affects myself at this moment as the senior Lieut. To you, sir, we all look up with confidence for protection and support in preserving unbroken the regular chain of promotion in the Regt. The many proofs we have already had of the interest you take in us tends to our advancement

either individually or as a Corps give me confident hopes that in the present instance your usual efforts will not be wanting on my behalf . . . The hope of promotion when it fairly comes to our turn is the strongest incentive we have to perform our duty with zeal and alacrity and to submit cheerfully to every privation incident to a military life, in this hope I rest satisfied that I shall in my turn benefit by your disinterested exertions in favour of your Rgts.

Before going abroad, Duncan was stationed in various barracks and camps along the south coast of England to guard against the possibility of invasion, but he kept closely in touch with affairs back home as well as trying to launch William. 'I am exceedingly happy to understand that the Sheep have held out so well this winter,' he wrote to his father in 1805.

I pray that the prices may answer next season better than they did last year. I am rejoiced to find you are pleased with the progress the Girls made while at Perth. Notwithstanding of Mrs Howall's Bill, I am convinced you never spent an equal sum that will afford both yourself and the whole family so much pleasure. At present a person is considered nothing without an education whatever their other qualities may be . . . It is with much pleasure I have it in my power to inform you that I am getting more and more closely into the good graces of my Brother officers, and particularly the Command Officer Lt Col Duff. Mr D Campbell gives fresh proof daily of the sincerity of his friendship. Col Duff has done me the favour of recommending William to Genl Reid, to be appointed Assist Surgeon to this regiment in lieu of our present Asst Surgeon . . . I appeared in yesterday's Gazette a Lieut in this Regt. It is of great consequence at present as we have a great number of Lieutenancies vacant. I am now the 14th Lieutenant and we should have 24 so that I shall have 10 after me very shortly. We are encamped here near the top of a high hill covered with heather. From the top of the hill we can see the French Coast as plain as you see Shehallien. We see at least fifty miles of the French coast, we hear nothing of Invasion now & indeed we trouble our heads very little about it. All is anxious expectation about Lord Nelson and the Combined fleets at present, nothing else is spoke of. The Duke of York is expected here soon to review the troops. We are at present busily preparing for him.

A few months later Duncan wrote again to his father.

I am happy to understand everything goes so well with you in Atholl this season. I hope your wedders will give a good price. We have had very fine weather here of late which makes the crops very abundant. I hope you have had an equally good season. I shall give a short account of the harvest in this part of the country. The oats and barley is not better than you have generally, and indeed the barley is not so good, nor has it all so good a colour, but the wheat is very good and all green crops are excellent. They are the worst farmers I ever saw tho, the whole of the oats is cut with a scythe and they leave it the same as you do. Hay is never bound up, they turn it with a rake once and after leaving it on the ground at least ten days, they collect it together in heaps and instantly carry it to the barnyard and stack it in long stacks exactly the same as you do. When the stack is made it is covered. It all shakes with corn, and sheaves fall like rain. They take a little better care with barley, the wheat is cut the same as with you but the stubble is higher than my knee always and in some places actually half as long as myself. They do not make stooks as you do, they put no head upon them, and they have not the same number of sheaves in them, some have four and some have ten or even fourteen without any head whatsoever. They are generally very bad shearers. One good shearer with you would cut as much as three of them. So much for the English farmers.

Duncan had proposed a partnership with his father.

I really cannot deny that your reasoning respecting partnership is very just. I will therefore cheerfully give up the idea for the present. My reason for proposing such a thing will appear obvious to you, that it proceeded wholly from the anxiety I must naturally feel for your interest . . . Auchleeks will be quite high now that he is Major. I suppose Shierglass is another. There will soon be nothing but majors and captains in that whole Country. I intend to write my Uncle upon his promotion to wish him joy, I will address him Captain Stewart. [The laird of Auchleeks was a Robertson, Shierglass a Stewart.] . . . I was ordered to Beachy Head Camp on duty and that very night the stable in which my horse was took fire and burned so rapidly that my horse and another was burnt to death, together with the saddle, bridle and all my other strappings. This was a loss of about £40 to me, you may be sure it put Malcolm Stewart's bill out of my head. It was about a fortnight after I met with this loss that I heard of my being allowed the 2s a day for the keep of a horse in the Atholls. This news came very seasonably, I ordered John Stewart to pay the £16 to a Capt Thomson of the 88th who was then at Perth and that he would bring it to me to enable me to purchase another horse. Capt Thomson has not yet joined but I suppose he has it for me as I direct. As I was on duty at the time I left my horse, I applied to government for an indemnification. I did not receive any answer until this morning when I heard by a letter from the Secretary of War that an account of the peculiar circumstances of my loss I was to be allowed 30 guineas. This was a glorious piece of news for me when I did not expect a single farthing on account of any loss. I made the application. This will make me comfortable again. With the £16 Capt Thomson has, it is more than what I lost. I did not like to mention the loss of the horse in my last letter to you, and indeed I would not have mentioned anything about it now were it not that I am allowed for him. It would be ridiculous to make you anxious and uneasy about a thing which could not be helped.

In early 1806, Duncan mentions 'the Death of Mr Pitt, your old favourite, and consequent change of Ministry will it is supposed occasion many changes in our present Military system. The Line will be considerably augmented it is thought, and the present Voluntary system will undergo some great changes. A short time must throw some light upon it. There is much said likewise about an increase in pay of Officers. This of all others the most welcome piece of news with us, let who will be Minister. I hope we shall get an increase in pay, for it is much wanted, with subaltern officers in particular'. Later on in the same letter he reveals that he is a close friend of David Stewart of Garth, at that stage still a major.

> I had a letter ten days ago from Major David Stewart Garth, from Gibraltar it was written fifteen days after his arrival there. The 42nd & 78th landed at Gibraltar all safe about the 16th Nov last. He desires to be remembered to you, my Mother and Miss J Stewart Bohally, Major D and me made a mutual promise at parting the last time I saw him to keep up a regular correspondence and he does not seem to have forgot it, nor will I either. I intend to write him in a few days.

One of Duncan's correspondents, Duncan Campbell, born in Rannoch and paymaster in the 88th, gives an insight into life back home. He was the son of a factor of the Forfeited Estate of Struan and elder brother of Sir Archibald Campbell of Ava. 'I had a fortnight's leave to go to Rannoch to see all my friends and concerns in that Quarter who I was happy to find all well but looking older than when I last saw them especially my mother and Strowan. [This was Alexander Robertso of Struan, the name-father of Sandy Irvine.] Strowan I think failing much and still living in the Barracks [Rannoch Barracks at the west end of the loch] a Bachelor. 2ndly as to Athole, the Gentry there are all dying or what is worse Mad.' Campbell goes on to say that he expects that Duncan will be sent on an expedition to Mauritius where 'you'll get some hard knocks with little prize money.'

But the destination was not to be Mauritius, as Duncan told his father in July.

> Just when I was sitting down to communicate to you an unexpected piece of intelligence, I received yours of the 30th ult. This Regiment received Orders yesterday from the Commander-in-Chief to prepare to embark for Foreign Service immediately and ordering all Officers absent to rejoin forthwith. This order was quite unexpected. We imagined that we should continue in our present quarters for this season. I understand that three Battalions, a Brigade of Guards and nine Battalions of this line, are to accompany us. It is pretty certain that we are going to the Mediterranean, that is either to Malta or Sicily, but most likely the latter place. Sicily is

the finest climate in the world and the cheapest place. Indeed every part of the Mediterranean is a fine Climate. We are all as happy as it is possible to make us at the Idea of getting to so fair a Country and the best of it is that Troops are never kept too long there, like the West Indies. In short we are happy to be sent any where to escape going to the West Indies. We expect an order to march in a week or ten days to whatever place we embark at. I am delighted at going. I shall meet where I go the 42nd, 35th & 78th Regts there. How happy I shall be to see Major David Stewart, Major G.D. Robertson [later a major general and the clan chief], Capt Dick, Dr Dick's son [Robert Dick of Tulliemet, across the Tummel from Logierait, distinguished himself at Quatre Bras and Waterloo and, as a major general, was killed leading a charge against Sikh entrenchments at Sobraon in 1846], all of whom are there, and also Sandy Robertson, Trinafour.

25

Fighting the French

Duncan participated in two battles. His first was a little-known disaster. The expeditionary force sailed south but not to the Mediterranean. It spent a month on the Cape Verde Islands and then on to the Cape of Good Hope. From there the convoy went to St Helena and arrived at Montevideo on 14 June and prepared to attack the Spanish colonies round the river Plate. Buenos Aires had been held for 46 days the previous year before the British were expelled. This was to be the second attempt. His letter describing this adventure is long, formal and full of detail, almost as though he believed his writing would reach a wide audience. He used it after his retirement in writing notes for a history of the 88th.

With the 88th at the head of the army, the British swept aside the Spanish forces opposing them and paused at the edge of Buenos Aires. Eventually, 4,500 British troops were drawn up on the edge of city and the 88th was ordered to march in two columns of 226 men apiece along two roads that led into the centre. They were forbidden to use firearms; the attack was to be carried out by bayonet alone.

> On entering the Town every thing was quiet not a soul to be seen. We penetrated into the very heart of it before a single Shot was fired. The first noise we heard was a heavy firing of the Musquetry on our left wing in the next Street. Immediately after a heavy firing of Cannon began on the left . . . We continued to advance until we came opposite to the Church that we were ordered to possess. We entered the outer Gates of it instantly under a dreadful fire but from want of proper Tools to break open the inner doors we could not get into the body of it to the Top. We then sallied out again leaving about 30 Men Killed & many wounded in the Gate way. We proceeded along the Street under a continued fire from the houses for some time until we were within 100 yards of the great square in front of the Citadel. Here we were brought to a stand for every one that advanced was killed or wounded. We turned off immediately to the left by a cross Street and broke into two houses with the assistance Butt end of the Mens Firelocks. We took possession of three houses and occupied the Tops of them by as many men as we could spare from the doors and Windows. Here we maintained ourselves for 3 hours in spite of what the Enemy could bring

against us. We commenced firing a little before we broke into the houses. I was wounded slightly in the Calf of the right leg by a Musquet Ball while in the Church Gate Way. I kept up with the men as if nothing happened untill we got into the houses. On perceiving it was slight I was quite happy. When it struck me I thought it went through my leg but it only took a bit out of the inside of the leg. It was a good deal bruised around the wound, which caused me to walk lame for about a Week but I am now as well as ever nearly. I left off when we entered the houses. We were pretty safe here for about half an hour until the Spaniards had time to collect on the Tops of houses that Commanded us, that is higher houses near us. For the last two hours and a half we remained we had very hard fighting, indeed of the kind latterly not a man could peep over the Top of the houses without being fired at by a number, not one or two. For the last quarter of an hour the men tumbled down as fast as they went up to replace another. At last we were completely surrounded and by such numbers that we began for the first time to think that matters were going on ill in other parts of the Town, otherwise the Enemy could not spare so many men to attack. In short after a short consultation amongst the officers we determined to surrender to save the lives of the few brave fellows who were yet able to stand by as by this time we lost one half of the whole number brought into action and had no hopes of any assistance. This was a dreadful moment.

The survivors of the 88th, the Rifle Corps and the Light Infantry were imprisoned in the citadel, 104 officers and their men.

'How was it possible that men without a Shot in their Musquets without Cannon and divided into such small bodies as we were could succeed?' wrote Duncan.

We were sent to be sacrificed to no purpose. There was not a man to be seen on the Streets. What was the use of our Bayonets therefore? There was nothing to charge but Brick Walls. Of the number the 88th brought into action we lost 109 Killed & 3 Officers and 15 Officers & 111 Wounded making in all 238 which is about the one half. The 87th Regt suffered severely likewise but nothing to what we did. They had about 650 men engaged of which they lost 50 Officers & 67 Killed & 13 & 108 Wounded, in all 193. The 88th lost as many as the rest of the Army put together leaving out the 87th. Had Genl Whitelock attacked the Town as any other man would have done which was to bombard it for a few hours with heavy Guns, it would have surrendered without losing one tenth of the men we lost. I hope there will be a strict inquiry into the Genls conduct. Indeed the whole of this Army cry out for it and if there is I shall be exceedingly surprised indeed if his head dont answer for it.

Lieutenant-General Sir Harry Smith, then an 18-year-old lieutenant in the 95th Regiment, was in the same column as Duncan and was also captured. He sums up the debacle in his memoirs:

Thus terminated one of the most sanguinary conflicts Britons were ever engaged in, and all owing to the stupidity of the General-in-chief and General Leveson-Gower. Liniers, a Frenchman by birth, who commanded, treated us prisoners tolerably well, but he had little to give us to eat, his citadel not being provisioned for a siege. We were three or four days in his hands, when, in consequence of the disgraceful convention entered into by General Whitelock, who agreed within two months to evacuate the territory altogether and to give up the fortress of Monte Video, we were released. The army re-embarked with all dispatch and sailed to Monte Video. Our wounded suffered dreadfully, many dying from slight wounds in the extremity of lockjaw.

To his chagrin, Duncan's father did not bother to reply to his account of the battle. Back in England at Ashford barracks, he wrote,

I have really lost all patience at not hearing from you. I feel the greatest anxiety in consequence. It is only natural I should when I see all my brother officers daily receiving letters from their friends, while I have not heard a syllable for the last sixteen months. I trust in providence that when I do hear from home it will end my anxiety by bringing good news. At present I am inclined to dread it. If yourself, my mother and all my sisters and brothers are alive and in health it is what I principally wish to hear, all other matters are but a secondary consideration . . . It is with the deepest regret that I acquaint you a Hospital Ship in which there were 2 Sergt & 24 Privates of this Regiment (all of them wounded men) has it is feared been totally lost. The Ship was very old and made much water before the Gale in which the Fleet separated, from which it is supposed she must have sunk during the gale as nothing has been heard of her since, and every other Ship of the Fleet has arrived 3 weeks ago. When the 88th landed in South America in June we were 808 Privates and now when all our disabled men are discharged we will not be above 500 strong, making a reduction of 300 men in a few months, indeed I may say in a few days, for the most of them were killed or rendered unfit for service in the four days in which we were engaged at and near Buenos Ayres. I trust however that the author of all our misfortunes (I mean the two generals that commanded) will meet with what they so justly deserve. I understand a Court Martial is already warned to try them the moment the one who is on his way home arrives. I am afraid you have had a severe winter hitherto, but we have had very fine weather here which I hope you have likewise. John McDonald (Dalchosnie) [later Lieutenant-General Sir John MacDonald] desires to be remembered to you. John and I live together at present and indeed have done so ever since Duncan Campbell left this Battn. Do not forget what I have urged in the beginning of this letter, but write to me the moment you receive it. With sincerest love to all, not forgetting Aunt Betty.

Duncan's disdain for the 'author' of the Buenos Aires debacle was soon satisfied when General Whitelock was court-martialled and dismissed from the service.

James, Duncan's father, had managed to write to his son before the receipt of this irritated letter with the news that the 'Athole Volunteers' of which Duncan had been adjutant had presented him with an inscribed gold watch. He was highly gratified.

> The second paragraph of your letter really surprised me. I mean that which communicates to me the distinguished honour conferred upon me by the officers of my late, and greatly esteemed Corps, the Athole Volunteers. It is a thing I never had the vanity to dream of. Their marked kindness and hospitality to me while amongst them, more than sufficiently rewarded any service that I was capable of rendering to them . . . and the Gift being presented to you for me at such a time, renders it doubly valuable in my estimation.

As usual, Duncan continues with advice on the management of the estate.

He was granted leave in early 1808 and wrote to his father from Perth on his way back to his regiment. He had encountered friends at Dunkeld, including the Irvines.

> Yesterday morning it was my intention to be off early for this Town but it was the day on which the Boys at the school of Dunkeld say their orations, I was detained in consequence and saw all the people that I wished to call upon in the Church hearing the Boys, among whom were Mr & Mrs Irvine and Miss Stewart Garth. I was informed by them that Major David had come off to Perth the evening before, but it seems he had to make some calls by the way as he is not yet arrived here. I expect him however here today, I intended to set off for Edinr this morning, but I wished to see Major Stewart first and I had some other business besides that detains me here today, I shall be off tomorrow morning positively. Major David will certainly be here today some time and I hope we will be able to manage matters so as to travel to London together.

And in his following letter from Danbury camp in Kent, Duncan records that David passes on his good wishes, and he had been promoted from Major David to Colonel David.

In this letter, September 1808, he states that he 'met Tom Stewart Blackhill in London. He told me he was going to accept of a Company in some English Militia Regt but I did not believe it.' The letters are peppered with mentions of his Atholl contemporaries. Tom Stewart of Blackhill [part of the Cluny estate], for example, pops up again in 1811, this time in a letter to Duncan from Sophia Stewart of Shierglass. She is further quoted later, and her spelling and punctuation is erratic, so for reasons of readability, her errors have been sometimes amended.

The good folks in Strathtay are all quite full of that odd creature Tom Blackhill's marriage which he says is to take place immediately, but to vouch for the truth of it is more than any person can in reason pretend to, as they have only his own authority for it. The report is that having gone to Edinr soon after his Father's death, and inspected the Will, he found that he could not be deprived of the estate but was not to get possession of it till he was married. On which happy intelligence he return'd to Perth, took a post chaise, set out for Crossmount in violent haste, where he arrived that night, put the Question to Margt, was happily answered in the affirmative, return'd immediately with the joyful news and told Mrs Menzies at Weem he would be back in a fortnight with his Wife!!! Whether we are obliged to Tom's inventive genius for the Whole Story except the part of his being at Crossmount a little time must determine, but I can hardly believe it possible that my friend Margt should be so infatuated as voluntarily to plunge into a depth of Misery from which death alone can free her. Yet, if almost any person could tolerate a life with such a confirmed ne'er-do-well as the Laird of Cluny unfortunately still is, I believe the Lady in question may. Her very Moderate share of sensibility and uncommon sweetness of temper will certainly make her suffer less than most others would in the same circumstances but I fear there is no great hopes of his reformation, with a person who is in general inanity itself, unless being Lady Cluny will make her exert her energies a little. The Blackhill Ladys are said to have £3000 portions each; the old gentleman was tolerably liberal of which I daresay the Misses will very soon feel the good effects in the increased number of their admirers.

Duncan's battalion joined the rest of the 88th in the peninsula. Vittoria was the second battle in which he was a participant, and his letter is worth quoting in full.

23rd June 1813, My Dear Father, Aware of the anxiety you will feel on my account when you hear of our doings for the last two or three days, I lose not a moment in acquainting you that I am safe and sound and never in better health after all our fatigues and dangers than I am at this instant. I had a few lines ready written to send off yesterday but I could get no opportunity. Having a little more time today I intend to make it something longer.

Lord Wellington's dispatch will give you a better idea of the battle of the 21st than is in the power of any individual to do who was merely a humble actor in the conflict but there are a few circumstances which may come to the knowledge of individuals that his Lordship will not dain to notice in his official dispatches though they may still be interesting. The 21st June has been one of the proudest days for Britain that is to be found in its history. The victory was certainly the greatest that Lord Wellington gained and the nature of the Battle was such as to prove to the whole world and to the Enemy in particular the superiority of British Troops over

French and I rejoice to say that both the Spanish and Portuguese Troops who were engaged fought like Lyons, nay some of the Portuguese Battalions showed both discipline and gallantry equal to any of the British even, I speak not from reports but from what I saw with my own eyes for two Portuguese regiments fought alongside us the whole day. I know not what the official dispatch will say as to the time the Battle lasted but this much I know full well that a distant cannonade commenced on our right at Eleven o'Clock from which moment the firing never ceased until night although the Battle cannot be said to have become general along our line until about half past twelve or one o' Clock. The greater part of our army had to cross a river to get at the Enemy. Our Division (the 3rd) under Sir Thomas Picton crossed the river in the face of the Enemy by a Bridge which our Brigade forced about half past 12 o'Clock. We crossed with such rapidity that altho the French had cannon placed to scour it and sharp shooters beyond calculation lining the whole opposite bank, we lost only a few men. Had the British been placed in the situation the French were to defend it no human power could have forced this Bridge. This first success put us all in high spirits, however the grand thing was yet to come. Our Brigade the 45th, 74th & 88th formed in three separate columns the moment we crossed the Bridge, and moved as quickly as possible to attack a round steep hill in front of us about 500 yards. The Enemy had a body of cavalry at the foot of it and a strong column of infantry hid behind the brink of it but our advance was so rapid and determined that the Enemy's cavalry first gave way and then the infantry without daring to show their faces. The 88th being the centre Rgt was posted opposite the middle of the steep hill where tremendous opposition was expected. However we were not long getting to the top of it. I had the honour to command the leading company of the Regt up this hill. When we got to the top we turned to our left where we saw the Enemy's grand line of Battle formed about half a mile off ready to receive us. A few moments after Lord Wellington came up from a height upon which he had stood in the rear and passed at full gallop to the left of the 88th where he stopped to view the Enemy's line. He had hardly looked at them when he ordered the 88th which was the nearest Regt to him to form a line and advance to attack a strong body of the Enemy formed in close column about 100 yards only in front of us, this column was covering the centre of the Enemy's principal line and seemed determined to make a hot stand. The moment we advanced it opened a tremendous fire upon us but at the same time began to waver and some even to run away. We gave them a Volley and intended to charge immediately after but the fellows did not wait for us and ran like a flock of sheep into a small straggling village something like Pitlochry. We followed them to the end of the village when our Genl ordered us to halt and wait the arrival of the other Divisions of the Army which were intended to form on the right and left of us, for at this moment we were quite alone and within 150 yards of the centre of the Enemy's main line which opened a truly tremendous fire of shot and shell upon us to drive us back from the village and the fellows who ran away picked up a little courage when we halted and annoyed us very much from behind walls and houses. The 74th very soon came up to support us and charged with a wing of the 88th through the Village out of which we drove the Enemy in an instant and occupied the whole of it. If our Genl (Brisbane) had not halted us we would have driven the Enemy out of this village at once without giving him time to do us any mischief. The 74th and us continued in this village in spite of the Enemy's efforts to drive us out of it until our line was complete and advanced to the village. When it came up to us we rushed forward and occupied our place in the general line of Battle. This moment was the most interesting of the day. It is impossible to give an idea of the steadiness and rapidity with which the British line advanced not heeding the Enemy's fire though vollies of cannon were fired at us. The Enemy's line very soon began to break and by the time we got fairly within about a hundred yards of its centre the whole gave way and ran for it, we followed as quickly as possible, the Enemy's second line soon showed itself but was forced to run as quickly as the first. We still continued advancing over hedges and ditches and fields of the finest corn I ever saw. The constant roar of cannon and musketry during this advance was awfully grand, perhaps not less than 200 pieces of cannon firing incessantly. At length we saw the Enemy's third and as we afterwards found out last line advantageously posted. The ranks of the 88th marched to the attack of the third line was as if we had set out from Grenich [the house on the hillside north of Loch Tummel where Duncan was born and his father still lived] and marched through your corn towards the Tullich on the top of which the Enemy line looked very formidable. Our general halted us as if at Wester Tomandrainach in a field of corn until the rest of our line should line up with us on our left and right. The Enemy fired incessantly at us during this little halt but we never fired a shot in return nor took any notice of him as we wished to preserve our means of destruction until we should be close up with him. When we were ordered to advance and charge the line on the hill, the fire from the Enemy became extremely hot indeed and as we were quite exposed we lost a great number of men. However this did not in the smallest degree check our progress. On the contrary we advanced all the quicker. When we were within 150 yards the Enemy's line gave way and fled as usual. We pursued almost out of breath. A good number of the French were killed here. This hill being forced the whole of the Enemy's third line fled. At this moment Lord Wellington galloped past to the front of our Brigade to view the State of the Enemy. Here he beheld one of the most gratifying sights he ever saw, the whole of the Enemy's army flying away in the greatest confusion, cavalry artillery and infantry all mixed. Our cavalry was now ordered to the front to complete the work of destruction. We rushed on as fast as our legs could carry us to support them. From that moment there was nothing but prisoners the Enemy abandoning artillery, baggage to facilitate his escape.

Night alone put an end to the pursuit. Our Division halted for the night about a league (three miles) beyond the city. The fruits of the Victory are the taking of 151 pieces of cannon 415 Ammunition wagons, the whole of King Joseph's carriages and baggage and cows and mules loaded with the plunder and Baggage of his officers beyond all calculation, besides the Military Chest with a great deal of Treasure. I was ordered here on duty the day after the action to pick up the wounded and to assist protecting the captured cannon and this gave the opportunity of seeing the extent of the Enemy's loss. The number of prisoners we have taken is by no means as great in proportion as the ordnance. Their killed and wounded are numerous and so are ours as you will observe by the Gazette account. The 88th lost nearly 250 men in killed and wounded, by far the greater part wounded in consequence of the great distance the Enemy took care to keep from us. We (the 88th) have only one officer killed, Ensign Saunders, & five wounded. All the Athole lads in this army are safe, I have seen every one of them in these few days & I heard of them this very day – I am to remain here some days and I shall write you again soon, God bless you all, D. ROBERTSON.

I have met

1 John McDonald Dalchosnie and his brother

2 Genl Campbell, Carie [The buyer of the Garth and Drumcharry estates in 1834]

3 James Stewart 42nd Duntanlich

4 Jno Stewart Kinnaird

5 John Stewart, son to Peter Stewart, Perth

6 Charles Stewart who was with Mr P Stewart many years, son to Donald Stewart Shierglass

I also saw this very day John Dow from Tomantaid

All these are well as our Q Master & Donald McDonald are quite well at this instant

DR

This battle was notorious for the plunder that disappeared into the pockets of the British Army from King Joseph's baggage train. Duncan makes no mention of his share, if any, but shortly after the war he commissioned a lavish set of silver cutlery with a 'K' for Kindrochit on each piece, as well as some fine mahogany dining-room furniture. The quality of land his father farmed is unlikely to have yielded sufficient spare cash for this, nor did his wife bring much of a dowry.

The 88th fought their way through Spain, across the Pyrenees and into France. The next letter from Duncan arrived in Atholl in July 1814.

I am really perfectly sick of this war and so are the whole Army with the exception of perhaps a few great men who look for either titles or promotions from a continuance of it through interest and not merit. The state in which we have been in since we entered France on the 10th of Nov last is enough to make those wish for peace who never did before. To describe it within the compass of a letter is quite impossible. I shall therefore not attempt it. The 88th has not had much to do in the fighting way of late although we have been present in every thing that happened . . . We find the French inhabitants in general very civil. The people in this part of France are much the same both in manner and dress as those Inhabitants of the other Side of the Pyrenean Mountains. All the inhabitants of the vallies of the Pyrenees and the Country bordering on them on both the Spanish and the French sides speak the same language. It is called Basque and is as different from both the French and Spanish as the Gaelic is from the English language and what is a little remarkable too, the men in all this extensive district wear blue bonnets precisely the same make and shape as those wore by the Low Country Farmers in Scotland but not quite so large . . . The Country here is very fertile and most beautiful. If it was summer weather we would do very well but nothing grows at present and our animals are nearly starved for want of forage. However I hope Peace will relieve us all soon. This would really be a heavenly country to live in time of Peace. The French Army and us are very polite to each other except when we are actually fighting. Our Sentries & theirs are posted within 50 yards of each other. We almost daily have conversations with their officers on duty on the neutral ground between the Sentries. On these occasions we entertain each other with a little Brandy or whatever else we have to spare and seem in short to vie with each other about who shall be most polite!! In half an hour after this friendly intercourse (as I saw it happen only a fortnight ago) perhaps one party receives orders to attack the other and we go to work directly to destroy each other by every means which our ingenuity can invent. For one who has time for reflection, this state of things must appear very unnatural but those accustomed to such scenes think nothing of it.

After Napoleon was exiled to Elba, the 88th were stationed at Valenciennes near the Dutch border. Duncan had been petitioning Wellington for leave ever since the army had entered France and this was finally granted. The regiment was then posted to Canada and missed Waterloo. After the war, it settled down to the tedium of peace-time soldiering.

26

Sophia

Duncan's wife was a long time coming. She was suggested by Colonel David in 1814 in a letter which also commiserated with Duncan over the demise of James, the second of the Kindrochit brothers. His death is described as 'a merciful release' but nothing else is known. The colonel wrote, 'Malcolm Stewart, Brother to Shierglass, is dead in Jamaica, so that if you and your old sweetheart, Miss Sophy Stewart make up matters you and yours may be Lairds of Shierglass, for I see no prospect of Shierglass marrying, nor of Capt Charles Stewart, nor Mrs Stewart, Derculich, having children, so that I would have you not delay too long like me, till I am too old, stiff and grey, and none of the young girls will look at me, and those of my own standing such as my old flame Miss Flemyng are something like myself – we have seen better days, and you are now in your prime, so don't lose your time and opportunity.'

One suspects Sophia can hardly have believed her luck when this officer and heir to Kindrochit proposed. They were both 32. 'I had allowed my affections to be irrevocably engaged long before an avowal of your sentiments,' she wrote in 1811, her first surviving letter to him.

She was born in the Netherlands. Her father Donald had blotted his copybook by killing his brother-in-law. Nestling sadly beneath a quarry on the south side of the A9 opposite Blair Atholl is the ruin of the mansion house of the Stewarts of Shierglass. Built about 1720, this is a typical example of the kind of dwelling built by the lairds in the 18th century. In 1765, the owner of the precipitous estate went to market at Moulin. In the evening he supped in the inn with his brother-in-law, the Stewart laird of Bonskeid. This man was locally feared and disliked since he forced his tenants and others to join the army so that he could collect the bounty money. During the evening an altercation erupted between the two men, who were almost certainly drunk. Shierglass was said to be eating cheese using his dirk and cut himself on the lip. Enraged by the laughter of the others, he lashed out with his knife, caught his brother-in-law beneath the chin and killed him.

It was believed that the ghost of a murdered man would haunt his assassin unless he paid homage at the victim's burial. Shierglass watched the funeral procession from the hillside before fleeing to Holland with his family to escape facing trial for murder. There he joined the Scots Brigade of the Prince of Orange. Eventually he returned home and the families were reconciled. This incident is referred to by Effie Stewart of Kynachan in the letter she wrote from Edinburgh after she had eloped. She wrote it three years after the event, which shows what a sensation the killing had created in Atholl.

At the beginning of the 19th century, the Stewarts of Shierglass were teetering on the edge of financial collapse and the property would be put on the market after the death of Sophia's brother in 1818. Like so many others, the final nail in the coffin would be legal bills – in this case the residue of a dispute with the Duke of Atholl over shooting rights which lasted five years and was won by the duke with costs.

A letter of 1806 to Elizabeth Robertson of Trinafour from her brother revealed that 'Miss Jean Stewart, Shierglass has presented her hand to the rich nabob, lately of India. Long may she reap the benefit of his substantial body and person. Both are unacquainted to me, and unquestionably my anxiety for them is but little. Duncan, Kindrochit, throws out a few words not agreeable to the proud nabob.'

The proud nabob inherited the estate of Derculich, one of that run of estates, which include Ballechin, Findynate, Cluny and Blackhill, along Strathtay. Sophia often stayed at Derculich, with her sister, and indeed it became her main residence after the sale of Shierglass but she was not particularly fond of her brother-in-law, Alexander Stewart. During the various disputes after the death of her brother, he displayed 'that inveterate spirit of opposition and annoyance which he seems resolved to show at every step of the proceedings.'

Duncan took Colonel David's advice. Since he was soldiering in far-flung places for most of this time, his courting was by letter. Sophia did not keep his letters; he kept hers, and this gives an opportunity for a local perspective. As she rightly observed in her first letter to him in 1811, she was conscious of the 'inferiority of my epistolary talents' and she can ramble on about the least interesting subjects, but she did her best to pass on gossip. To be fair she 'did not well know what to write, for tho generally employed, there is that sameness in my life here that "every day is still but as the first" seeing very few people and in the literal sense of the word hearing nothing affords little opportunity of communicating any thing new'. Hers was the kind of life that features in Jane Austen's novels – with rather nastier weather.

Apart from the familiar social round, the general occupation for her and her circle was spinning. Flax had long been an important cash crop and it was turned into thread at home on the Saxony wheel, the typical device of imagination, before being woven into linen by machine. At certain times of the year the 'muckle wheel' would be employed to turn wool into yarn for homespun clothes. Of an evening the household would sit round the fire and spin. Sometimes one of their number, or perhaps a stray man, would read to the spinners from the newspaper, a novel or some improving religious work. They might just gossip, or sing. One can see why Sophia found it hard to fill her letters.

> You have frequently My Dear friend remarked that I never could be at loss for subject when writing you, as every incident that occurs in this country cannot fail of interesting you – but pray consider what incidents either trivial or important are likely to arise in the confined circle in which I of necessity move especially while the weather is such that we feel little inclination to leave our own fireside, and every body else seems equally fond of theirs.

Her style takes some swallowing. Judging by the way she responds to Duncan's letters, so did his.

> I rejoice to find that the benediction of your goddess arrived so opportunely. But Ah! My friend instead of your goddess permit me for a few moments to assume the more useful character of Monitress and begin with advising you to beware of flattering her who looks for nothing but reciprocal sincerity.

Duncan must have toned down his passion, since her next letter states,

> The style delights me and its adoption, in preference to the rather too impassioned language of your former epistle, is to me a most flattering proof of your attention to my wishes. Far, very far be it from me to suspect you of insincerity.

In this letter she says she had spent a couple of days at Grenich with his family which cannot have been wholly straightforward as their intended union was a secret – of sorts. She visited the Stewart Menzieses of Foss, the parents of Sandy Irvine's first wife, and Lady Foss teased her about Duncan.

> I was much pleased with our visit to Foss, even though I did suffer a little from Mrs Stewart's raillery, but as she spares nobody I didn't mind it much, tho certainly Mrs S M's remarks and queries have sometimes a freedom in them almost approaching to rudeness, which puts one to the disagreeable necessity of sacrificing their veracity or telling what she has no right to know. Indeed I think her manner altogether has rather too much of the 'ease which marks security to please'. We must not therefore quarrel altho for the present she is pleased to play off a few livelinesses at our expense.

To keep Duncan in the picture she lists the people she sees – the
Trinafour estate a few miles up the glen from Kindrochit had been bought
by a Robertson who had prospered on marrying the heiress of a Devon
squire. He would later buy Auchleeks from his cousin Duncan in 1821,
thus keeping at bay a John Stewart who 'is talked of as a very determined
offerer for Auchleeks, but I hope no such plebeian will succeed the
respectable family that so long possessed it'. 'The Fincastle Misses' were
Stewarts and about to lose their estate; a couple of generations earlier
Henry of Fincastle married Bonnie Jeannie Mercer's sister. The Urrard
family [Charlotte Stewart of Urrard had married Major James Alston
who was now laird of the estate, which was at the centre of the battle of
Killiecrankie. Their son was later in the 79th, and David Irvine reported
him 'being carried out mortal' from a private dinner in Glasgow], Mrs
Revd John Stewart, wife of the minister of Blair Atholl, who also
preached at Struan Kirk within sight of Kindrochit, Duncan's Stewart
cousins from Dalchalloch as well as a roll call of the families of the
lairds of Crossmount, Strathgarry, Findynate, Killiechassie, Edradynate,
Bonskeid, Ballechin, Duneaves, Lude, Bolfracks, Kinnaird, Auchleeks,
Weem, Cluny, Blackhill, Donavourd, Orchil, Frenich, Foss, Drumcharry
and Balnakeilly.

The Duke of Atholl and his kin seemed not to have been part of this
circle, although they were seen by Sophia 'almost every day visiting their
new purchase opposite to us. I understand they admire it very much'. This
was the Kirktown of Struan, which the duke had bought from Robertson
of Lude. This ancient family was in the process of financial collapse – legal
bills again – and Charles McInroy, one of the nabobs into the origins of
whose fortune it was unwise to look too closely, would buy their estate
from under the duke's nose. Local tradition held that he paid for Lude
with gold stashed in the nosebag of the horse on which he entered Atholl.
His son would later purchase Shierglass from the Stewarts.

As well as visiting – and marrying – each other, the entire community
gathered for the Great Event, the Sacrament of Holy Communion, which
was held four times a year and rotated between the parish churches in
Highland Perthshire. In August 1811, Sophia had, she told Duncan, 'the
pleasure of seeing your father and sisters at Blair Sunday last, being the
Sacrament day all the Country were as usual assembled. My Brother had
the felicity of escorting no fewer than nine young ladies to the Church
door but unfortunately they all deserted him there.'

A couple of months later she

had the pleasure of being a night at Grenich for which Lady Foss says I
am turned perfectly impudent and barefaced. Every trifling circumstance

will again be laid hold of as 'confirmation strong' of a report, the truth of which has been much debated betwixt some of our too busy neighbours since you left the Country, but my anxiety to get your sister Betsy home with me induced me not to sacrifice too much to mere punctilio. I am now most happy, as Betsy was good enough to come with me and I hope will be prevailed with to stay for some time. I need not say your Sister sends you her love, but I may with truth say she could not with greater sincerity than does, My Dear Friend, your Sophia Stewart.

Soon after this, with Duncan's sister Elizabeth – Betsy – then staying with Sophia at Shierglass where she kept house for her brother John, she wrote that they

were favoured a few days ago with a visit from Miss Betty, Orchil, who was as usual most particular in her enquiries for you. She was kind enough to introduce to us a very agreeable young lady, a Miss Sweedland, a connection of Mrs McDuffs of whom you may perhaps have heard. Miss S. is very lively and very accomplished but the airs and graces of a high bred Londoner were so entirely novel to us natives that they have afforded ample subject of conversation ever since, especially to Betsy, whose good humour and lively remarks are a constant fund of entertainment. What do you think of Trinafour leaving the Country, without once looking in upon us? Was he not very unkind indeed? Betsy is quite inconsolable and I you may suppose not a little mortified at such a falling off. I have not seen our friends at Derculich this long time. They are both well, but will not I fear be prevailed upon to cross the Boat of Tummel again this winter. They made a narrow escape in going home from here, some time ago, by the temporary Bridge across the Mill lead at Logierait giving way under their Gig. Providentially neither Mr or Mrs Stewart had got into it after crossing the Ferry, and the servant and horse were got out without material injury.

Perhaps one of the obstacles to a wedding was her brother. Sophia felt it her duty to look after him, with the help of a small troop of servants, and would have to find him a substitute for her should she get married. She wrote to Duncan in Edinburgh, on his way back to his regiment after leave.

Mr Keay's Maiden Sisters are not old – I am told they are very amiable, and though no beauties, I have a positive plot on one of these young ladies for a sister-in-law though you must know I never saw either of them, and whenever I can gain influence enough over my obstinate brother to make him spend a winter in Edinr I will certainly endeavour to turn Match Maker and persuade him to marry and be happy with one of the fair ladies in question. I would ask you to forward my plan by speaking a good word for him now, but I suspect you would be rather a dangerous deputy in such an affair. You may suppose from this I have lost all hope of succeeding with

Miss Stewart Urrard. By the bye, we ought to have been there Monday last, the 11th of Novr, being the anniversary of their happy day. The Major still delights to honor it by collecting as many of his friends as he can, but unfortunately the day was unfavourable, and in place of the expected Gala were obliged to content themselves with apologies from Balnakeilly, Derculich &c &c &c. Betsy and I were as lazy as the rest, and considered more inexcusable, being somewhat nearer. Mr Stewart Strathgarry and my Brother were the only two that attended. Betsy is quite well. She does not surely suspect that I write you, whatever else she may guess, but she has so often heard me reprobate the custom of Misses corresponding with their swains that I should feel a little ashamed were my own practice known to differ so much from my favourite theory.

27

Darling Doff

The year 1812 began with a sniffy note from Sophia. Duncan had been posted to Banff. 'I must take it for granted you arrived in safety, and are pleased with your new quarters much, and agreeably engaged no doubt when you could not spare one half hour to an absent friend.' Amongst the attractions of Banff for Duncan was the proximity of his influential friend General Sir Alexander Duff, who was about to be married to the daughter of James Stein of Kilbogie. Duff, son of the Earl of Fife, had been in command of the 88th in South America. Duncan must have overdone his description of her, for Sophia's response dripped with jealousy.

> Whatever a few fastidious people may say of a trifling disparity of rank or want of fortune it will be impossible for anyone not to admire this new acquaintance of yours. Let me consider now if ever I met with such an assemblage of good qualities in the limited circle in which I have moved – amiable, intelligent, unaffected and affable. Beautiful in person, Graceful and interesting in Manners. All these, combined in one lovely object, form I must own a Being of a very superior order to those we generally meet with in the common walk of life and, when bestowed as 'Heaven's best gift' on any favored Mortal, cannot fail of contributing largely to their happiness.

Times were changing – what times do not? Although the estates were still largely held by their ancient possessors, the softer attractions of Perth and Edinburgh were beckoning. 'I would not be surprised that in a few years there would be as few residing proprietors in Strathtay as there is in this already nearly forsaken Strath. You would hear that Ballechin has resolved upon leaving his beautiful residence and it is currently reported that Mr Izett wishes to let his house and return to the South, but from the very high value he puts upon it, it is not improbable he will be allowed to inhabit it himself. Five hundred a year would be paying pretty high even for the beauties of Kinnaird.'

Their marriage contract was dated 12 April 1816. Drawn up by a Dalchalloch cousin, Duncan Stewart, a lawyer in Edinburgh, it was witnessed by James Robertson esquire of Kindrochit and Lieutenant-Colonel John Macdonald of Dalchosnie.

A five-year break in Sophia's letters ended in 1817. Duncan was still in the army, involved in peace-time soldiering with the occasional spell in Ireland, the news of which posting was received with 'astonishment and dismay' by Sophia as it has been for more recent generations of military wives. The most obvious change in Sophia's letters was that her husband graduated from being 'My Dear Friend' to 'My Dear Duncan'. She was also more secure and assertive.

'All friends at Findynate are well, John dined here yesterday after visiting his patient the young wife at Edradynate who has been obliged to undergo the terrible operation of having a tooth drawn already which has fortunately relieved her for the present.' When Sophia uses the word 'friend', she always means a relative. Both she and Jessie Irvine also used it when writing to their future spouses. Anyone described as 'poor' was usually dead. In this case the mother of Dr John Stewart of Findynate was a daughter of William Stewart in Dalchalloch. Her sister was Duncan's mother. Dr John married Grace Stewart who, like the Irvines, was descended from the Stewarts of Kynachan. He had been a naval surgeon and taken part in a dramatic frigate action, capturing the Banda Islands in the Dutch East Indies.

Sophia recounted a visit of the future chief of the Clan Donnachaidh in 1818, again giving an insight into the style of life of the leading families in Atholl. She actually got his rank wrong. He was a retired army captain, not a colonel. 'We had a visit from Col. Robertson and all his family from Duneaves, they came to dinner Monday and stayed all night on their way to Strathgroy. The Col. really makes a most Patriarchal appearance trudging along beside his covered cart containing his wife, his three children, and two servants.'

A month later she was writing to Duncan at Banff about fish.

> I believe you disapproved of sending the salted fish I wanted but I still wish for it notwithstanding, Barny will be a good judge of it. If you would make him buy three or four good ones and bind them on the top of the trunk, they will be safer and cheaper than if in a separate package. Make him cut off their heads as they are of no use and add to the weight.

The fish arrived. 'I put you to a great deal of trouble, and I fear to more expense than I intended for my dried fish which I thought were always cheap in Aberdeen, however they seem admirable fish if you paid high for them.'

On 21 February 1821, Dr John Stewart wrote to Duncan. 'It was most gratifying to me and every one of the family to hear of Mrs Robertson being safely delivered of a daughter.' This was to be their only offspring, named Sophia Jane Stewart Robertson but known as Sophy. The child was the centre of Sophia's life – and Duncan's. Her godfather was the Sheriff, Duncan's nephew James. In 1821, Sophia was writing from Derculich in Strathtay.

> I must say that travelling with my little darling is a charge greater than I ever had . . . Our young traveller bore the journey well and is I thank God healthy and lively, altho her teeth have already begun to be troublesome. She has already got one and another is cutting the gum, poor little thing. This is the beginning of her trials but I have great reason to be thankful that it has been made so easy to her as yet.

The Stewarts of Ballechin were one of those families that were now only visiting their estates in summer. 'The Ballechins were all here a few days ago. They were inquiring very particularly for you. Ballechin seems quite a New Man on having got back to the Land of his fathers again but the Lady is at heart a Southron and will continue so. The crops look much better on this side of the Hill than in Athole, tho even here they will be very short, but there they are very much burnt up. Indeed, such a long tract of dry weather has destroyed the hay and pasture lands irrecoverably I fear this season.'

In August 1821 Duncan was stationed in Manchester – a couple of years after the military had charged a crowd, killing 15 in the Peterloo Massacre – and they were wondering if the time had come for him to resign his commission. But there was no living in Atholl for him. Kindrochit was still his father's estate, and Sophia divided her time between her brother-in-law's house at Derculich and Shierglass, which was on the market. August was the time for seaside holidays. Kirkcaldy, Portobello, Rothesay, Helensburgh or the Isle of Man were talked of as suitable resorts.

However, her baby, and a little clucking, was what Sophia's letters were largely about.

> Oh My Dear Duncan, could you know how very much I long to place my little pet in your arms? I often fear you forget her altogether, but when you see her, she is so completely your own, you 'cannot choose but love her', such a lively interesting little thing, but I must not raise your expectations too much for she is neither very stout nor very pretty, but you will easily believe that I am very partial and that I wish to bespeak your partiality likewise.
>
> I do not My Dear Duncan at all like the idea of your being in these, so very new, Barracks. They must be excessively damp. You certainly ought to have fire in your room during the day, and take care not to place your Bed near the wall. I trust you will not consider these precautions unworthy

of your notice. We know well there is nothing more dangerous than this damp of New Buildings.

In 1823, Duncan had some leave before returning to Ireland. His wife wrote from Derculich.

We left Kindrochit about a fortnight after you did and, after staying a few days at Shierglass, came over here. Our little pet I am happy to say enjoyed the drive here much, and was not a bit the worse of it. She seemed perfectly at home the moment she came in and appeared to recognise every person and thing she saw our friends from Shierglass came here a few days after I did, the Ladies stayed ten days, Miss Stewart Crossmount was also here, and before they left us the Blair Manse girls came, who, with Catherine Stewart from Perth, are still with us. All these young folks with Sophy make a little more noise than is quite agreeable sometimes, and make me wish I had deferred my visit a little longer, but as the weather generally admits of her being out she does not upon the whole give much annoyance and is as lively and restless as ever you saw her and often asking when Papa is coming back with a Coachy and cock robins for his 'Darling Doff'.

Auchleeks House was being demolished, and a new mansion would replace it. Sophia went to the dispersal sale.

Your sisters and I went to Auchleeks roup, the things did not sell high, but they were not at all so good as I thought. We did not purchase many things but what we got were good bargains. The Trinafour people it seems had no intention of taking the furniture for the new house and bought very little only some beds which they got for half price.

A couple of months later Sophia mentions the Trinafours again.

I was surprised to find when we came through Perth that Trinafour and his English Lady had gone up to the Highlands. Peter Stewart says she is a most intolerable Cockney and very unfit for a place like Trinafour in its best state, and in its present state I think she can hardly suppose it fit for her. It was certainly inconsiderate in the Laird to expose himself so much to the ridicule of his Lady, a compliment I understand she is rather ready to bestow upon him without so much cause as he has now given her.

Duncan and his siblings had been brought up at the rented farm of Grenich on Loch Tummel. Presumably this was due to the lack of a suitable mansion house on Kindrochit. But now this was to be put right.

I heard from Betsy yesterday and am glad to find they are all well at Kindrochit. Sim comes over here almost every week and gives me regular accounts of the progress they make. Sim is so partial to his own plan that he torments me about the roof and the windows, which he insists will never look or answer so well as them he recommended. However I am glad to hear they are making good work, and his looking at them occasionally is a great advantage. He says your Father is quite taken up with the house and is in constant attendance every day. Pray was it the beginning of July or August that they engaged to have it ready? However it does not signify which for they can scarcely have it done now either the one or the other.

A month later, she wrote,

The walls of your Father's house was to be finished as this day, and I begged of them to lose no time in harling it while the weather was so good. I see the garret windows are aligned from the gable to the front, as in the original plan. It seems Sim said they could not conveniently be placed in the Gable owing to the two chimneys. I certainly think it would be better to abide by the Regiment till you were ordered Abroad, provided you could then leave it. Your little Darling Doff is I am thankful to say in the best possible health at present. She had another bad cold just about the time I last wrote you, but she got perfectly the better of it, indeed I never saw her more vigorous and lively than she is at present. Sophy desires me to tell 'Papa that she is a very good girl, and wishes very much to see Papa' in which wish I most sincerely join her.

And in August 1823 from Derculich Sophia is worried about the damp of the new once again.

I do not think your Father's house can be dry enough for them this season. Indeed My Dear Duncan I wish we had another home for the winter. It will be painful in the extreme for all partys our being in the house when they leave it whatever time it happens. It is so like turning people out that the idea is quite distressing, and I really wish it could be avoided. It would be no great expense taking a small lodging in Perth for the winter: – tell me what you think upon this Subject and I will remain in Perth or here till I hear from you.

28

Clan affairs

As Dr Stewart reported, James Robertson of Kindrochit died in 1823.

Aug 25. Kindrochit Sunday 10am. My Dear Duncan, With the deepest grief I have to acquaint you that your worthy old father is extremely ill. On Monday last he felt slight pain in his throat but continued going about as usual until Friday following when the pain got worse with some difficulty in swallowing but not such a degree as to alarm your sisters or himself. About 10 o'clock last night he suddenly became alarmingly ill. I arrived here about 6 o'clock this morning & found him very distressed. His breathing very laborious with great difficulty in swallowing, pains in different parts of his chest. I immediately applied a mustard sinapism to his throat which has blistered it already, but I am sorry to add without offering the slightest relief, he is getting hourly worse & from his present alarming state, unless he soon gets relief which I must reluctantly confess to you that there is very little hope of, he cannot sustain many hours. This unexpected distress has plunged your poor sisters into the greatest grief. I need not say how extremely anxious they are that you should endeavour to be here as soon as possible. There is nothing to be expected from present appearance so you & them must be prepared for the worst. Helen has your letter of the 15th instant a few hours after writing to you. Mr & Mrs Stewart arrived at Derculich on Friday in high health and spirits from Portobello where they left your Lady and little Sophy as well as you could wish . . . [26 August] Monday 8am. It is with pain and sincere grief I have now to tell you that he expired about thru 8 o'clock this morning like an infant going to sleep. He was perfectly sensible and recollected all day and down to the last hour he could swallow & did not seem to be suffering much pain. The funeral is to take place on Saturday. Your poor sisters who had too much experience in like melancholy occasions hope they will be able to conduct everything to your entire satisfaction. They are perfectly aware that it is impossible for you to be here. Mrs Robertson is expected in the course of the week. All here unite with me in affectionate regard to you. I am, yours affectionately, Jno Stewart

And, with one more letter, Sophia's correspondence ceases.

You will before this reaches you have received the Mournful tidings of the Death of your affectionate and worthy Parent, an event which, when I last wrote, I little imagined was so near us and which, however long delayed must when it comes bring pain and grief to the hearts of an affectionate family. Yet My Dear Duncan we have all great cause of thankfulness that your Father's sufferings were so short and his transition from this world to the next so easy. Your Sisters I am thankful to say are as well as you could possibly expect to see them. I left Porto Bello as soon as I possibly could after receiving the first accounts from here, but as I was obliged to stay a day in Perth, I did not arrive here till Friday. The Interment took place Saturday, and it will be gratifying to you to know that everything was conducted with the greatest regularity and propriety every person asked attended, except two or three. The day was good and all was got over in good time. John Robertson Milton [tenant of Milton of Invervack who married Duncan's sister Margaret and fathered, amongst others, the diarist and Sheriff James Robertson] signed the funeral letters and your excellent worthy cousin John Findynate officiated for you at Dinner. Indeed his considerate and kind attentions on this occasion can never be forgot. Tho certainly My Dearest Duncan no other person could make up to us for your absence, he did all he could, and much more than any other person would think of, to supply your place.

The Sheriff was a regular correspondent of both Duncan and the Irvines – and devoted to little Sophy all her life. Then a lawyer in Edinburgh, he wrote to Duncan on his father's death.

My Dear Uncle . . . I had a letter from my brother to day of yesterday's date; he says the funeral is proposed to be on Saturday. Mrs Robertson and Soffy are going off to morrow at 6 o'clock in the morning. They are both in good health. Mrs R wishes me to say that, as you cannot be at home before the funeral, nor indeed till every thing is settled, you had better not come over until you get your affairs put in proper order, particularly if you will be obliged to go back again to Ireland to do so. Forgive me my Dear Uncle if I also advise you to remain. I know how anxious your poor sisters will be to see you and how anxious you will feel to come home; still the immense trouble and expense of travelling so far to no purpose almost but to see them is a great sacrifice, and when you intend too to be home in the latter end of next month. Yours most affectionately, James Robertson. P.S. John Stewart Garth is at home. I suppose both he and the Colonel will attend the funeral.

Duncan took half pay on 4 December 1823 and settled at Kindrochit. Evidence of his interests beyond those of a small country gentleman is scant, but he became deeply involved in Clan affairs. This was a year after his friend Colonel David had achieved a national sensation with his *Sketches of the Highlanders* and had further raised the profile of the Highlands in helping Sir Walter Scott with the tartan extravaganza of the King's visit to Edinburgh.

The Sheriff wrote to Duncan from Edinburgh in May 1824.

> The Clan Dinner went off this year rather heavily. There were only about 16 or 17 present. I could not attend. You will have heard of an intended Club of the name for the institution of which principally the Clan were called together. There was a Secretary to it appointed with powers to call a meeting or take any other step he might think conducive to promote the object in view. This Secretary is your friend James S. Robertson. He was Croupier at the Dinner. 'Secretaryship and all, thou hast it now'. He is a keen clansman & a good fellow notwithstanding. He has been hitherto so much engaged in business (Whitsunday term) that he has not called a meeting of the Committee, or done any thing else instead except having written to the Chancellor of the Exchequer requesting him to become president of our Society. I have seen the answer couched in most polite terms – but declining on account of nonresidence in Scotland . . . By the bye Mr McInroy was asked and thought proper not to honor us with his presence. We are all in high dudgeon of course. You should not ask him to dine with you at Blair. I shall write you immediately after the first meeting of the Committee. They have already anticipated the funds of the Club by paying away £10.10 for a bagpipe to the piper Alexr Robertson from Strathbrane.

That same summer was formed the Association of Atholemen. Duncan and Colonel David seem to have been its engine. The Association's first minutes read:

> At a Meeting of the Clan Robertson in Athole held on the 8th June 1824, it was suggested by their chief Capt Robertson of Strowan, that it would be a most desirable event to form an association with the Clan Stewart within the bounds of Athole, as in ancient times, for the purpose of promoting and cementing a generous, manly, and Brotherly friendship between the two Clans, such as subsisted between their ancestors, also to revive and cherish a proper Highland spirit and feeling among the members of the two Clans, and give encouragement to every species of industry, for which this part of the Country is well adapted, and especially the manufacture at home and the general adoption of dress of those fabricks which have ever been peculiar to the Highlands, namely Tartans, Plaids, and Bonnets.
>
> The meeting unanimously approved of the proposed association and a few gentlemen of the name of Stewart present (the representatives of some of the Stewart families of Athole) gave their cordial assent to the proposition also.
>
> Col Stewart of Garth, one of the Gentlemen present, recommended that some of the Gentlemen of each Clan should be nominated to act as a

Committee for the purpose of making the necessary arrangements for the intended meeting, as he could not anticipate any objection on the part of his Clan to the immediate adoption of the plan now proposed.

The following gentlemen were accordingly named to compose the Committee viz Captain Robertson of Strowan. Col Stewart of Garth, Mr McInroy or Robertson of Lude, Mr Stewart of Foss, Mr Robertson of Auchleeks, Dr Stewart of Bonskeid, Capt Robertson of Edradynate, Mr Stewart of Derculich, Mr Alex Robertson Auchanree, Capt Stewart of Shierglass, Capt G. Stewart Allain, Capt Robertson Kindrochit.

The first meeting of the Committee to take place on the 12th of Nov next – Col Stewart of Garth, Capt Robertson Kindrochit convenors. Capt Robertson Kindrochit was requested to forward a copy of the minutes of the proceedings of the present meeting to each of the Gentlemen now named, and in the name of the meeting to elicit their assent and co-operation.

This was to be the organising committee of the Highland Games, which is still held at Blair Atholl each summer. It had been started by Colonel David in 1822 at Dunkeld, and, after the 1826 meeting, the duke's factor wrote:

> There was yesterday a most indecent exhibition of the Highland Society raised by Col David Stewart . . . They went to assemble in Inver park, and, among other indecencies, several of them stripped to the shirt to run races . . . The Society is becoming so riotous and dangerous, particularly since they have a teacher of fencing, for which prizes are given, that your Grace may wish the carrying of arms at least to be prohibited.

By 1835 it was highly respectable. The duke died in 1830. His son was insane and the late duke's brother Lord Glenlyon took over at Blair and became patron of 'The Athole Gathering'. Duncan was secretary and treasurer. He also became secretary of the Clan Donnachaidh Society, which was based in Edinburgh.

On the death of Captain Robertson of Struan in 1830, Duncan advised his sister about the clan relics, and she wrote with gratitude. 'I had a letter from General Robertson for the Stone of Colours [the Clach na Brataich, the charm stone of the Clan, unearthed by Duncan Reamhar, the chief, during a campaign against the MacDougalls of Lorne in the 1330s and now on view at the Clan Centre at Bruar] and the Seal with the Robertson Arms etc etc to be forwarded by the Coach and to get Box Booked. Where shall I send it to meet the Coach and get it booked? I trust in your indulgence for the trouble I give at present. Indeed I know not sufficiently to express my gratitude for all the obligations I am under to you.'

The new chief was General George Robertson. Duncan and his nephew James handled the succession of the Struan estate. Alexander, the Jacobite poet chief who had been a contemporary of John Stewart of Kynachan, left his lands in Rannoch and Glen Errochty encumbered by debt and, after the Annexed Estates Commission had handed the estates back in 1784, the debts were still outstanding. Trustees had control, and General Robertson battled to oust them. He wrote to Duncan in 1830, 'There is not any person whose opinion I would sooner have than yours . . . My dear Sir I again beg to repeat to you my most grateful thanks for your powerful aid on this occasion.' The general initially settled in Elgin but a close friendship was struck between his family and Duncan's. The general's daughter Frances, known as Frankie, would become Sophy's closest friend.

29

Sophy goes to school

In 1837, Duncan died. David Irvine made reference to this in a letter to his brother Sandy, then minister of Foss. 'Kindrochit's death shocked me. He can be ill wanted in the Country and I am afraid he was but little prepared for another world.' Whether his lack of preparation means that he died suddenly in apparent good health, or that he retained some wicked ways that needed repentance is not known.

His heir was his daughter Sophy. Aged 16, pretty, vivacious, she embodied both an ancient cadet family of the Clan Chiefs and a modest estate. The latter was put in the hands of trustees on her behalf. The most prominent was the Sheriff, Sophy's cousin and godfather. Duncan's father had borrowed money in 1818, and this was still unpaid, so preparations were made to let the house to a shooting tenant, Captain John Drummond. The unmarried sisters Anne, Betsy and Helen moved a couple of hundred yards east into Kindrochit Cottage; Sophia went to Derculich with her sister and the nabob, and Sophy went to school in Edinburgh for a year to learn ladylike accomplishments and also to introduce herself into Society, although most of the people she mentions are Atholl families 'in town' for various reasons. A short run of letters from Edinburgh from Sophy to her mother survives and a couple from some five years later. Two are to her trustee, the Sheriff.

Sophy arrived in Edinburgh in October 1838. Her first letter to her mother at Derculich came a fortnight later.

> 25 Royal Circus, Edinburgh. Octbr 20th 1838, My own dearest Mama, Will you think me in rather too great a hurry for I have not allowed quite a fortnight to elapse? However I hope you are beginning to long for a letter from poor me. Oh dear Mama, how happy & thankful I was to receive your letter. I hope you reached Derculich in health & happiness on Friday. All our party have made their appearance at last. Miss Emma Duglas the last arrival appears to be a nice lady-like girl. She is not a general favorite, but as yet I have found her very agreeable. She is past sixteen, & is an orphan poor thing, so I intend trying to be kind to her.

I like the Miss Learmonths better every day. They are so kind, not the least like Governesses. Miss Mary the second is everybody's favorite, but I have found them all very kind & Miss Amor also. We had our first lesson this season from Mr Turnbull the dancing-master on Tuesday. He is the oddest fat little man I ever saw. It is perfectly impossible to refrain from laughing. He makes such odd remarks & talks incessantly. However he is a good teacher & attends more to the figures &c than to the mere steps. The two Miss MacEwans & Miss Duglas learn dancing so I am by no means the only great girl in the hopping class. I like Mr Cooper the writing master very much; Oh how much nicer a Master is for writing & arithmetic than a Mistress. He makes every thing so clear and easily understood. I hope I shall improve in my writing, for Mr Cooper always says 'A very nice copy Maam, very neat.' Miss Shindley also says that I am attentive & is to send me a pretty new piece before my next lesson. I think I hear you say 'What a vain little monkey.' However it was but a lapsus &c & I don't intend being vain any more, but the hope of being able to play you a tune decently when I go home pleases me greatly. Mr Riccarton appears to be a very good French master & I have enough of work to occupy my time without being the least hurried.

I have got my stays at last & they fit very well, Miss Learmonth had paid the woman before I knew of her being there, but having the cash I shall pay for my work &c so it will be the same thing at last. I wish you or Auntie would try to think of some work for me; I have finished my purses and the bag is very nearly done. However I will just take to my old friend the trimming and fag away at it. I wish I had thought of asking Aunt to have the kindness to send me some apples for New Hallowed Even. I am sure she would not have been angry. However it is too late now, for the Edinburgh carrier leaves Perth on Thursday I believe. At least he is here on Saturday.

I dined at the Strowans. The Nickles, Frances & I went to the Gardens last Saturday. The Nickles sent me an invitation to dine with them, which I was obliged to decline being pre engaged at the Strowans. [General Robertson of Struan's mental health had broken down and, aged 72, he was living in an asylum in Morningside. He died in 1842, leaving an only son and heir also named George Duncan Robertson who had been born in 1816. His daughter Frances was a close friend of Sophy; his son was not. The Nickles were the family of Major later Major-Gen. Sir Robert Nickle 1786–1855, formerly in the 88th Regiment, in which Sophy's father had served.] However we spent a nice forenoon together, & I hope to go some other time. I shall not finish this epistle till to-morrow for Frankie & I dine at Mrs Bell's to-morrow & she calls for me at twelve. I must bid you good night dearest Mama & will finish my letter to-morrow if possible. Good night & joy be with you all. Sophy.

Saturday morning. Good morning! Dearest Mama! I have recommended scribbling this most sensible & interesting epistle tho' I am sure it will tax your patience to read it but as nobody looks at any of our letters I can scribble away as if I were talking to you. Mr Cooper gave us pens to mend last night & I am writing with them to-day, so I hope you will find me capable of being useful in that line, when I go home. Miss Learmonth has been very poorly for some time. She is now better & with her sisters desires her best compliments to you.

Dr Bell has been vaccinating some of the children. Would you wish me to undergo the operation once more? Miss Greig my room fellow has not been at all well poor thing, her stomach has plagued her very much, she is getting better, but several of the girls have had slight colds &c, and I have been the healthiest & strongest body in the house & have had no greater ailment than a slight headache since you left Edinburgh.

By the bye dear Mama please to send me one of my work boxes, as soon as you conveniently can, for I require it very much. I do not mind which you send, only if my Aunts can get at the one Carry gave me it would not scratch the table so much because as how it has no feet.

I think I have now said all I have got to say & an unconnected mixture of stuff it is, but this being Saturday the noise of tongues &c by which I am surrounded is most uncommon. Besides I have a great number of my old enemies, in the shape of cotton stockings, to repair and have no good Mama to help me now. Little Anne Cunningham called out to me, 'give my love to your Mama', so I declared that down it would go. Tuesday is the birthday of two of the girls but I do not intend setting the fashion of birthday gifts as there would be no end to it. We do not think we shall have any great fun till Hallow'even – alas for a saunag [a Gaelic sing-song]. I have not left myself room for questions, besides it is better to tell you all about what you don't know is it not? & in your letter be sure to tell me every thing about every body. Give my best love to the Edras [the Stewart Robertson family, who lived at Edradynate, an ancestral property in Strathtay less than half a mile to the west of Derculich]. I hope they will remember to write to me. Give twenty thousand loves to dear dear Aunt. I shall write to her next. Give my love also to Uncle & to my home Aunts when you write. How is Mr Robertson? Quite well I hope, remember me to him. How is old Miss Menzies?

You said I should send for Davie when I wanted a coach, but who do you think Miss Learmonth employs? No other than Donald Stewart, Couldaloskin; he knew me the other day & grinned in my face, till I turned & stared at him & thinking he had a Couldaloskin face I nodded. I afterwards found out who he was. [Couldaloskin, now Cuiltaloskin is a farm a couple of miles up Glen Errochty from Kindrochit.]

Do you not think I shall become quite a scribbler when I pester you with such long letters? I must leave a corner, in case Frankie will have some news. Do write to me soon, I shall weary dreadfully before the end of a fortnight, much less a month. It is not cold enough for worsted stockings yet, but I will get some by & bye.

Pray dear Mama excuse errors for I cannot think of going carefully over such a long epistle. Poor Mama to have to decipher it all. By the bye do not ask the Glen to carry any letters or messages for me if he comes here. Frankie sends her love. Believe me my beloved Mama your own affectionate Sophy.

The Glen to whom Sophy refers was Alexander Stewart of Glencripesdale, which lies on the south side of Loch Sunart in Morvern. Dr John Stewart of Findynate had married his mother's sister. Nicknamed Glenstool, he later married the beautiful Clementina McDiarmid of Bohally, descended from Charles Stewart of Bohally and Clementina of Kynachan, and they played host to Clemmie Irvine and Amelia Stewart on their jaunt in 1838. Amelia called her 'Athole's Fair Champion'.

Sophy's letters are filled with social events and names. In her next she talks about the Sheriff.

I had a note from James the other day desiring me to tell you that he had had an epistle from Capt Drummond who has been so careless as to lose the Inventory of furniture at Kindrochit which I had such trouble in writing for him. James says that his note was a very civil one & he requests you to send another copy as soon as you can. James amuses me by his solicitude about my wants, every time I see him he says 'now are you quite sure that you do not require pocket money or any thing'. However I have more than two pounds of pocket money remaining. I have got my ring, it is a very pretty one & by far the most highly valued of all my ornaments. I also had a very kind letter from Miss Irvine [Clementina, who died on the voyage to Australia]. I was greatly astonished some time ago by the receipt of an epistle from Clemy Stewart Glenlyon House, by Post too. I have not answered it, nor am I at all sure about doing so, for I think of Glenlyon & every thing belonging to it as seldom as possible & with anything but pleasurable sensations.

Clemy at Glenlyon House was Glenstool's sister. Another indication of the extraordinary kinship web in Atholl is that this Clemy married her cousin Charles McDiarmid, whose first wife, Clementina Irvine, is mentioned in Sophy's previous sentence.

In her next letter Sophy reveals the reason for her dislike of Glenstool. She is trying to decide whether or not to stay in Edinburgh for the next three months,

But the real great consideration which has most weight in making me wish to remain another three months is the hope of tiring out that pest – I was greatly inclined to call him a worse name – Glencripesdale & the dread of being once more subjected to Dr Stewart's intrusive & indelicate interference. I love the Dr very much but certainly will not submit again to his management.

Dr Stewart of Findynate had been trying a bit of matchmaking between his heiress niece and his nephew. Glenstool must have been less than subtle in his advances at Glenlyon House. In May 1839, she mentions him again. Her mother had succeeded in putting him off in some way.

I cannot close my letter without thanking you Oh! how gratefully about that toad Alie Stewart, but poor soul he has offended me in no way since I came here. Oh dear no, my dislike to him is all of Genuine Strath Tay growth. I am going to dine with the Strowans to-morrow & I am happy to have at last been able to accept one of the Dallas' many invitations to take tea with them.

William Dallas was a lawyer whose daughter married General Nickle.

The Sheriff met Glenstool in Tobermory in 1843 and wrote about it in his diary. One can see why Sophy might have found him unattractive.

On my arrival at Springbank I found Sandy Stewart Glencripesdale with his pretty bride, and his brother in law Niel Stewart, Foss, and a young Edinburgh lad, Bob Renton, sitting round the Table with a quantity of biscuits, glasses and an empty Wine decanter before them. I procured a reinforcement of solids and liquids, and we passed an hour or two very jovially. Mrs Stewart retired at half past 11 and Niel and his young friend went down to the Inn at the same time to roost. Sandy took his three tumblers of Toddy and enlarged wisely and emphatically on the incomparable felicity of the married state which he strongly recommended to my consideration and adoption.

Wednesday 9 August 1843. When I was dressing Glenstool came in to my room looking drumly and unrefreshed; he complained of our late Sederunt last night. I denied the premises, upon which he exclaimed hurriedly: 'aye aye its well for you to say so, but mind – I had to give a horn to the wife after I went to bed – mind that, mind that – that makes the difference, you see', rubbing his hands and winking on me à la Liston. [John Liston (1776–1846) was famous for playing comic parts on the London stage.]

Another young man who failed to meet with Sophy's approval was George Robertson, Frankie's brother and next chief of Sophy's clan. 'By the by I quite forgot to say that living with the Strowans is quite out of the question. I would not live there while George is in the house for anything I ever saw. Besides I have not been asked. George leaves in the beginning of April, & if they choose to invite me then I shall be delighted to go.' Concerning George, the Sheriff thought 'the boy was spoilt by overindulgence'.

Money was tight for Sophy.

Are you not surprised to see another letter from me after the voluminous epistle which I suppose you received last week? But you know my last packet did not go by post so I feel no compunction in sending this so closely on its heels. The because however of my writing so soon is Mr Oliphant leaves off his class next week, I shall then have nothing but music & an hour of writing to attend to with Masters. Miss Mary & Granny alias Miss Learmonth keep croak croaking about idleness, waste of time, the pity of paying for staying here & doing nothing but what we could do at home viz read & work & a deal to the same purpose. The Learmonths wished me to begin drawing last quarter but I thought you would not wish it. Besides I do not like Chalk heads with cherry lips &c & Simpson's style of landscape is not a pretty one. Now, however, that the composition class is over they have begun again the same story, so I just resolved upon writing you at once on the question of painting or no painting lessons. I wish we were rich Mama! Then I would get lessons in singing & painting too, but as we are not I shall be content without either if you think it necessary. I would not have mentioned the subject had not Miss Mary hinted & hinted till in an evil hour I promised to mention to you & certainly painting flowers from nature would be a nice amusement in the country. Miss Mary desires me to say that we all require an elocution master for a few lessons. I agree with her for in truth most of us read horribly. That will not be at all an expensive, though a very useful, class, so I hope I may attend it. It will be more serviceable than painting or singing.

I have not mentioned any thing about the Learmonths wishes or my own to James, for he cannot bear to refuse me any thing, at least he never does so but says I am by no means extravagant. By the by, should I learn painting Aunt's kind present will enable me to buy a drawing box with every requisite & leave me some pocket money besides so that will be no additional expense to you.

Sophy was allowed to paint.

I have been as busy as a bee this quarter. My half-quarter of painting & singing will be about one quarter of Drawing in expense I mean between them. It is a desperate business to procure an account in this house. Miss Bird got my paint-box, & Miss Mary says as the account has not come in, it will be better to let James settle that matter when he pays other accounts, so I have to be even with her. I have taken summer dresses into my own hands and pay for them on the spot. I wish I knew if my pink muslin is let downable, as if it is I shall get one fewer. As for nightgowns & indeed slips, I shall return to you in rags or next thing to it. I have got a by no means expensive straw bonnet & have trimmed it myself. That is my best bonnet, & the white silk shall be dyed if worth it, which I think it is, & will do for a while before winter cleeding [clothing] commences. I have got Lyle thread gloves for 6d & ditto mitts. They are capital things for the garden &c. Work I have little or no time for. I have just finished a collar. When you write to my dear Kindrochit Aunts please tell them that I would have written by Sandy Cameron's wife but she was off ere I knew of it.

In a letter of June 1839, still to her mother at Derculich, Sophy goes into detail about Clementina Irvine's forthcoming marriage.

I received a very very kind letter from my dear Miss Irvine yesterday, announcing her marriage at last & inviting me to be her bridesmaid. It was an old Kindrochit promise which I never expected her to remember, but she expresses a very particular wish to have me & I am sure I shall be delighted to go if you have no objections. The misfortune is Clementina says the day, tho' not quite fixed, will probably be before the end of this month, so going North in time will not only deprive me of nearly a week's lessons but will prevent me from paying a short visit to the Strowans. However when her wedding's in the case I would gladly let all other things give place.

To be sure I shall be sorry not to see more of the Strowans & I wonder that Clementina has not invited Frances to her bridal but I don't think she intends doing so, for she has charged me to announce the event to the Strowans & to them alone. Missie says she was to write to you immediately & I trust dearest Mama that you will let me hear from you in double quick time as I wish much to let Clementina know what my plans are, for she says she will not ask any bridesmaid till she hears from me.

By the by, that Crook in my lot Glencripesdale is to be bridegroom's man. How horrid, but even that I would put up with rather than not see Miss Irvine 'ere she goes to Australia, for it is by no means improbable that we may never meet again, as neither she nor I are the most robust people in the world.

I should like to make some little present to Miss Irvine, whether I be her bridesmaid or not. Do you think I should work a white satin bag in chenille, or net one of those little Devil purses, white with silver pins & ring which would cost 3 shillings? No very costly gift, but every Lady need not know the price.

In your letter tell me how I am to address Missie, as Clementina which I never called her or Miss Irvine. I am so taken up about this marriage that I cannot write about any thing else with any pleasure. She was always such a favorite of yours & of my dear dear Father's as well as of my own, that I am as interested in her welfare as though she were what she never never never will be: my cousin.

If you write on Friday I shall have your letter I think by nine on Saturday, then if I write to Missie on Saturday she will have time in case of my declining her invite to provide herself with another damsel equally or nearly so capable of drawing the snow white glove off her lily hand. If I do go I shan't get any new frock, the one which was worn only at my chief's nuptials may surely do, after it is washed, for anyone who cannot boast the longevity of our clan.

Young George of Struan had been married in April.

Sophy returned home to Atholl. Over the next few years she and the

Sheriff corresponded and she refers to him as 'my dear and respected God Father' and teases him gently about being stuffy. He occasionally makes reference to her in his diary. In one entry he mentions her 'popping the question', so the subject of her marriage – or his – was certainly on his agenda. As her godfather and a trustee of Kindrochit he felt he had a legitimate interest in her future, but his plans for her would all turn to ashes.

30

Sophy's marriage

The Sheriff, James Robertson, had known the Irvine family all his life. He lent money to David Irvine. He advised the family on the break-up of the Garth and Drumcharry estates and he further gave advice to Sandy Irvine during one of his campaigns to find a better parish than Foss.

> 1st Oct 1838. My dear Irvine, I have this moment heard that the Minister of Blair has had another attack. If I can make it out I will attend Lord Glenlyon's dinner on the 5th. I made a sort of promise to Condie [a Perth lawyer] to that effect but I fear I shall not be able to keep it. Do you however make a point of being there, and if possible have a few minutes conversation with Condie on the subject of the Blair Church. They have you in view – yet you must not allow them for a moment to forget your claims. Let your brother William write to me when any decisive change takes place in Mr Stewart's health.

Referred to, behind his back, as 'The Pope of Blair', the Revd John Stewart still had more than four years to go, before dying on 22 March 1843. On that occasion, Sandy at last succeeded in being promoted to the richest parish in the presbytery by being translared from Fortingall to Blair Atholl and Struan. The Sheriff was appointed Sheriff Substitute of Ross-shire at Stornoway in June 1841. In March 1842 he moved to Tobermory as Sheriff Substitute of North Argyll. He remained there until March 1846, when he was appointed Sheriff Substitute of Orkney and transferred to Kirkwall. He started keeping a journal on 21 July 1841, and wrote a daily entry until November 1875, a couple of months before he died.

Every summer he returned to Atholl to visit his parents and old friends. He called on Sandy in September of 1843.

> After breakfast called on Alexander Irvine at the Manse of Blair, and I did feel most heartily glad to see him there for the first time. Saw also his good old mother, the only remaining relic of the kindly Stewarts of Garth, God bless her, and his daughter, an intelligent girl of nine, with a sunny countenance, who welcomed me with both hands and an exclamation of 'I am very glad to see you'. This scene gave me unalloyed pleasure. Walked

with Irvine round the glebe, through the garden and house. Dined at home and walked to Kindrochit after.

The journal entry continues, 'Dined at home and walked to Kindrochit after. Mrs Robertson, Sophy and William Canada were just arrived from Auchleeks; took tea first at the Cottage and again with Mrs Robertson. I saw no great change in any of my aunts, though age is stealing on all and especially poor Aunt Helen.' William was one of the sons of Dr William Robertson of Montreal. The entire family had been over in Scotland earlier that year.

Thursday 21 September 1843. A calm and very hot day. Sunny. Donald and Wm went to Kindrochit. I rode first to Killiecrankie Cottage to call on Mrs Hay of Seggieden and thank her for giving the use of her Pew at Strowan Church to my father and his family. Afterwards called at Lude where I found Mrs McInroy at home, the Laird himself being at Perth Races. She took me through the house which is now completely finished and furnished and certainly very handsome. After dinner Emily rode to Kindrochit and I accompanied Irvine in his Gig to Cluny Cottage. His brother Dr Irvine was from home.

Friday 22 September 1843. Another calm hot sunny day. Irvine drove me to Dunkeld where he was to officiate at the Induction of Mr Whitlaw to that living. William Irvine had arrived during the night but was called off again before we got up in the morning. Dunkeld looked beautiful. Went to Church. Irvine gave an admirable discourse, and his address to Mr Whitlaw and to the people, especially that to the latter, was of a very high rate of excellence. Irvine afterwards presided at the dinner and acquitted himself almost equally well as in Church, and let me say here that he is certainly in many respects improved. He is patient, forbearing and considerate towards his parishioners; visits them frequently without distinction of Seceder or Churchman, and he never on any occasion introduces the subject of Church politics to them. I anticipate that by this time next year the secession at Blair will be the shadow of a shade. [The Disruption of the Church of Scotland took place in May, four months earlier, with seceding Free Churches set up all over Scotland.] 255 communicated at Blair last Sunday. I dined with the Presbytery of Dunkeld. Irvine spoke well. Whitlaw returned thanks and proposed healths but never spoke a word more than one sentence on each occasion; this is literally true and I think the man acted wisely and well. He appears more of a gentleman than the generality of Scotch Clergy; but Irvine in that Presbytery is a Triton among the Minnows. Drove home principally after dark. Overtook Willy Irvine on the road below Pitlochry. Long talk with him and Dr John at Pitlochry. Nice fellow. Boat off the Garry and slept at Manse, after eating 'an enormous quantity' of Grouse Pye which the good old Lady [Jessie Stewart or Irvine, Sandy's mother] provided for us.

Sunday 24 September 1843. Another fine day. To Church; my father there. Donald in his kilt sat with Mrs Irvine in the Minister's Pew. I sat with our own family in Mrs Hay's Pew. My father went out with Aunt Betsy at the end of the English service. All the rest remained to hear the Gaelic. Irvine excellent in both. He announced that he is to Lecture at Blair at 5 o'clock. Home to dinner.

Monday 25 September 1843. Another fine day, sunny but chilly. Breakfasted early at Milton. Bade adieu to my dear father and mother, and left with Emily for Kindrochit. After a world of trouble we set out about 11 o'clock; that is to say, Donald, William Canada, Sophy and Emily resolved to accompany me as far as Killin and clapped themselves along with me in the double seated Kindrochit [gig] and with Donald as our guide and head, and John's Brown mare as our cavalry, we set out joyfully on our journey. Called at Dalchalloch and saw the good old Lady there; Hot work in walking up the long hills. Went through Fortingall for the first time since the Garth Estate was sold and the Irvines left Drumcharry. The lower hills looked higher and greener and steeper than my recollection of them. Saw the modern house built on the old site of Drumcharry by Sir Archibald Campbell for the first time, and gave many a sigh to the memory of kind old General Stewart; and in passing Duneaves thought with equal sorrow of old Strowan whom I visited there in the autumn of 1823 when I was in higher health and strength and hope than I ever was before or since. But let that pass. Corned the brown mare and took a chop ourselves at Fortingall. Examined the celebrated old yew tree in the Church yard, the remains of which are still green and flourishing. The place is surrounded by a high wall and the Garth family are buried around and apparently among the old stems and roots.

Expatiated to William Canada and Sophy about Fernan and made them join me in denouncing the grasping and greedy Breadalbane family who obtained a grant of these lands from the Crown when the Estate of Strowan was in the hands of Government under the forfeiture of 1748 as late as the time of George III. Sent for Charles McDiarmid younger of Bohally who is settled there now as a medical man and who gave us a long account of Australia, and a sad catalogue of mishaps and failures befalling our acquaintances there. Charley is somewhat improved.

At this stage the Sheriff liked and respected Sandy – and they exchanged waspish letters about the failings of the seceding clergy and church – but this was soon to change. Sophy, it becomes apparent, was supposed to marry Donald, the Sheriff's younger brother, but the Journal entry of 15 May 1844 reads, 'Letter from Emily; she says that there is a serious flirtation between A R I [Sandy] and Sophia K! I do not like it at all, and never expected it. Sophy should do better, and I will feel disappointed if she and Donald do not make a match of it.' And he forthwith wrote to

Donald saying that he 'is wrong in not speaking plainly and manfully out,' and that he 'should declare himself to Sophy', adding, 'I wd speak to Sophy for him.'

In June 1844 the Sheriff made his annual visitation, staying with his parents at Milton of Invervack.

> Emily and I went to Kindrochit to Tea. Found no great difference in my aunts, Mrs Robertson or Sophy. After Tea Mrs Robertson called me out and announced that Sophy and Sandy Irvine are engaged to be married in Autumn. I knew of a flirtation, but did not anticipate that matters had gone this length. She asked my opinion. I answered generally. Sophy cried and hoped I did not disapprove. I said rather coldly that I did not, for which she thanked God, and again cried on my shoulder. I never felt less inclined for a scene. My aunts looked very gloomy.

Sophy was 23, Sandy a 38-year-old widower with a 10-year-old daughter. Now in his journal the Sheriff starts to use a nickname for Sandy – Fraochan, which means bilberry or blaeberry. The following day the Sheriff

> Went to Blair Atholl Manse. Saw Irvine in his Study. Talked over marriage settlements. Found him very reasonable. Returned to Milton. He went to Kindrochit. I wrote to Donald about how matters stand between Sophy and A R I. Dined at Manse. Walked with Irvine through his farm.
>
> 15th June 1844. Wrote to Donald farther about Marriage, settlements, &c &c. Went to Kindrochit to Tea. Long talk with my aunts [at Kindrochit Cottage] who are exceedingly sore about Sophy's marriage. Afterwards went up [to Kindrochit House] and took tea alone with Sophy and Mrs Robertson. Talk about settlements. Sophy left room. She went down with us to Kindrochit Cottage, and Aunt Anne accompanied me to Milton at night.

The next day was Sunday. Sandy preached at Moulin and James gloomily sorted through details of their marriage contract.

> Got note from Mrs Robertson Kindrochit to meet her half way to Kindrochit which I did. She wished that £2000 should be settled on Sophy and A R I in liferent, and failing a family, to go to her heirs.
>
> 18th June. Called at [Blair Atholl] Manse, and arranged farther about Contract. Irvine agreed to everything I proposed. Saw his mother who came up with him that day. Went to Cottage and Kindrochit; farther talk with Aunts. Aunt Betsy relenting. Took tea alone at Kindrochit; Mrs Robertson and Sophy very affectionate at taking leave.
>
> 29th Aug. [Tobermory] Wrote to Donald Edinburgh; about Fraochan; bad marriages; Strowan, William and Sophy; I will renounce Fraochans. Queen coming to Blair Atholl!!!
>
> 21st Sept. [Tobermory] Queen in Atholl; Sophy K's marriage; Inveraray Meeting. Letter from William. The Queen went to Blair Church last

Sunday! Irvine preached, and the Newspapers describe his discourse as plain, lucid and earnest. Just so.

24th Sept. [Tobermory] Sophy Kindrochit married today.

There are a couple more entries in the Journal concerning Sophy. In September 1847, James 'Went down to the Manse and saw Mrs Robertson of Kindrochit looking old and gray. Old Mrs Irvine looking well. Irvine somewhat gray and faded. Sophy thin, her two children strong, healthy and plain, and Elizabeth Irvine forward and precocious. Dined with them; Alastair Foss, George Stewart and William Irvine there.' And, in May 1850, in Edinburgh, 'The Irvines with Donald; Sophy looks thin and ill, and so does the Parson. The Irvines dined with us . . . poor Sophy, she seems very anxious to be intimate with us.'

Sophy died in January 1856, aged 35, with her husband at her bedside. Her death certificate reads 'Neuralgia 3 weeks. Haemorrhage from the bowels 36 hours'. Willie Irvine, her brother-in-law, attended her. She was buried at Struan. Her three-month-old daughter joined here there a fortnight later. In his journal James wrote,

Poor, poor Sophy! . . . I wish from my heart that I had seen her before her death. Dear Sophy, I loved her for her father's sake – I like her mother too – God help her – As for her husband, I cannot esteem the man. And this is the end of Sophy Kindrochet whose prospects at one time promised so fairly, so brightly. It wrings my heart to think of it all.

Her mother moved into the manse and reared her five surviving grandchildren.

The Sheriff was in Atholl in 1867 when Sandy died and, rather cold-bloodedly, recorded the details of his demise.

Found Irvine going about when I called to look out his papers & we were going over them when he ordered lunch. Just as we had sat down, & he had put a bit of mutton chop in his mouth he choked in swallowing it & went to his bedroom. We followed him – His daughter stood at the door. I put my finger down his throat & he put up the bit of mutton – but he continued to wretch [we] put our fingers in his mouth repeatedly. Nothing further came up but phlegm. He stood before a looking glass the image of death & we thought he would die among our hands. He got a little better however, & in an hour his brother came & administered opiate & put him to bed. We left at 4 – Dr Wm Irvine left at ½p 5. And at ½p 6 I had a note from Alister that his father was dead!

Perhaps one further letter is worth quoting. The writer was Elizabeth Irvine, daughter of Sandy by his first wife, passing on family information to Canadian relations in 1859, and it gives a picture of Sandy and Sophy's children. Elizabeth would marry Francis Fraser of Findrack.

And now to a little of home news, that is to say, a sort of family sketch of our own very selves, as Gran [Sophia Robertson, nee Stewart of Shierglass d.1861] says she is sure that will interest you. She herself is wonderfully strong and active, looking very much better than she did last year. In short you may tell your father that his aunt is a very wonderful person for her years, both mentally and physically for she is now past 79. The children are in name and age as follows: Sophie 14, Alister 12, Clementina 10, Duncan 8, and Robert 6. Sophie, your namesake, is both tall and stout. She is, we think, more like her Shierglass relatives than anyone else belonging to her. She had at one time a look of her mama, but that she has completely lost. She will not be the least pretty, but promises to be handsome, what you Canadians call fine-looking, I believe, and lady-looking & she promises to have too, what is of far more importance, her mother's amiable and gentle temper. [She married John Robertson, the factor to the Duke of Atholl.]

Alister [Great-grandfather Alexander] has always had a general look of Papa's uncle, General Stewart, whom I am sure your Papa remembers, but he is very big now & instead of being a little man promises to be a very tall one & broad too. He is at school at St Andrews & has been for two years, & when his holidays are over returns there for a third.

I don't exactly know who to say Clementina is like, not much like anyone, but a sort of mixture of all her relatives & a funny old-fashioned piece of goods she is. [She became Mrs Charles Winchester.] Duncan is a regular Kindrochit & ridiculously like his cousin Duncan in Canada. Sometimes he moves and laughs so like Duncan I can hardly keep my gravity. [He emigrated to South Africa.]

Robert is much stouter than Dochie & is the only one of us the least like Papa, I think. [He became a doctor with his uncle in Pitlochry. A great athlete, 'Bulldog' Irvine captained the Scottish rugby team. He would train by running from Pitlochry to Edinburgh.] Papa is much thinner than he used to be, & grey too, but years will tell on everyone.

My grandmother, old Mrs Irvine [Jessie Stewart of Garth d.1865, aged 89], is still wonderfully well & lives in a little cottage close to her son the doctor. Your father, Gran says, always inquires very kindly after the former family here.

The Stewarts of Derculich will, I daresay, remain permanently in Perth, as Mrs Stewart's health is so much improved since going to reside there.

The ladies at Kindrochit Cottage are very well. [These are the maiden sisters of Captain Duncan Robertson.] Your father will be glad to hear of them for they were old acquaintances of his. He will also remember the Stewarts of Dalchalloch. They left that place several years ago, but lived for some time at Middle Bridges, a place not far from Blair. The brothers went to Australia where they are very comfortably settled in the Sydney district, but about a year and a half ago the two unmarried sisters Jane and Betsy, followed them. We have heard of little more than their safe arrival.

If your father remembers the family of Auchleeks Robertson, please tell him that the old laird is dead. His widow and family live in the south of England. The young laird is also obliged to live there as his wife's health is too delicate to live here. General Macdonald's new house, a palace rather, is getting on very fast. He is very lame owing to an accident when hunting, but otherwise in good health. Strowan [George, Sophy's acquaintance], not content with selling Mount Alexander to the General, has advertised for sale all the rest of his unentailed estate, the new house he built at Dall and all the rest. He will still have a corner left with the Barracks at the west end of Loch Rannoch for a residence. 'Sic transit' the Strowan estate & the glory of the chief of his Clan Donnochy. It has caused great regret here.

After his father's death, Great-grandfather Alexander changed his name to Irvine Robertson in accordance with the requirements of a Trust Disposition of 1824 by Duncan Robertson of Kindrochit to 'assume the name and carry the Arms of Robertson of Kindrochit' – not that there were any arms to carry. He sold Kindrochit to the Duke of Atholl in 1883 for £16,000. He would become minister of Clackmannan, a doctor of divinity like his father and grandfather, and finally sever the family connection with Atholl.

And they all lived happily ever after.

Appendix 1

On the death of John Stewart of Kynachan in 1733, from a Perth kinsman, John Smyth, a merchant and supplier of funeral accessories.

To David Stewart esquire at Kynachan, Sir, The melancholy accounts of the death of so worthy so good and honest a friend could not but affect me in a very sensible manner, but this being a debt we have all to pay we ought to submit cheerfully and make a right use of this hidden summons namely to be in a readiness to pay this debt ourselves when it shall please God to call on us.

I heartily sympathise with your mother on this doleful occasion, and pray that God who is a husband to the Widow may support her under this very heavy affliction, and make her children dutiful and comfortable friends to her.

I have sent my apprentice David Carr with a cerecloth which I believe will be needful since the weather is warm and the burial not sooner than Thursday, he will give directions anent rimming the coffin, and leave perfuming oils to rub over the coffin the day of the interment a little before lifting the corpse. The sooner he is put in the coffin the better.

My wife has given orders to the baker who will have everything ready tomorrow forenoon, and she has sent several things by this bearer in case that any of them do not fit or please you they may be returned tomorrow with David Carr, so as they may be changed and others sent in their place. There is sent a pair of stockings, hat and cape, gloves, buckles and buttons.

Your linings shall be ready according to direction against Tuesday morning early against which time the tailor has engaged to have your clothes ready and Toschach has promised to have your shoes very soon.

There will be a suit of fashionable linings for your mother and sisters, ready in a day, but I'll take no more off but one suit for each of them til my wife get their particular directions, and as for their gowns it is not practicable to make them til either their measures or a gown for every one that suits or fits them best be sent for the tailor's direction, and let him know if they have black petticoats already or if there's occasion to take to Killicranky for new ones for your sisters, but your mother's must be either cloth or flannel as she pleases, but they must send the length of their petticoats and aprons.

I have sent two patches of flannel to your mother for choice for her gown, and send either the measures or a gown of your mother's and one of every one of your sisters.

I spoke to Mr Wood about the clothes and we both agree that if the burial is not sooner than Thursday it will be soon enough to fit the clothes Tuesday morning and your horses may be here to go off Tuesday night and travel all night, and they'll be home in time enough, but if you want to have the clothes sooner send word with David Carr. If possibly I can get away I'll endeavour to be with you Wednesday night but cannot positively promise. My wife and all here join in making offer of our humble service to your mother and family and I am

Your Affetc friend and humble servant, JN: SMYTH,

After writing, my wife thinks needless to send patches of flannel, for the finest is what my wife thinks the only one that's proper, there is three pairs of mourning gloves but if any of them do not fit, return them. Perth. (Mon) May 25th, 1733.

Appendix 2

The coarse satirist Allan Stewart of Innerhadden here describes Robert Stewart of Garth's room at university in the 1770s. He is using 'Divinity' descriptively – and ironically.

A College Room of Divinity

I strolld one day into a room
When honest Bob was not at home
But as his key was in the door
I sat me down for half an hour.
When round the room I cast my eyes
A medley of such objects rise
That straight away to employ my time
I thus described them all in rhyme.
A table first which was made of oak
Had one leg short, another broke:
As much of it as well could stand
Was filled with papers, pen and sand,
While various books confusdly lie
Scotch songs with deep philosophy.
Foul pipes and mugs together lay
With boxes of best Virginia
The newest method for the fiddle
A violin broken in the middle
With great variety of prints
Of copper plates and metzatints.
Here phaeton from heaven was hurld
And here the wonders of the world.
The cartoons mixd wih arateens
With heads of British Kings and Queens
Joan with her consort punchanello

With Vernon's siege of Portobello.
Here Drake that glorious English tar
With Ormond and the Russian czar.
A cat without a tail or ear
Lay sleeping by a mug of beer.
Along with her upon the hearth
Lay Pope's new Dunciad and Garth
Who did not dread the harmless fire
Which just was going to expire.
Upon the floor was careless thrown
A dirty shirt and tattered gown
An Homer never meant to look on
A wooden desk to set a book on.
Two globes: twas difficult to find
Which was for heaven or earth designd
A pair of bellows and a broom
And a bureau adornd his room.
In bottle neck was fixd a candle
An earthen jug without a handle.
Two or three ribs of iron
Was never designed to make a fire in
So much decayd and full of holes
It would not hold a pan of coals.
Upon a little table stood
A china bason full of blood
A tweezer case, a dirty towel,
A pitcher of hot water gravel,
A glass which some unlucky stroke
Hade in a dozen pieces broke.
A chest half full of right bohea
With proper furniture for tea
Had not the cups and saucers been
Some blue and white, some red and green,
Some large enough to hold a gill
While others scarce a spoon would fill.
Here lays a female's fan and gloves
The trophies of his former loves.
To Chloe lay an open letter
In which he owed himself her debtor
But could not her requests fulfill
He had not yet received his bill.

Upon the window stood a bowl
With relick of a roasted fowl.
A College plate with dirty dishes
A powder horn and net for fishes.
A rusty gun without a lock
A racket and a Shuttle cock
With Oil and combes and powdring block.
A canister and a pair of Shoes
A pistle never designed to use
A Coffie-mill and perfumd ball
A Chamber-pot and that was all.

Appendix 3

Memorandum of the Military Service of Colonel David Stewart C.B.

In Autumn 1793, Lieutenant in the 42nd Regiment, and embark with my Regiment for Flanders – Served under the Duke of York – Relief of Newport in November, and returned to England.

In January 1794 the Regiment joined an Expedition to the Coast of France under the Earl of Moira – Return to England, and embark in June under the same Commander for Flanders –s campaigns under Duke of York in Winter 1794 and Spring 1795. Return to England.

In October 1795 embark for the West Indies under Sir Ralph Abercromby – In April 1796 Expedition against St Lucia – During the Operations stationed seventeen days with an Officer and sixty men on an out post on the right of the army, commanding an important pass, close to the Enemy – No exchange of this duty 'Because' in the words of Sir Ralph Abercromby 'an intelligent Officer in whom he placed confidence was requir'd for that Post' – On an Occasion when the Enemy threatened to attack this Detachment, it was proposed to send a reinforcement, when the General said, 'it is not necessary; Captain D. Stewart and a part of the 42nd occupies the Post and will defend themselves'. After the surrender of St Lucia, embark for the Island of St Vincent. The 42nd led the attack on the 10th of June 1796 on the strong and supposed inaccessible position of the Enemy. – Four Redoubts in succession were to be taken – When our Troops got possession of three Redoubts they halted – I pushed forward with about Ninety Men of my Regiment, and placed them so close under the fourth redoubt that the Enemy could not bring their Guns to bear upon us. – We lay there ready to assault when followed up and supported by the Troops, but the General understanding that the Enemy were disposed to surrender without standing the chance of an Assault, I was recalled – After the Enemy had marched out as Prisoners, it was discovered, that the Position could have been attacked, and carried with little loss from the place I had occupied – We also learned that the near approach of this Party so alarmed the Enemy that they proposed to surrender without further resistance.

It was four months before the Enemy was dispossessed of all their strongholds in other parts of the Island – I was in constant activity and never lost an hour's duty by sickness, altho' I had the duties of Commanding Officer, Adjutant Quarter-Master, and Paymaster; as all the Officers except two and myself were totally disabled by sickness and debility. – A detail of the various skirmishes and duties is unnecessary – In one instance I attacked a Post with a detachment of my Regiment, and carried it with trifling loss; it had been twice attempted before unsuccessfully – On another occasion I discovered a secret path, thro' the woods and mountains, and getting round the Enemy, surprised a small Post in their Rear – Thus when they found that they could be attacked on that side on which they thought themselves secure, they surrendered at discretion.

Expedition to Porto Rico in 1797, Sir Ralph Abercromby commanding – Always under his immediate notice, and employed by him in all confidential Duties – When the conquest of the Moro (the Gibraltar of the West Indies) was found impracticable, and the troops ordered to embark, I was stationed by the General on a Bridge – a most important post – as being the only Communication by which the Enemy, now getting more daring, could disturb the embarkation.

Return to England in 1797. Gibraltar and Expedition in 1798, against Minorca, under Sir Charles Stuart, the Spaniards surrendered without firing a Shot – Expedition against Cadiz in 1800 – Egypt in 1801. After the landing was effected on the 8th of March I pushed forward with two Companies to drive back three Field Pieces which galled the Troops exceedingly; when ordered by General Oakes to retire upon the Regiment to wait till the other Troops had landed, I had some difficulty in getting the men to retire, as they were eager to follow the Enemy.

In the Action of the thirteenth the 42nd was ordered close up under the Enemies position – Having sustained some loss, General Moore ordered the Regiment to take ground to the right, beyond the reach of Fire, – and I remained behind with a few men, and carried away the wounded, and thus saved them from destruction, the Enemy having kept up a fire upon them as they lay on the ground unable to move.

I was stationed on the right Wing of the 42nd regiment on the 21st March; – The Morning was pitch black when the Battle commenced, and no object could be discovered at the distance of six yards – Suspecting that the enemy would advance from a certain direction I ran out to reconnoitre, and more by the murmuring noise of the movement of a great solid column, and by the clank of their arms, than by Vision, I discovered the near approach of what was called the 'Invincible Column' and thus giving timely notice to my commanding officer, the charge with the Bayonet which followed, shewed that this Corps had then lost its claim to the proud title of 'Invincible' – I was wounded at that moment, but not being immediately disabled, I kept with my Men till faint with the loss of blood and exertion I was incapable of farther movement; but not allowing myself to be carried to the rear, I was placed on the right of the Regiment, where I saw all that passed better perhaps, than those who were in constant movement – The wound disabled me for the rest of this Campaign.

In 1802 returned to England. Appointed in 1803 to receive the balloted men of the Army of Reserve from the Highland Counties and to form them into the 2d Battalion of the 42d regiment in Fort George – In this duty I met with several difficulties too long to detail; I shall only notice that by a little knowledge of the Highland Character and of the manner of managing Soldiers, I prevented a threatened Mutiny, proceeding from some well grounded complaints of non performance of promises.

In 1804 appointed Major in the 78th regiment. For this promotion I recruited 118 Men. In 1805 stationed under General Moore in Kent, Ordered to join the 1st Battalion of my Regiment in India; this Order was countermanded in consequence of a particular occurrence – an extraordinary degree of attachment displayed by the Soldiers, and of sorrow at the idea of my being separated from them.

October 1805 embarked for Gibraltar – Appointed by General Fox to command and discipline in an uniform manner a Corps composed of all the Light Infantry in the Garrison – May 1806 sail for Sicily – in July land in Calabria – Battle of Maida – In this Action I had an opportunity of performing an important piece of service – Personal attachment and regard for the memory of Officers whose Character might suffer by my stating the particular circumstances of this affair, prevent me from doing so – I have had the same feeling from the day of the Battle; and I not only have avoided writing on the subject but even speaking of it except to those who were present and knew the whole – It was from this feeling that I requested of Sir John Stuart not to mention the circumstances in his Dispatches, although he was very desirous to do so in justice to me – He was also fully sensible of the great and important piece of Service rendered to him; which turned on the point whether to be a victorious or beaten general; to prove a forerunner and a good sample of the reverses which the French afterwards sustained – Actuated as I have always been by a delicacy towards the memory of my friends, who are dead, I cannot now enter into a detail of circumstances and only state generally that, by a prompt and decided interference I checked a retrograde movement (more properly a retreat) of my regiment in the very heat and most important moment of the Contest; which would have left the centre of our Line clear for the Enemy to pierce through – Thus taking each of our wings in flank and in front – movements for which General Regnier was fully prepared – our Troops so exposed could not withstand the Shock and would with ease be driven off the field before the second line could come to their assistance – The proposed Retreat of my Regiment, which would have had such deplorable consequences, proceeded from a misapprehension of Orders, the confusion of the Officers who carried and delivered them, and from other causes which need not be detailed. – How quickly our brave young Soldiers recovered from the panic with which they were struck, when they saw themselves running away from those who had previously fled before them with terror and precipitation, was soon proved by their rapid and irresistible charge on a veteran Enemy so much more numerous.

Immediately after this Charge which completely overturned an Enemy who from the previous movement had calculated on no resistance and an easy conquest, I was wounded, but, being able to walk, I kept the field till all was over; and then, as at Alexandria, had an opportunity of observing every movement and event during the subsequent part of the Action. Returned to England in 1806 in consequence of the wound which has long been most troublesome.

In 1808 was promoted to the Royal West India Rangers and sailed for Barbados. In 1809 commanding that Garrison consisting upwards of 3000 Men. In 1810 commanded a Light Infantry Brigade on the expedition against Guadeloupe. Attached to the division commanded by Major General Harcourt, who, after the failure of an attack he had ordered on the principal Post of the Enemy, said, 'If I had employed Colonel Stewart on this Service, I would have had the happiness of seeing Guadeloupe conquered and the Garrison surrender to the Troops under my immediate Command.'

Removed to Trinidad in 1811 and returned to England in 1813. – Thus my tour of duty being at a distance from the great scenes of Action in the Peninsula I unfortunately lost that opportunity of improving myself; but in the internal Duties of a Garrison and a Corps I had full scope for acquiring experience. This was in the Command of Men whose punishment for Crimes and Military Offences had been commuted to a Service for life in the West Indies. – These men were considered irreclaimable and dismissed from their former Corps as incurable and ordered to join the West India Rangers. – In my former Regiments, the 42nd and 78th, we had few or no punishments. The Contrast in my new Corps was melancholy – The day previous to my assuming the Command

36 Men received heavy Corporal Punishment – 307 Men deserted in eight months – 295 died of fever and various diseases, and the unprincipled depravity exhibited by two thirds of the Men was horrible. It would be inconsistent with the brevity of these memorandums to explain the means by which I endeavoured to reclaim and reform these men, to check crimes and desertion, and by new habits of regularity, and change of Manners, to prevent the occurrence of diseases incident to dissolute and intemperate depravity. I shall therefore only state the result as was seen in the conduct of the Soldiers. – By punishing with the last severity when necessary (two soldiers were tried and shot, and three hanged), but preventing by every possible endeavour the commission of Crimes; encouraging and rewarding every symptom of improvement; so contented with their Situation, and so regular had the Men become, that during the last eighteen months I had charge of them, desertion had disappeared, the number of deaths was reduced to the usual proportions in that Climate – Punishments were very unfrequent, and then only quite slight; and altho' quartered in an open Barrack, in a populous neighbourhood, with many objects of temptation, there was not a complaint from any Inhabitant against a Soldier during a period of eleven months, and thus their conduct proved the gratifying change in their habits and principles. – By this contrast which I witnessed in the Command and direction of Soldiers in two Corps of a high scale of moral rectitude; and of other Soldiers without principle and debased by many vices; my own knowledge of human nature was increased, and many new lights afforded me for discovering the best modes of preserving the primitive habits and character of good men, and of improving the dissolute and hardened.

London July 18th 1823. David Stewart, Colonel

Appendix 4

From *Recollections of William Stewart Irvine, M.D., F.R.C.S.E.*
by E. Molyneux (Edinburgh: David Douglas 1896)

In former days, no one could be long in the Vale of Athole without hearing
the name of Dr. Irvine as a household word; and thus it was that some
time before actually meeting him I seemed to know the 'old Doctor,' as
he was affectionately called. The Doctor's word was, in those days, as a
law to the country people, his advice authoritative, his voucher a complete
character in itself. 'The Doctor knows me well,' was often the one and
only testimonial thought necessary on either side. And well might it
be so, for fifty years of family histories came within his own personal
experience, and behind them lay a great store of inherited knowledge and
tradition. He stood, as it were, at the parting of the ways between the old
clannish life of the Highlands, full of individuality and local colouring,
of wild poetry and loyal, long-cherished devotions, and the new order of
things advancing slowly, steadily, like a rising flood that submerges old
landmarks, obliterates old traces, and levels old barriers, until those who
knew the land from childhood would wander as strangers through it. So
is the old order passing away, year by year, in the Highlands, though the
change may be stayed here and there by special efforts or conditions. But
in Dr. Irvine's keen, retentive memory one could read as in a mirror the
life of days gone by for ever, could trace the origin and growth of lingering
customs, the meaning of certain characteristics in fact, could share in
hopes and fears that are now no more than survivals, could, as has been
well said, 'behold the series of the generations' and 'weigh with surprise
the momentous and nugatory gift of life.' Yes; and he himself, was he not
the embodiment of much that is found nowhere but in these Highlands?
Was he not the life of their life, in the best sense?

Shrewd, sagacious, hardy and enduring, faithful and laborious, with a
fire of enthusiasm, a vein of unconscious poetry that ran glancing through
all his talk, and made every word of it interesting. Never have I heard from

him a commonplace or colourless remark; whatever might be the subject, it suggested to his mind an experience, an anecdote, an illustration touched with humour and pathos, and, best of all, *drawn from life*. No second-hand talk, no borrowed opinions, no thought of effect, but just the outpouring of a sagacious, sympathetic mind, stored with facts of human life. The many distinguished men he had known, either professionally or otherwise, were brought before you by a few graphic touches, some salient trait given that told more than a page of generalities, and there was the man before you whom Dr. Irvine had known and whom you henceforth knew. It is wonderful to see how people and events live on in such a mind as his.

But what avails description of a real character like Dr. Irvine? How can I show the man himself who was the soul of all he said? No more than I can picture for others the rugged, benevolent face, strong, square-browed, bearing the impress of thought and power; the deep-set grey eyes that could gleam with humour and glow with enthusiasm; the rare, genial, sympathetic smile straight from the heart; all, in fact, that blended in his aspect the strong and the lovable.

Dr. Irvine's descent, on the mother's side, was from an old Highland family, the Stewarts of Garth, and in face he bore a strong resemblance to his famous uncle, General Stewart of Garth, author of *Sketches of the Highlands*, etc. etc. The ruined stronghold of the family still stands at the head of the Keltney Burn, some way from Aberfeldy, a grey, massive keep, isolated and impressive even in its decay. Dr. Irvine was also linked with the most romantic episode of Scottish history through his great-grandfather, Mr. Stewart of Kynachan, who followed Prince Charlie, and was imprisoned at Carlisle for his share in the uprising. [The author here confuses the generations. David followed Prince Charlie, John his father, and his was the portrait.] I have heard Dr. Irvine relate how some friends managed to convey relief to the captive by sending a large snuff-box full of snuff, but so remarkably weighty that his great-grandfather, on investigation found at the bottom of it golden guineas with which he bribed his gaoler to loosen his chains so far as to allow of his lying down! He was subsequently released, and returned home with a new acquisition in a 'viol de gamba,' which he had learnt to play in prison.

The portrait of this ancestor hung in the dining-room at Craigatin (the house which Dr. Irvine built for himself at Pitlochry), along with a fine Raeburn of his grandfather and other interesting portraits, and one could not but feel in intercourse with him that he had inherited, not merely the memories, but much of the innermost life of a remarkable race.

Besides his strong and distinctively Scottish qualities, there were in him ideals that came from an age more poetic than ours. The old world courtesy, so unfailing, the self-devotion to a cause, regardless of consequences (in his case the cause was the claims of his profession taken in the noblest sense), the loyalty to all who trusted him, the fatherly care for all who depended on him, the fine enthusiasm for principles and disregard of personal advancement, these attributes, which ought to be among the plainest signs of good descent, were the great attractions of his character. 'Spirits are not finely touched but to fine issues,' and the influence of any such man during a long life of work can never be estimated, but it is not often that circumstances combine, as in this case, to develop the utmost resources of a rich nature.

When Dr. Irvine first came to Pitlochry in 1833 the district was comparatively unknown and unvisited. Communication was slow and difficult in the absence of a railway or of roads like the present splendid highway. His responsibility as parish doctor extended over forty-five miles of country, much of it wild moorland only to be reached by rough, precipitous roads, almost impassable for weeks at a time in winter. This wide district he had to traverse on horseback, and often far beyond its bounds he was called for private practice or consultation. Single-handed he had to struggle with difficulties that would have dismayed a far stronger man than he was physically, but which in time only served to develop that high courage which is the groundwork of every virtue, the backbone of every principle. Little or no professional help was to be had, and often, in the early years of his practice, he was summoned to some distant farm or croft to fight a disease he had perhaps had no previous opportunity of studying. There, in the wilds, far from all resources, he had to rely on his own penetration and sagacity, with no efficient nursing, nothing on his side in the battle save the calm endurance of the children of toil and their faith in him. In a case of this kind he would leave minute directions for the nursing during the following day or two, foreseeing every contingency and knowing the impossibility of returning earlier; then would ride home, without rest maybe, to find an urgent summons in another direction. Utterly exhausted, he would perhaps fling himself down on the hearthrug for an hour or two of rest, then take a light meal and start off for another long ride. At such times he was hardly seen by his own family for days together. After some years, when he had prevailed upon other doctors to settle down at different outlying points of this extensive district, things became easier, but a life of continuous and unremitting toil was his until threescore and ten had been reached and passed.

Imagine the power for good of a man of this stamp in his daily familiar intercourse with the people. Speaking their own Gaelic, familiar with their ways of thinking, he was trusted as few are ever trusted in this world, and this nobly earned trust enabled him to render services quite apart from his profession. He knew the daily lives, the needs, the hopes and fears of the people as if they had all been of his own family; he was the trusted friend, the helper in need of all who sought his aid.

When he first began work in it, the country was still under the influence of old ideals and memories, still ignorant of King Demos and all his ways. Poor the people were, deplorably 'narrow,' no doubt (according to modern notions), and wanting in the most elementary ideas of creature comfort, but in the main independent, reverent, holding fast by antiquated beliefs in righteous retribution and reward, and having a certain originality which is the portion of those who think their own thoughts and are in daily contact with the powers of Nature. The few books they possessed were really mastered; the art of conversation was valued and practised in a way that would shame some of the 'highest circles' and in every glen was to be found someone with a retentive memory to hand down the legends and songs and ballads of far-gone days. Gifts of song or story-telling were highly valued at the Ceilidh or friendly gathering of several families round one fireside during the long winter evenings, when the women brought their knitting, and spinning-wheels, the men busied themselves with creel-making and other handiwork, while first one and then another kept up the 'flow of soul' by music or recitation.

From Dr. Irvine's strong, vivid memory and his picturesque phraseology what a book of reminiscences might have been produced! But he never could find time to write down any notes during his busy life, and when the leisure came with advancing years, he was too tired! Speaking one day of the changes that had gradually come about in the country within his own recollection, he gave the following facts: 'My recollections,' he said, 'are of the primitive times, which were times of starvation. I remember, at a certain meeting of the Turnpike Trustees, there were two old men present, one a guest, the other a treasurer of the Trust. The former mentioned that in bringing up meal for the supply of the country (before 1810) only one boll of meal could be carried at a time in a cart because of the badness of the roads. The other man said, "If your memory had carried you further back, you'd have remembered when no cart could come up; when one man led a horse or pony which had six or eight others tied together behind each with a sack of meal on his back, and only thus could they get the meal up into the country." The population was too large for the produce of the country. When I came here in 1833 the population of Moulin parish was 2,300; now, in 1891, it is about 2000, notwithstanding the growth of Pitlochry. The meal always ran down before the end of the season while the people were at the shielings. The time spent at the shielings was between sowing their crop (in May) until they returned to reap late in autumn. An old woman in my time remembered that there was often only enough meal remaining to take to the shieling to feed the baby of the house, and the others fed on salt meat and kippered salmon (so abundant in the rivers, which were not preserved) and milk; the milk kept them from dying of scurvy. Potatoes were not then largely used, in fact were scarcely known. Near the end of the last century they began to grow potatoes, and from that time food was more abundant, and the ravages of scurvy were stayed.

'The people were very active, but not very powerful; they have become, in my observation, a finer race physically, but I don't think more talented. I don't think the mixing with the Saxon has improved their intellect, but it has improved them in two ways: First, in regard to bodily size and strength; second, the Saxon prudence has controlled the Celtic impetuosity. Want of steadiness of purpose characterises the Celt. I have known so many young fellows who got on well, and showed marked ability in a certain line; but then made a dash at something they did not know, failed, lost heart, and were ruined.'

Dr. Irvine here alludes to the native cleverness of the Highlanders, and he used to tell many stories illustrative of their ingenuity and imagination. For instance, the story of a ghillie on one of the Perthshire shootings who was very enthusiastic about the Jacobite rising, and whose forefathers had taken an active part in it. He was being badgered by the 'Sassenach' shooting tenants, and had endured hearing the campaign and all who took part in it held up to ridicule for some time. At last he said quietly to one of the gentlemen who were standing on a piece of rising ground, 'Would you be so kind, sir, as to step down from that knowe?' 'Why?' was the query; 'what do you mean?' 'I think, sir, it will be best if you will be stepping down from that knowe; for it is a very dangerous place; people will not be able to speak the truth while they are standing there.' That certainly was the retort courteous!

Many a man, finding himself so much isolated as Dr. Irvine was in the early days of his practice, would have sunk down into a mere jog-trot existence, and never been heard of beyond the bounds of his own district. He, on the contrary, kept pace with the times by systematic reading, and kept in touch with the great world through his warm friendships. Pitlochry, though comparatively unknown as a health resort forty or fifty years ago, was yet frequented by some select spirits, men of science or of power in some line who resorted to it for summer quarters. In this way Dr. Irvine became acquainted with some of his warmest friends. Among them were Dr. John Brown, Principal Forbes, Norman Macleod, and many others long since passed away: friends who afforded him the stimulus of a society of pure intellect and heart, of plain living and high thinking such as mere outward prosperity and so-called 'advantages' cannot always command. The reputation of his skill as a doctor induced many invalids to adventure themselves thus far in the Highlands, and by degrees the value of Pitlochry air, and the charms of its surroundings, became generally known. Few perhaps realise how much of the present prosperity of the place is due to the steadfast labours and high personal attainments of one man, and herein is the saying true 'One soweth and another reapeth.' His unaffected simplicity and naturalness of character prevented him from estimating or understanding the extent of his power and influence, and in fact, from his own point of view, his life was chiefly remarkable for the kindness and goodness of his numerous friends, and the many blessings bestowed on him by Heaven. He took little account of the lives saved and the homes blessed by his skill and sympathy.

Dr. Irvine was the son of a Highland minister well known in his day, and a brother of the still well-remembered Dr. Irvine, minister of Blair-Athole. He was himself a devoted adherent of the Church of Scotland, and, in his last years, when released from pressing professional claims, he became an elder, in order, as he said, 'to be still of some little use'. Many will long remember the frail, venerable form, Sunday by Sunday, passing down the Parish Church with the collecting-bag, and will recall the kindly gleam that shot from time to time from his eyes, softened by time and trouble.

And now that he has passed away from the place that knew him so long, it seems to have lost its animating and unifying spirit, and to be resolved into more prosaic elements. But he was weary, and longed for rest. His work was done, and, to such a man, what is life without work? – a lingering death! The last few years of his life had been marked by severe trials, and in the early part of 1893 came the death of his wife, which left him for the first time face to face with loneliness. This supreme trial he met with Christian fortitude and resignation, but his strength and life ebbed away, and 'to depart in peace' became thenceforth his one desire and prayer. *Home* for him meant no longer his beloved Vale of Athole, nor even the well-known house by the banks of the Tummel, but the Father's house of many mansions – the 'Land o' the Leal'.

Appendix 5

Dr John Stewart of Findynate was the pre-eminent medical practitioner in Atholl in his day, in which post he was to be succeeded by Dr William Irvine. Stewart died in 1844 by which time he had entered local legend. He was written up by Duncan Campbell in his *Reminiscences and Reflections of an Octogenarian Highlander* (Inverness, 1910).

Dr John Stewart of Findynate had been a navy surgeon for many years, and when he came home to reside on his small ancestral property in Strathtay, and to establish for himself a medical practice over a large district, he was found still to be a Highlander of Highlanders in language and sympathies. He was one of the small lairds of long descent who helped much to link all classes together and to sweeten the social life of their locality and their age. He gave the tinkers a camping-place on his property, where they took care to comport themselves so well that no fault could be justly found with them by Justices of the Peace – of which body he was himself a member – nor by ministers, kirk sessions, or the country people. When they encamped on his ground he looked to it that they should send their children to school well cleaned, and as decently clothed as circumstances allowed. The camping ground was open to bands of all surnames, but if two bands came at the same time they had to keep the peace among themselves, or woe to the offenders. The tinkers who used the royal surname of Stewart – and they were numerous – looked up to Findynate as their special or almost heaven-born Chief, and those of other surnames were not much behind them in their devotion and obedience to him. When the country had no rural police, and kilns were numerous, and there was a large and steady demand for horn spoons and tinsmith's work, the tinkers had a tolerably good time of it, although their old silversmith work had come to an end with the eighteenth century in most places. As his part of the country was as orderly and as law-abiding as could be wished, Findynate did not see the necessity for Sir Robert Peel's blue-coated police. He soon came into collision with the one who was stationed at Aberfeldy. He was driving in his dogcart one day to visit a patient whose house was some twenty miles up the country, and when he reached the Weem toll-bar he met the new policeman with a little tinker widow woman in tow. She was a daughter of old Duncan, and her proper name was Jean MacArthur, but she was known on both sides of the Grampians by the nickname of 'Co-leaic,' whatever that strange compound word might mean. Amazed at seeing the harmless Co-leaic interfered with, Findynate pulled up his horse, and in fiery wrath – for his just indignation at anything which looked to him like oppression of the weak flared up like kindled tow – shouted to the policeman, 'Let that woman go. Why have you dared to stop her?' 'I have stopped her,' replied the policeman, 'because she is a vagrant.' 'She is,' was the stern retort, 'what she was born to be. She was at school with me. She has brave Sons in the British army. I know her history, and will be her warrant that she has always been a decent harmless body. Let her go at once if you do not want to get into trouble for being over officious.' Then turning to the Co-leaic he asked her, 'Where were you going when this man stopped you?' She mentioned a farm some miles further up the water. 'I'll be driving past it,' said he, 'so get up on the back seat and I'll take you there.' In this manner demure little Jean was carried off triumphantly and the over-zealous policeman was left discomfited.

Politically a Tory of the Tories our worthy doctor was practically a democratic feudalist with a sympathetic heart, unpaid services, an open hand and a loud voice in denunciation of oppression and persuasive in pleading for the poor and afflicted. To take the tinker class as the lowest I verily believe he did more good among them by blending kindness with scoldings and quarter-deck discipline than any of the agencies for redeeming them which have been since then set on foot. And they repaid him with reverential devotion and worshipful loyalty. I had in later years, when schoolmaster and registrar at Fortingall a singularly touching proof of the feelings his tinker people entertained towards him. On a winter day, when the roads were slushy after a heavy fall of snow and showers were still falling, a young sprightly tinker girl of twenty or thereabouts who, if well washed and dressed, would have been called a pretty girl anywhere, came to my house. She had a newly-born, well-wrapt babe clasped to her bosom, and her errand was to get it registered. She sat by the kitchen fire crooning in the pride of young motherhood to the pink morsel of humanity while I went for the register, and my sister made tea for her. When questioned as to the date of birth and other usual particulars, the story, in all respects a true one, which she had to tell was an amazing one. The child was not yet 48 hours old, and yet she had, through the slushy roads, walked with it that day four long Scotch miles to get it registered. She made quite light

of that feat of hardihood, but shuddered a little in telling what preceded
the child's birth. She and her young husband were with the band to which
they belonged in Bunrannoch when she began to think that it was nearly
her time, and insisted on going away with her man at once, that their
child might be born on Findynate's land, where she had been born herself.
'When more than half way over the hill, the snowstorm,' she said, 'burst
suddenly upon us and after struggling for a while with the storm, I became
weary-worn, and my trouble began. Happily the hill barn above the Garth
farmhouses was near, and my lad, the dear fellow, carried me and laid
me therein. He ran himself – "le anail na uchd" – to the farmhouses for
help. And good women, with blankets and lights, for it was no mirk night,
came to me, and could not have been kinder if they had been angels from
heaven. My bairn was born in the barn, but they soon carried us both to a
comfortable bed and warm fireside. It is a pity that the bairn was not born
at Findynate, but it is a mercy he is a boy, and that he is to be baptised John
Stewart.' 'But,' I hinted, 'your husband does not call himself a Stewart?'
'Well,' she replied, 'I am a Stewart and my first-born is to be baptised John
Stewart.' When the entry was completed, she was getting her second cup
of tea, and I asked her if she would like an ember in it. 'Oh,' she said, 'I
want to be a strictly sober woman all my life, but today a drop of spirits
would go down – deas-toabh mo chleibh – the right side of my heart.' So
the second cup was laced with whisky, and having merrily thanked us and
drunk it up, she went on her way rejoicing.

Bibliography

Atholl, Duke of, *Chronicles of the Atholl and Tullibardine Families* (Edinburgh, 1908)

Broster, D.K., *A Jacobite Trilogy: Flight of the Heron, Gleam in the North* and *Dark Mile* (London: Penguin, 1984)

Campbell, Duncan, *Book of Garth and Fortingall* (Inverness, 1888)

———, *Reminiscences and Reflections of an Octogenarian Highlander* (Inverness, 1910)

Gillies, William A., *In Famed Breadalbane* (Perth, 1938)

Grattan, William, *Adventures With the Connaught Rangers, 1809–1814* (London: Greenhill Books, 1989)

Hopkins, Paul, *Glencoe and the End of the Highland War* (Edinburgh: John Donald, 1986)

Irvine, Alexander, *An Inquiry into the causes and effects of Emigration from the Highlands and Western Islands of Scotland, with Observations for the Means to be Employed for Preventing it* (Edinburgh: Peter Hill; London: Longman & Rees, 1802)

Irvine Robertson, James, *Atholl in the Rebellion of 1745* (Aberfeldy: Heartland Publishing, 1994)

———, *The First Highlander* (Edinburgh: Tuckwell Press, 1999)

———, *The Lady of Kynachan* (London: Corgi Books, 1995)

———, *Scotland's Heartland* (Aberfeldy: Heartland Publishers, 2001)

———, *The Robertsons. Clan Donnachaidh in Atholl* (Kinloss: Librario, 2005)

Kennedy, James, *Folklore and Reminiscences of Strathtay and Grandtully* (Perth, 1927)

Kerr, John, *Church and Social History of Atholl* (Perth and Kinross Libraries, 1998)

MacGregor, Gordon, *The Red Book of Perthshire* (Perthshire Heritage [www.perthshireheritage.co.uk], 2008)

Overlee, Vern & Drummond, Henry, *The Psychic* (Canaan, Vermont: Mora Press, 1983)

Sinton, Thomas, *Family and Genealogical Sketches* (Inverness, 1911)

Stewart, Charles Poyntz, *Memorials of the Stewarts of Fothergill* (Edinburgh, 1879)

Stewart, David, *Sketches of the Character, Manners, and Present State of the Highlanders of Scotland with Details of the Military Service of the Highland Regiments.* (Edinburgh: Archibald Constable, 1822)

Tullibardine, Marchioness of, *A Military History of Perthshire, 1660–1902* (Perth: R.A. & J. Hay, 1908)

Clan Donnachaidh Annuals (The Clan Donnachaidh Centre, Bruar, Pitlochry, Perthshire, PH18 5TW)

The Stewarts, Journals of the Stewart Society (The Stewart Society, 53 George Street, Edinburgh, EH2 2HT)

For transcriptions of documents cited in the text, see www.jamesirvinerobertson.co.uk.

Index